The Politics of Urban Renewal

THE POLITICS
OF URBAN RENEWAL

THE CHICAGO FINDINGS

Peter H. Rossi and Robert A. Dentler

WITH THE ASSISTANCE OF *Nelson W. Polsby,*
Patricia Denton, Carolyn Huson, and Peter C. Pineo

GREENWOOD PRESS, PUBLISHERS
WESTPORT, CONNECTICUT

Library of Congress Cataloging in Publication Data

Rossi, Peter Henry, 1921-
   The politics of urban renewal.

   Reprint. Originally published: New York : Free Press,
1961.
   Bibliography: p.
   Includes index.
   1. Urban renewal--Illinois--Chicago. 2. Urban re-
newal--Illinois--Chicago--Citizen participation.
I. Dentler, Robert A., 1928-   . II. Title.
[HT177.C5R6 1981]   307.7'6'0977311   81-6327
ISBN 0-313-22780-2 (lib. bdg.)   AACR2

Reprinted with the permission of Free Press, a division
of Macmillan Publishing Co., Inc.

Reprinted in 1981 by Greenwood Press
A division of Congressional Information Service, Inc.
88 Post Road West, Westport, Connecticut 06881

Printed in the United States of America

10 9 8 7 6 5 4 3 2 1

To those dedicated citizens of Hyde Park–Kenwood who gave so much time, effort, and devotion to finding new ways of rebuilding their part of a city.

Preface

*T*he research reported in this volume was supported by a grant from the Urban Renewal Administration of the Housing and Home Finance Agency of the federal government. The Community Conservation Board of the City of Chicago contracted with the Agency to conduct the research as a Demonstration Project (Hyde Park–Kenwood Demonstration Project, Illinois D-2, CCB 319.1 AD). Although the Community Conservation Board at all times remained close to the research activities and aided in many ways, the actual responsibility for the Demonstration Project was subcontracted to the Hyde Park–Kenwood Community Conference, a nonprofit civic association dedicated to the improvement of neighborhood conditions in the Hyde Park–Kenwood areas of Chicago.

As subcontractors, the Conference engaged the authors to design and carry out the study. It is another tribute to the integrity of this organization that it sought outside its own ranks for personnel to conduct the research, hoping in this fashion to insure an objective view. Furthermore, the Conference insisted upon the necessity for complete autonomy and freedom for the research staff, giving us free access to its records and facilitating contacts with other organizations. We hope that this report lives up to the responsibility and trust that the Conference leaders showed in engaging the research team.

This volume is the product of team-research. The Conference engaged Peter H. Rossi, a sociologist on the faculty of the University of Chicago, as a consultant to provide over-all direction and guidance to the research, and Robert A. Dentler, an advanced graduate student in sociology, as project director

[*vii*]

to provide day-to-day supervision of research activities. The two senior members of the research team collected much of the original data underlying this report and collaborated closely in writing and revising the several versions of this final report.

The senior members of the research team engaged several others to help carry out the task. Nelson Polsby, then a graduate student in political science at Yale University, was appointed as research associate. Mr. Polsby carried a large part of the burden of field work, contributed much to the interpretation of findings, and wrote a portion of the initial report.

Patricia Denton collected and analyzed the mass of materials which form the basis for the two case studies reported in Chapters 6 and 7, although final responsibility for the interpretations rests with the senior authors.

Carolyn Huson served the project as general coordinator of collected data—coding and classifying it—and carried much of the burden of preparation of the statistical data contained in Chapters 2 and 5 and in the appendix. She also served as a trained observer at organization meetings and public hearings.

Peter C. Pineo collected, reviewed, and consolidated a wide range of published data on local population trends, crime rates, and economic conditions. A portion of his labors is reflected in Chapter 2 of this report. Barbara Whitlock, a British social service worker and an American Friends Service Committee Interne in Community Service, volunteered her services full time during the summer of 1958. She extracted materials from the Conference records and provided the staff with important documentary data. Marjorie Piercy served for more than a year as project secretary. A professional writer herself, Miss Piercy contributed valuable editorial suggestions and prepared the index as well.

Many individuals contributed to this study by their wholehearted voluntary cooperation, for which we are very grateful. Among these we should like to single out for special attention the following: Jessamine Cobb, Dean Swartzel, Douglass Turner, and Philip Hauser, all of whom served on an Advisory Committee for the project; James V. Cunningham, Executive Director of the Hyde Park–Kenwood Community Conference, who showed great patience and responsiveness to the needs of researchers; and Julia Abrahamson, former Executive Director of the Conference, who provided extraordinary assistance by reviewing the bulk of the manuscript and suggesting many corrections in factual items that strengthened the veracity of the narrative.

Irving Horwitz, former Conference Block Director, also reviewed portions of the study and made many valuable suggestions, as did William Frederick, former Chairman of the Conference Planning Committee. Commissioner J. Paul Holland and Donald Hansen of the Community Conservation Board took an active part in facilitating the work of the research team, as did D. E. Mackelmann.

The editing and preparation of the final version of this report was aided considerably by a Faculty Research Grant to the senior author from the Social Science Research Council. The Council's contribution to this report is hereby gratefully acknowledged.

Although we have had the benefit of the cooperation and willing assistance of the persons and organizations listed above, as well as many others, the responsibility for the content of this report rests solely on the authors. Without the aid we have received this report would not be possible. It is a pleasure to acknowledge this help.

Peter H. Rossi
Robert A. Dentler

Chicago: June, 1959

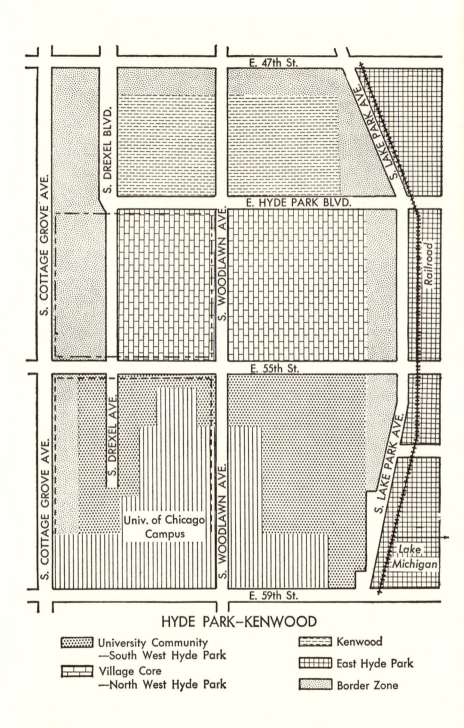

E. 47th St.

S. DREXEL BLVD.

E. HYDE PARK BLVD.

S. COTTAGE GROVE AVE.

S. WOODLAWN AVE.

S. LAKE PARK AVE.

Railroad

E. 55th St.

S. DREXEL AVE.

S. COTTAGE GROVE AVE.

S. WOODLAWN AVE.

S. LAKE PARK AVE.

Univ. of Chicago
Campus

Lake
Michigan

E. 59th St.

HYDE PARK-KENWOOD

University Community
—South West Hyde Park

Village Core
—North West Hyde Park

Kenwood

East Hyde Park

Border Zone

Contents

CHAPTER 1

Purposes and Procedures

*T*his study of social action—the deliberate organization of human effort for a common purpose—reports the drama of how citizens in a deteriorating community on the South Side of Chicago developed ways to halt blight by helping to create a workable plan for the conservation and renewal of the physical plant of this community.

Federal and state laws require that renewal planning spring in part from community-wide citizen participation and endorsement. A successful renewal program therefore hinges in part on the active involvement of local residents in the planning process. The laws make it clear that this involvement must include not only willing compliance with but also sharing in the planning. Grounded in the premise that decisions about the right of eminent domain and the expenditure of public funds must be made in the public interest, the laws specify that this interest must be shaped through open communication between officials and citizens.

The democratic character of this legislation is evident. Practical considerations also support use of citizen participation: public apathy might obstruct execution of a renewal program; citizen resistance could prevent political consensus where controversy deepened into conflict; and public confusion could prove costly in an already expensive undertaking. When the program is essentially one of conservation rather than of slum clearance, these possibilities become more salient, for neighborhood conservation requires residential stability and a social climate of optimism.

This study of citizen participation in urban renewal planning begins where urban renewal legislation leaves off. We have taken the effects of citizen participation as problematic, and we seek in this study to understand the part *actually* played by citizens in affecting renewal planning in a particular instance. Other researches under Demonstration Grants have been concerned with how to enlist the support and participation of citizens in an urban renewal effort.[1] In contrast, we will concern ourselves with the end product of participation, the contributions that citizens can make to an urban renewal plan.

To accomplish this end, we have had to consider the roles played by citizens in contrast to the parts played by the many other interests and organizations that can have a stake in renewal. Citizen participation is viewed as one among many elements active in the process of planning. Thus, in order properly to assess how citizens affect the planning process, we have been forced to enlarge our concern to include many other primary forces that have affected urban renewal in Hyde Park–Kenwood.

The central question of this study is what did citizens contribute to an urban renewal planning operation in Hyde Park–Kenwood. The term "citizen" is used in its broadest sense, as including all residents and the organizations through which they acted. In actual practice not all citizens could be studied. Only those who participated through the channels of participation that were established left a sufficient trace of their activities to be considered. Inactive citizens, undoubtedly the large majority, are a consideration in this report only as they are reflected through the views of the active participants.

At the other end of the participation scale, it is also difficult to distinguish between citizens and officials. Many of the influential residents of Hyde Park–Kenwood wore more than one hat. Lines of authority and responsibility can scarcely be expected to be clearly defined in the first urban renewal project.

Our solution to the difficulties of defining what is to be meant by the term "citizen" has been to use it loosely and to

---

1. William C. Loring, Frank L. Sweetser, and Charles F. Ernst, *Community Organization for Citizen Participation in Urban Renewal* (Cambridge, Mass.: Cambridge Press, Inc., 1957). William Bishop Nixon and Joseph M. Boyd, *Citizen Participation in Urban Renewal* (Nashville: Tennessee State Planning Commission, 1957).

study the actions of citizens mainly as reflected through the actions of those groups which undertook to speak on behalf of a general citizenry. For this and other reasons, we have given primary attention to the Hyde Park–Kenwood Community Conference, a mass-membership civic association widely recognized as speaking for and on the behalf of the citizens of Hyde Park–Kenwood. We recognize that the feelings and ideas of many of the residents of Hyde Park–Kenwood were not channeled through the Conference, and our study obviously neglects to some degree this unorganized group.

The Hyde Park–Kenwood Urban Renewal Plan is the first of its kind. Locally, it represents a step in the city's program of conserving and revitalizing the middle-aged communities of Chicago. Nationally, it is a new departure in attending to urban problems. The Housing and Home Finance Agency of the federal government reserved $28,312,062 for investment in this operation, and the City of Chicago reserved bond funds totaling $1,847,755. The City of Chicago is also committed to contribute grants-in-aid (public facilities) worth about $9 million. These funds are to be used to provide for additional recreational space, additional community facilities, expansion and strengthening of institutions in the area, modernization of an obsolete commercial pattern, rerouting of through traffic onto major arteries avoiding residential streets, and providing for new private housing and some public housing. More than 100 acres are scheduled for acquisition, within which approximately 644 parcels will be acquired for demolition, totaling some 5,900 dwelling units. About four-fifths of the community's physical plant will be left standing, subject to rehabilitation through about $30 million in private investments. An additional estimated $60 million will be invested by private developers of cleared land, including the University of Chicago.

The task of this study has been to analyze the part played by organized citizens in preparing this workable program. We have asked: How did renewal become important to sectors of the public? What did citizens seek to gain through renewal planning? How did citizens group themselves to achieve these goals?

These questions required that we look into the parts played by other groups, by the owners of commercial facilities in the community, by institutions such as the University of Chicago, which dominates this particular neighborhood physically and culturally, and by municipal officials.

The contribution of citizens was thus studied within a context of a set of intersecting interests. Each chapter of this study develops a selected facet of this context in an effort to treat citizen action in a rounded and sensitive fashion.

Citizen action tends to take on a style characteristic of a community's dominant cultural themes. Chapter 2 of this study gives a concise history of Hyde Park–Kenwood and reviews its social characteristics in order to gain a clear sense of some of the qualities unique to this community. This chapter shows how the faculty of the University of Chicago have settled in the area, attracting as fellow residents a population of highly educated professionals and businessmen. It describes as well the ways in which growth in the surrounding city have posed challenges for Hyde Park–Kenwood as it became transformed from an early railroad suburb into a metropolitan sector hemmed in on all sides by the growth of the city. For twenty years, the dominant cultural themes of Hyde Park have been liberalism and intellectualism complete with all the organizations and activities embodying these themes. Chapter 2 accounts for the emergence of these themes.

Renewal planning may be looked at as a form of decision-making, with certain gains and penalties accruing to each decision made along the path toward action. Chapter 3 takes this view, surveying the alternative roads to renewal open to planners and citizens under the circumstances laid down in Chapter 2. It limits the terms under which renewal planning appears to have been feasible in Hyde Park–Kenwood. Certain conflicts are endemic to renewal activities—for example, the conflict between the need for increased housing and the need for reduced population density in deteriorating areas. Similarly, there are economic limitations on any plan; middle-income housing may prove impossible to achieve without subsidies, for example. Such realities modify the course of citizen action in planning and have therefore been reviewed in advance.

The central part played by the University of Chicago in planning the renewal of Hyde Park–Kenwood is described in great detail in Chapter 4. This institution unquestionably as-

sumed the role of prime mover in the planning process. How
its leadership handled this role and the effects of this performance on citizen participation are of interest in themselves, for
it appears likely that conservation programs are most easily
achieved in communities which include one or more dominant
and wealthy institutions. This story is also essential to any
attempt to understand the forms that organized citizen activity took in Hyde Park.

The rather extraordinary character of Hyde Park–Kenwood is perhaps best understood through knowledge of the
civic association which its residents have formed and manned,
the Hyde Park–Kenwood Community Conference. This organization was the first group in the community to concern itself
effectively with planned renewal. It was the first to devise ways
of communicating about renewal to and with the residents of
the community. The machinery created by the Conference to
facilitate citizen participation is the major focus of this study;
it is described in Chapter 5.

A history of the Conference is contained in Julia Abrahamson's book, *A Neighborhood Finds Itself* (New York: Harper
& Brothers, 1959), upon which we have drawn for many details.
Our concern centers on the period from 1956 to 1958, when
renewal planning was under way. In these three years, the
Conference became the primary vehicle for citizen involvement
in planning.

The Conference stimulated citizen participation in the
planning process in order to so affect the planning process that
the planners would produce a plan more closely attuned to
the felt needs and desires of residents. Widespread citizen participation produced equally widespread public acceptance of the
plan. While it is clear that the Conference achieved much, it
also experienced failures. To gain insights into the factors
which contribute to success, we analyze in some detail two case
studies—one in which the Conference successfully played a role
of mediation between the citizens and the planners and another
in which its role was not successful. These case studies are
given in Chapters 6 and 7.

Urban renewal planning is only partly a local matter. The
city and the metropolitan region are also involved. The scene
of action in the final phases of planning during 1958 shifted

from Hyde Park to downtown Chicago. Chapter 8 analyzes the tactics of a metropolitan opponent to particulars in the local plan, the Cardinal's Committee on Conservation, an agency of the Catholic Archdiocese of Chicago. This chapter seeks to explain why this opposition, like the local opposition voiced by a Tenant and Home Owners Association, failed to modify the plan seriously.

Citizen participation represents but one side of a two-way exchange. Chapter 9 describes briefly the part played by city officials and municipal agencies in responding to local interests. In a way, the final significance of citizen action depends upon the attention public officials give to local expressions and demands. Our effort has been to consider this feature of city government in particular, rather than to review the total complex of administrative and legislative procedures. We have concerned ourselves with the way in which city officials responded to the interests of a particular community of voters and how they managed to reconcile this with the needs of the total metropolitan region.

This study is primarily analytical and secondarily descriptive. The analysis proceeds in terms of organizational antecedents and their consequences. Our key problems, for example, were as follows: (1) What organizational machinery was developed in Hyde Park–Kenwood to provide for the participation of citizens in urban renewal planning? (2) How, specifically, did citizen action affect the planning process? Did public involvement lead to production of a "better plan"? Did it increase public acceptance and understanding of planning? (3) Did citizen participation affect the response of city officials to the plan? (4) How in this instance did citizen participation fit into the total planning process? What functions did citizens assume in contrast to those assumed by other organized interests?

Chapter 10 summarizes the answers to these questions as we came to understand them. It also reaches toward the larger overriding question: What may be learned from the experience of Hyde Park–Kenwood that may be of use in other neighborhoods and communities?

Research Procedures

The research strategy selected was intended to trace the influences of citizen participation upon decisions made within the renewal planning process, as well as to achieve a clear image of the setting within which this contribution took place. Materials for the study were collected between May and October of 1958, *after* the plan itself had been released for public consideration and after many official hearings on the plan had been held throughout the local community. The strategy had to be one of careful reconstruction of the processes by which actions were taken and decisions made, although the final phases of the process could be observed directly.[2]

First, about eighty interviews were obtained with individuals reportedly most active in local planning and solving community problems. The interviewees were selected by the chain process of beginning with persons holding key committee positions, (for example, William Frederick, 1958 chairman of the Community Conference Planning Committee) and working outward to include coverage of individuals and groups referred to as influential by other respondents. Simultaneously, samples of organizational leaders were added directly to the interview list, as influential persons within the Conference, the South East Chicago Commission, and many other groups became known through the review of documents.

The interviews followed no set pattern of questioning but were each individually tailored to fit what was known in advance from documents or other interviews about the respondent's role in the urban renewal planning process. The interviews were

---

2. This is perhaps the only way a study of political participation could be made in any event if the decisions concern urban renewal in a very large metropolis, where the financial stakes are great and where every level of government is involved. Urban renewal programs are inherently political because they include coordinated allocation of scarce public resources, the use of governmental machinery, and choices between public and private purposes. Political actors are far more willing to be candid about their participation after a decision than during its deliberation.

The application for a demonstration grant was made by the Community Conservation Board early in 1957 at the suggestion of the Hyde Park–Kenwood Community Conference, who helped prepare the application. The Community Conservation Board subcontracted with the Conference to carry out the terms of the grant.

conducted under the usual guarantees of anonymity, either in the respondent's home or at his place of business. This guarantee of anonymity turned out to be a severe handicap in the analysis, since at many points it would be of great help to the reader in judging our analysis to know what were the specific sources for our statements. Because the respondents were so central in the events, it is not possible either to quote from the interviews or to paraphrase their content without in most cases revealing the identity of the person. Most of the interviews were about an hour long, with some lasting as much as three hours. The interviewers made notes during the interview which formed the basis of a reconstruction.

It is hard to evaluate these respondents for their completeness as a set. We believe we interviewed almost everyone who played an important role; only a few persons whom we attempted to interview refused to see us. Though some interviews were far from models of frankness, modesty, or objectivity, the majority of respondents were candid, objective, and informative. Some apparently enjoyed this opportunity to speak analytically and anonymously about their activities and those of others. We are grateful to those men and women, obviously busy and overburdened, who gave so freely of their time to tell us about the roles they and their organizations played in the urban renewal planning process.

Conference records of its Planning Committee, Board of Directors meetings, and Executive Committee meetings were examined systematically, and pertinent extracts were made. The Hyde Park *Herald* and other newspapers were handled in a similar manner, with coverage of issues going back to 1953. Metropolitan dailies were clipped, classified, and filed for general coverage of current renewal affairs.

The National Opinion Research Center contributed to the research about forty intensive interviews with Block Group leaders as well as a set of interviews with a sample of residents that included questions about individual knowledge of the renewal plan, participation in block organizations, and the like.

Staff observation of public information meetings, block group meetings, public hearings, committee meetings, and the City Council, from late April through the Council sessions of

September, 1958, provided a third means for gathering data on citizen participation.

An effort was made to trace visible changes in the contents of the renewal plans themselves, from their tentative beginnings in the Metropolitan Housing and Planning Council's publication *Conservation* (1953), through the official preliminary and final plans. Where possible, changes in the plans were related to efforts by citizens to effect such modifications.

Aside from supplementary maps, records, questionnaires, and administrative memoranda, all information collected in the study was transcribed, coded according to prescribed categories, and then reproduced in the number of copies required for rather elaborate cross-classification in a master file. The data were then filed by topic, person, and organization, providing easy access to all references on a given subject.

Because existing data seemed so contradictory, we were also forced to review the mass of published data on population, crime reports, housing surveys, and the like.

The different sources of data tended to complement each other. The documents provided the basic factual accounts of events, and the interviews and observations provided the insights into the meanings of events as seen by the participants. Of course, meanings and facts are almost inextricably intertwined in both documents and interviews, although one ordinarily prefers the former as a source of facts. The combination of interviews and documents enabled us to make what we consider to be reasonably accurate reconstructions of the course of events along with the affect and meanings given to those events by the major participants.

CHAPTER 2

The Community Setting

*T*he task of describing a community is a difficult one. Nevertheless, we must provide some clues to the nature of Hyde Park–Kenwood that will enable the reader to apprehend the character of this neighborhood and to judge its similarity to other urban neighborhoods of his acquaintance. This is the task of this chapter. Since, in the space we have, no definitive history of the area nor extended description of the present population or social structure can be given, the account presented here provides only gross outlines.

The residents of an urban neighborhood supply images of it varying with their experiences, needs, and life postures. The Census Bureau provides another approach, with standard categories and considerable precision. Other documentary sources provide ways of transcending fallible memories and partial perceptions, to give some historical depth to a description.

We attempt here to weave together the data provided by several modes of investigation. Our account is partly historical but concentrates on the events of the last decade, which brought Hyde Park–Kenwood to the threshold of urban renewal. The greater part of this chapter will be devoted to the description of Hyde Park–Kenwood as it was in the 1950's.

Specifically, we present in this chapter three major topics: first, a summary of the history of the area; secondly, a description of the economic and demographic changes which precipitated the community's efforts to renew itself; and, third, an attempt to characterize the social structure of the area,

The demographic analysis in this chapter was made by Mr. Peter Pineo of the Project staff. Dr. Beverly Duncan of the Chicago Community Inventory kindly gave freely of her advice, for which we are grateful.

paying special attention to the organizations that existed in the area since before 1949 (the year the Hyde Park–Kenwood Community Conference was founded).

Historical Origins

The planning of Hyde Park–Kenwood as a residential neighborhood began 100 years after the first settlement of the area by Europeans. In the 1850's Chicago already showed signs of becoming an important railway center. Fingers of growth crept out from the center along the major railroads, pushed by a population boom. Hyde Park was perhaps the first truly suburban settlement to the south of the Loop, largely influenced in its placement on the lake shore by the location of the main line of the Illinois Central.

The opening of a railway station at 54th Street and Lake Park Avenue in 1856 stimulated the growth of Hyde Park Village. A second station, opened in 1859 at 47th Street, was followed by the erection of the first set of mansions in Kenwood. Paul Cornell, a first-rank citizen of Hyde Park for many years, erected in 1857 a commodious frame hotel, Hyde Park House, east of the Illinois Central tracks at 53rd Street, where a cluster of hotels have been located ever since. Hyde Park Village was incorporated in 1861 and included a forty-eight square-mile area running as far south as Calumet City.

An era of great financial prosperity in Chicago following the Civil War gave City Hall sufficient optimism to plan in 1869 a ring of expensive parks, including Washington Park, which became the western boundary of Hyde Park, and Jackson Park, the southeastern boundary.

The Chicago fire of 1871 and the decade of land speculation and rapid urban growth which then occurred generated an explosive building up of Hyde Park and Kenwood. The first wave of extensive building took place in the 1870's. A second wave during the 1880's introduced apartment buildings in great number for the first time. Many of the 1880 structures were, incidentally, cheaply built and promptly became overcrowded.

What began as a village nestled against a double-line railroad was in 1885 a pleasantly dispersed community of single-family residences ranging from costly mansions to inexpensive cottages and farms, interspered with occasional two-story flats and three-story walk-up apartments, bordered by a handful of hotels near Lake Michigan and two handsome, heavily forested parks on the west and southeast. Patterns of future habitation and activity were already visible. During these first three decades a tennis club, a Kenwood Social Club, the Hyde Park Literary Society, a Lyceum and Philosophical Society, and similar local sources of adult education emerged and flourished. In 1890 this suburb announced itself the largest village in the world, the census of that year yielding a population count of 85,000.[1]

The conditions for engulfment by the metropolis were well under way by 1880, though hardly apparent from within Hyde Park. Rapid population growth, the extended limits of the Village to the south, and the location of manufacturing and processing industries to the south of Hyde Park underlay its ultimate absorption by the city.

The first indications of this fate came with the vote on the issue of annexation to the city in 1889. Many villagers opposed annexation on the grounds that existing liquor controls would not be enforceable, a point of view toward urban influence which has echoed persistently to the present. But the vote in the Calumet area (the southernmost sector of the Village) for uncontrolled liquor and for the benefits of municipal incorporation carried the day.

Because of the public parks and resort-like character of the former Village, Hyde Park was chosen as the site of the 1893 Columbian Exposition. In preparation for this event, streetcar lines along Cottage Grove Avenue (the western boundary) were extended to 63rd Street, where an elevated railroad reaching from the Loop was extended to the lake. Hyde Park sparkled between 1889 and 1893 with civic and commercial optimism, and land speculators and builders rapidly exploited vacant properties in anticipation of vast crowds of Exposition visitors. Apartment hotels were built in all sections of the former village core, particularly along the streets closest to the Illinois Central tracks and 55th Street.

---

1. That is, 85,000 in the forty-eight-square-mile village, but about 7,000 in the roughly two-square-mile tract that equaled the contemporary community of more than 70,000.

The disappointing turnout for the Exposition produced widespread temporary unemployment, and many of the apartment hotels passed into receiverships by 1895. The population growth of greater Chicago continued, however, and by 1900 additional vacant sections of central Hyde Park (specifically, Drexel Avenue, Hyde Park Boulevard, and the Cornell Avenue lake front) had been built up, chiefly with three-story walk-ups. These apartment houses contained spacious apartments and were well constructed; but, because land was at a premium, they were built so close together as to give some streets in Hyde Park the appearance of brick canyons. Later apartment houses continued this pattern of overuse of the land, accentuating its urban appearance.

The apartment building in Hyde Park took place in spurts until most of the readily available vacant land was exhausted around 1925. The initial wave of building sparked by the Columbian Exposition died out in the first decade of the new century. The building surge of the second decade was characterized by a vogue of "sunparlor apartments," adding more three-story walk-ups to Hyde Park. The last burst of construction from 1920 to 1924 consisted mostly of tall apartments along the lake front and some walk-ups inland. This all but completed the residential plant of the area.[2]

Retail and other commercial building coincided with these seven waves of physical growth from 1860 through 1924. This expansion took a form typical of Chicago. Retail shops strung themselves out in ribbon fashion along 47th, 53rd, and 55th Streets, slicing the grid plan into residential sectors rectangular in shape and bounded by shops on the north and the south sides. Businesses and shops further encircled the natural boundaries of the entire community by hugging the transportation routes—the streetcar lines along Cottage Grove on the west and the railroad tracks to the east. By 1925 business and commercial developments had settled into the positions they would occupy until redevelopment would alter radically their locations in the area.

Residential construction brought a population which was far from the bottom of the social heap. Kenwood developed as

2. After 1946 a handful of high-rise apartment buildings were added.

one of the top residential areas of the city, as attested to by its fine homes laid out in large plots on tree-lined avenues. Upper-middle-class businessmen and professionals settled into the spacious apartments in Hyde Park, and the apartment hotels close to the lake filled up with the families of the same economic bracket. Industrial workers and their families moved in along the business and commercial strips. Only a minute fraction of the population was Negro until the end of World War II.

Hyde Park–Kenwood was strongly conditioned by the institutions that settled in the area. In 1892 John D. Rockefeller made a gift to the University of Chicago of two strips of land one block wide and located on either side of the Midway. Construction of the University buildings was well under way by the time of the Columbian Exposition. Aided by this and other gifts from Rockefeller and under the guidance of William Rainey Harper, the University rapidly developed into one of the high-ranking universities in the United States. By the early twenties its place in the academic procession was close to the head, a position it has maintained since.

The University occupies a large block of land on the southern border of Hyde Park. Graduate students and faculty, now numbering 5,000 mostly live in Hyde Park. An additional 2,500 undergraduates live mainly in dormitories scattered over the campus, with some portion commuting from residences nearby or from other areas of the city.

Closely associated with the University are a cluster of seminaries whose faculty and students also contribute to Hyde Park's residential population. Among the other institutions which settled in the Hyde Park area are The American School, a famous correspondence school; George Williams College, once Chicago's YMCA college and now primarily a training school for YMCA workers; an Osteopathic hospital and school; and a social agency. In the southeastern corner of Hyde Park is located Chicago's famous Museum of Science and Industry. On the Midway are the headquarters of the American Bar Association, the Public Administration Service, the International City Manager's association, and the famous Sonia Schenkman Orthogenic School.

Although clearly overshadowed by the University of Chi-

cago, these institutions add to the impression of Hyde Park–
Kenwood as a national center of learning, research, and professional activity. In turn, the neighborhood provides the
institutions with the living arrangements for their personnel,
knitting the fates of neighborhood and institutions closely
together.

Hyde Park–Kenwood Today

Because each growth wave added its distinctive kind of
physical structures to Hyde Park and Kenwood, the total area
is far from homogeneous in appearance and occupancy. Indeed,
the neighborhood is perhaps best viewed as a set of sectors and
border zones, each set off from the other primarily by boundaries—the ribbonlike commercial strips, the railroad and the
main thoroughfares such as the Midway. We have been able to
distinguish four sectors plus a number of border zones formed
by these boundaries, each with its distinctive population and
physical appearance. (See Frontispiece Map.)

Starting from the north, the first sector, Kenwood, is the
most distinctive in appearance. Running from 48th Street to
Hyde Park Boulevard and from Drexel to Lake Park, Kenwood
is bounded by commercial property to the north and east and
by a complex of apartment dwellings on the west and south
sides. Within these natural walls, Kenwood emerged as a cluster
of very large, expensively built single-family dwellings penetrated at points by attached stone single-family dwellings and
three-story walk-ups. From 1890 through 1929 Kenwood became known as one of Chicago's favorite building grounds for
millionaires.[3]

Kenwood became an exclusive residential area in part because of its original land usage. The core was laid out as a

---

3. South Park Avenue, a street which connects the South Side with the
Loop, was planned to include large bridle paths to enable commuters to
gallop to their banks, law firms, and brokerage houses on LaSalle in quick
time. Open space in Kenwood was abetted by two factors; first, the
uniquely large individual properties purchased as settlings for the mansions,
and second, the curious duration of a Farmer's Field, extending several
square blocks, near the center of the sector, which under a "stubborn
will" was restricted in use as a cow pasture only, from its purchase in
1869 to release of the will through death in 1928.

garden estate in the 1860's, a single tract of property land-scaped to approximate the estates of landed proprietors in Ireland. Its owner, Dr. William B. Egan, intended to subdivide and sell similar properties nearby. Although his real estate scheme failed commercially, his plan to make the neighborhood an "aristocratic" one succeeded. More than a third of Kenwood today remains an area of elm-shaded streets lined with very large, expensive homes. Only the border streets show any deterioration.

A second sector might be called the University Community, located between 55th Street and the Midway (built as a vast carnival esplanade for the Columbian Exposition and serving as a natural southern barrier thereafter) and lying between Cottage Grove Avenue and the Illinois Central tracks. Inspection of the map will indicate the dominance of the physical plant of the University of Chicago over the extent of this sector. Surrounding the University buildings in this sector are clustered, as if for protection, a number of institutions—including churches, museums, special schools, and foundations—and blocks of single-family dwellings and apartment buildings.

One cluster of single-family dwellings is best known for the university and related professional attachments of its residents. "The Golden Square," as some call it, lies between University and Harper Avenues, from 55th Street to the Midway. This area contains well-built commodious dwellings, erected for the most part between 1880 and 1915. Although more than middle-aged, they have been well maintained; here the Hyde Park Improvement Association cleans the streets and alleys, supplementing city services on a private subscription budget of more than $15,000 annually.

In 1939 about 60 per cent of the University of Chicago faculty lived [4] within the University community sector, although most "old timers" on the faculty believed that the percentage in "those days" was closer to 90. As we shall show later on, this proportion has since declined, but the nature of the sector as the major habitat of the faculty has changed only slightly in more than two decades.

Unlike many metropolitan universities whose faculties com-

---

4. Computed from the telephone directory of the University for the academic year 1939-1940.

mute from the peripheral suburbs, the University of Chicago professors are housed within easy walking distance of the classrooms, laboratories, and offices. The University provides a rich cultural life through the activities centered on the campus and in the faculty community. Indeed, the University is often cited as the feature which kept Kenwood attractive to its wealthy population during the period from 1920 to the present, when the North Shore became the locus of the upper socio-economic class, in preference to once fashionable South Shore areas.

The cultural attraction—perhaps mostly a matter of potentialities, reflected prestige, and chance for contact with the academic community—not only held important segments of the Kenwood community intact; it also contributed directly to the growth of a colony of artists and bohemians in Hyde Park. The Columbian Exposition left a legacy of artist-citizens, who chose to remain in Hyde Park and parts of Kenwood long after the Fair was closed. The Loredo Taft Midway Studios were the most prominent result of this growth. (Taft's Studio later was used by the University of Chicago for instruction in the fine arts.) Gingerbread shacks built to house the souvenir stands, peanut vendors, and restaurants lined the path from the Illinois Central station to the Fair grounds. When the concessions left from 1893 to 1925, the buildings housed many of Chicago's most famous artists and bohemians, including Edgar Lee Masters, Theodore Dreiser, Carl Sandburg, Sherwood Anderson, and Thorstein Veblen. Built without electricity, central heating, or gas outlets, these one-story shacks became the center for a bohemian colony which extended toward the central areas of Hyde Park. The buildings persist shakily to this day, presently housing a miscellany of shops selling antiques, landscapes, and live bait and awaiting ultimate demolition under the Final Renewal Plan.

However, Kenwood and the University Community house only a minority of the total area's population, though their flavor and style dominate. The two other sectors contain the majority of the population. Lying along the lake front is East Hyde Park, segregated from the remainder by the Illinois Central tracks. Hyde Park–Kenwood as a whole contains about twenty hotels and about sixty apartment hotels, most of them

located in East Hyde Park. East Hyde Park has always consisted primarily of upper-income residents dwelling in spacious
luxury apartments or expensively serviced hotels. East Hyde
Park, compared to the rest of the area, includes a dispropor-
tionate population of widows and divorcees. In addition, it
has since 1920 attracted a growing proportion of professional-
class Jewish couples and families.[5]

The final sector—which we shall designate the "Village
Core"—is that falling roughly between Kenwood and the University Community, 55th Street to 51st Street (Hyde Park
Boulevard). This sector is least amenable to easy characterization, for it includes, as it has since the turn of the century,
long blocks of apartment houses along some of the thoroughfares, scattered collections of old frame dwellings left standing
since the 1880's, when the Village of Hyde Park had this sector
as its core, and a conglomerate of small businesses of all kinds.
This oldest section of the community has posed some of the
most difficult problems for renewal planning. It contains many
residents with strong identifications with the community; yet
its unplanned physical growth fostered the most extreme deterioration and provided open channels for in-migrants.

As a consequence, the Village Core developed considerable
ethnic and occupational heterogeneity. It houses a Roman
Catholic parish and parochial school and three Jewish congregations, and for a time it contained a Buddhist Church. Workers from the stockyards lived there along with hundreds of
skilled blue-collar and white-collar families, mixed in with professors, married graduate students and professionals. It also
had some institutions: George Williams College and the Chicago
Osteopathic Hospital and College have always been located in
the Village Core, the former since 1890.

Around the perimeter of Hyde Park–Kenwood and in between the sectors are areas best labeled as "border zones."
Though each border zone differs from the next, we may nevertheless consider the border zones separately, because the zones
do show common effects of certain social and ecological proc-

5. See Louis Wirth, *The Ghetto* (Chicago: University of Chicago Press,
Phoenix edition, reprint, 1956), pp. 257-261, for a full description of how
this area and related portions of Hyde Park served as migration outlets
for upwardly mobile, formerly ghetto-ized Jews in Chicago.

esses, and because each border is unlike the sector which it surrounds. Historically, 47th Street probably became the line of demarcation for Kenwood because the private estate of Dr. Egan, described earlier, had its gates and entry road situated there. This northern border street developed as a retail commercial strip as early as the turn of the century, at least along its northern side, although large apartment units lined the southern side.

This northern border and Lake Park Avenue, which adjoins the Illinois Central tracks to form an eastern border (exclusive of East Hyde Park) for Kenwood, were among the first portions of the community to experience physical deterioration, with the concomitants of declining property values, code violations, and exodus of stable segments of the population. Both borders suffered from contradictory land uses from an early period, foreshadowing their deterioration. On Lake Park Avenue land values and usage were determined by the adjoining tracks of the Illinois Central. Values declined as traffic increased from an average of ten trains daily in 1890 to about forty in 1956. The stone row dwellings interspersed with commercial and institutional sites and large apartment structures were never as desirable as those located on interior streets.

Another major border zone is constituted by Cottage Grove Avenue and Washington Park on the western edge of Hyde Park–Kenwood. Until the 1940's Cottage Grove Avenue served as a natural barrier to the expansion of the Negro "ghetto" to the west. Negroes did not cross this zone in significant numbers until after World War II. The physical characteristics of the Avenue contributed to a process of deterioration that had set in before the influx of Negroes, for Cottage Grove had long been zoned for commercial use to include gas stations, warehouses, wholesale outlets, and service shops.

The post-1940 Negro residential movement into Hyde Park–Kenwood penetrated and went beyond border zones of 47th Street, Lake Park, and Cottage Grove Avenues. The movements were patterned—at first, to fill these border areas and then to extend inward—especially in the northwest and southwest of the community—to a depth of one or two blocks. The community's southern border zone, the Midway, surrounded by

University-owned land, did not lend itself to use as an invasion route.[6]

Three border zones, then, and the partial border zones created by the commercial streets between the several sectors of the community are relatively alike in their unstable land uses, progressive deterioration, and support of transient and invading residential populations, and in their depressing effect on the housing areas immediately adjacent to them. They are also distinctively unlike the University Community, Kenwood, East Hyde Park, and the Village Core areas which they define and bound.

Table 2.1—Characteristics of Sectors and Zones of Hyde Park–Kenwood in 1950 *

	University Community	East Hyde Park	Kenwood	Village Core	Border Zones
Median years of schooling	14.0	12.6	12.4	12.2	11.9
Professional or technical workers	33%	22%	19%	20%	19%
Owner occupied	12	9	11	9	9
Widowed or divorced	12	19	15	14	13
Jewish (1946) †	17	51	40	53	53

Source: U.S. Census, 1950.

* Data in this table were obtained by averaging individual tract data by combining tracts along the following lines:
  University Community: Census tracts 617, 618, 619, and 620
  East Hyde Park: Census tracts 611, 612, 621, 622
  Kenwood: Census tracts 596, 597, 598, 599
  Village Core: Census tracts 608, 609, 610, 613, 614, 615, and 616
  Border Zones: Census tracts 596, 597, 608, 616

† Source of this estimate of Jewish population: Erich Rosenthal, *Estimated Jewish Population of Chicago, Illinois* (Chicago Community Inventory, University of Chicago, 1954).

The over-all characteristics of these four sectors and the border zones can be seen from the 1950 census data, as shown in Table 2.1. Unfortunately, it is not possible to rearrange the

6. As with border areas generally, however, the Midway, with its trees and broad parklike greens, is known locally as off-bounds after sundown for most university community students and families, because it has been the arena for muggings, purse-snatchings, and armed robberies on so many occasions—deeds often committed by criminals (particularly desperate dope addicts) who live south of Hyde Park in deteriorating sections of Woodlawn. At one time, University administrators sought to include in the renewal plans a scheme for widening 61st Street into an expressway, which would stand as a barrier to the south.

census area classifications to coincide exactly with the boundary lines as we have drawn them in the last few pages. Table 2.1 is made up by classifying census tracts into groups closely approximating the areas we have designated above. We have chosen 1950 as the base year in order to represent the situation before the major postwar changes occurred.

Hyde Park–Kenwood since World War II

The portrait of Hyde Park–Kenwood developed in the last few pages applies primarily to the period before 1950 when the community was predominantly upper middle class or better and almost entirely white. The dramatic population changes that began to occur in Chicago during World War II had their delayed impact on Hyde Park–Kenwood in the postwar period. These changes constituted a threat to the maintenance of the area at its prewar level of living.

The war brought to Chicago, as it did to all of the major northern cities, a tremendous stream of migrants from the southern states. A large proportion of the migrants were Negroes, who piled by the thousands into Chicago's "Black Belt" to the northwest of Hyde Park–Kenwood. In response, the areas of Negro settlement began to expand with gathering momentum when in 1947 the Supreme Court outlawed restrictive covenants.

In 1940 the borders of the "Black Belt" had reached within a mile of Hyde Park–Kenwood. By the census of 1950, the areas to the north and west of Kenwood were rapidly being consolidated as Negro neighborhoods and Hyde Park–Kenwood itself was in the process of being entered.[7] The Supreme Court decision had broken the dam, and the flood had begun to trickle along the border zones and down the commercial streets. In 1940 less than 4 per cent of the area residents were Negro. This increased but slightly in 1950, to 6 per cent, but then jumped tremendously to 36 per cent in 1956.[8] Furthermore, it is likely that the proportion of Negroes in the

7. O. D. Duncan and B. Duncan, *The Negro Population of Chicago* (Chicago: University of Chicago Press, 1957).

8. National Opinion Research Center, *The Hyde Park–Kenwood Urban Renewal Survey* (mimeographed, Chicago, 1956).

population has increased still further in the years since the 1956 estimate.

Between 1950 and 1956, 20,000 whites abandoned the area and 23,000 nonwhites moved in, according to the best estimates.[9] These are net migration figures which probably seriously underestimate the total amount of changeover in the area. The incoming Negroes were not evenly distributed throughout the area, but the pattern of entry was to fill up solid blocks, particularly in the northwest area of Hyde Park–Kenwood. The whites were crowded, as it were, into the east and south.

The most easily perceived characteristic of the newcomers was their color; but more important to the predominantly liberal, intellectually oriented white residents were the changes that accompanied their arrival. The density of Hyde Park–Kenwood increased as real-estate speculators crowded many more Negroes into the apartments vacated by whites. Parking became an increasing problem, and overtaxed municipal services could not keep the streets as clean as in the past. Other trends also tended to make the area less attractive as a residential neighborhood: the maintenance of the physical plant declined as landlords overcrowded their holdings and were confronted by less demand for services that whites took for granted.

In short, Hyde Park–Kenwood experienced "blight" as the class composition shifted toward the lower end of the spectrum. These changes can be seen dramatically in the shifts in population types occupying the area in the period 1950-1956.

In order to establish a base line against which recent changes in Hyde Park–Kenwood can be evaluated, we will first compare the area trends as of the decade 1940-1950 and then see how the area changed in the flood tide of transition during the period since 1950. Since the major sources of data were the censuses of 1940 and 1950 and a survey conducted by the National Opinion Research Center in 1956, the analysis is primarily in terms of gross population and socio-economic characteristics. These data do not reflect how these changes were received by the established residents. For these reactions we will have recourse to the interviews with informants (see Appendix).

9. Other estimates range as high as 28,400 for the net out-migration of whites.

In comparing the study area with the city, and also in measuring the strength of certain trends, we use an "index of dissimilarity" that reflects the differences between two frequency distributions.[10] An example is given below:

Percentage in Various Occupational Groups, 1940

	Hyde Park	Chicago	Absolute Difference
Professional, Technical, etc.	20%	8%	12%
Managers, official, proprietors	16	8	8
Clerical and sales	33	27	6
Other (operatives, manual, service)	31	57	26

$$\frac{\text{Sum of the absolute differences}}{2} = 26 = \text{Index of Dissimilarity}$$

The index of 26 indicates a considerable difference between the study area and the city with regard to occupational status, stating that at least 26 per cent of the area's workers would have to change to another occupation status for the two distributions to become identical.

Hyde Park–Kenwood 1940–1950

In 1950 the median family income for the total area was estimated at $4,312. In comparison with the city median at this time ($3,956), Hyde Park–Kenwood was 9 per cent higher.

10. The index of dissimilarity has certain advantages and disadvantages. Its major advantage is that it is sensitive to differences not only of major tendency but also in the amount of variability between the categories of the distributions. Its major fault is that it is dependent upon the number of categories used—and generally speaking, the more categories the higher the index, within limits. As well, it is wholly a descriptive technique, not lending itself to statistical inference tests. Care must be taken, above all, in comparing the indices produced by two different measures, such as years of schooling and occupational type. Without controlling the number of categories used, it would be possible to misrank the measures in terms of the extent to which they are the *essence* of the Hyde Park–Kenwood area's distinctiveness. For example, using seven rather than four categories of occupation type in 1940 produces an index of 29 rather than 26. However, the change is not sufficient to raise the measured dissimilarity of occupational type beyond that of years of schooling. The index ranges between 0—in the case of identical distributions—and 100—in the limiting case where all of one group falls in categories in which none of the other group does.

The Hyde Park section of the study—roughly the area to the south of Hyde Park Boulevard—was over 20 per cent higher than the city as a whole, even with nonwhites included. Hyde Park–Kenwood was in 1950 an area of demonstrably high socio-economic status. This observation is reinforced by indices of dissimilarity of roughly 26 for occupational type and 28 for years of school completed.

These indices may be compared in magnitude with, for example, the age distribution of the area. The study area was in both 1940 and 1950 somewhat "older" than the rest of the city, but the indices of dissimilarity are only 8 for 1940 and 7 for 1950.

This matter of high socio-economic status was probably the most distinctive characteristic of the area and an extremely important element in the renewal problem. Among other things, it turned the nonwhite in-migration into a class problem, since it was impossible for Chicago's Negro population to "send in" many migrants matching the average Hyde Park–Kenwood resident in socio-economic status.

The community had two other distinctive features. In the first place, the population was slightly older than the city as a whole. For example, in 1950 20 per cent of the women in the area were widowed or divorced, while only 16 per cent in the city as a whole were. Secondly, the population has certain characteristics of a university community. There are many single people, for instance—29 per cent of the males and 25 per cent of the females in the study area, as compared to 26 per cent male and 21 per cent female in the city in 1950.

There is an extremely high tenancy rate (in 1950 only 9.4 per cent of the units in the area were owner-occupied, as opposed to 29.8 per cent in the city) and a relatively high mobility rate (only 78.8 per cent reported the same dwelling place in 1950 as 1949 in the area, while 87.2 per cent did in the city). Tenancy and mobility are characteristic of a university population.

A few other observations support the statement of the high social and economic character of the neighborhood. The indices of dissimilarity in contract rent paid in the area and the city were 34 in 1940 and 30 in 1950. Phrased another way, the median rent in the area was $41.20 in 1940 and $50.50 in 1950;

in the city it was $31.51 in 1940 and $44.08 in 1950. Secondly, the values of the few single-family dwellings in the area were extremely high. The indices of dissimilarity with the city were 40 in 1940 and 34 in 1950.

The physical characteristics of the dwelling units in the study area can easily be inferred from the high tenancy rate. In 1950, 91 per cent of the dwelling units in the area were apartments in structures housing three or more family units, as compared to only 60 per cent in the city as a whole. The same situation pertained in 1940. Despite the fact that we use only two categories in this table, the indices of dissimilarity for structural type are high—32 for 1940 and 31 for 1950. Similarly, the dwelling units in the area were provided with central heating in 98 per cent of all cases, while this was true for only 72 per cent (1940) and 77 per cent (1950) in the city as a whole.

Using the 1950 census definition of "dilapidated" which included dwelling units with no running water or no bath, 16 per cent of the dwelling units in the study area were so classified, in comparison to 20 per cent in the city as a whole. In some areas of the city the percentage dilapidated in 1950 was as high as 76 per cent.

In age the buildings resembled the rest of Chicago: 63 per cent of those in the city as a whole were constructed prior to 1920, compared with 64 per cent of those in the study area. (However, recent construction of high-rise apartment buildings near the lake may have altered this average.) Hyde Park–Kenwood west of Illinois Central tracks is somewhat older, with nearly 75 per cent of all dwelling units more than thirty-eight years old, which means that the buildings in the core area are roughly the same age as in the bulk of those tracts which constituted the Negro "ghetto" in 1950. By a similar argument, dilapidation rates ought to be higher for the area "west of the tracks." In fact, when the three most northeasterly tracts on the lake are excluded, the dilapidation rate does climb to 18 per cent.

The number of individuals per dwelling unit for the study area was lower than the city median in both 1940 and 1950. The indices of dissimilarity for the study area were 14 in 1940 and 17 in 1950. In both cases Hyde Park–Kenwood had smaller numbers than the city as a whole. This may not be taken to be a measure of crowding, however, because dwelling units differ in size. Crowding may be defined as having more than one and a half persons per room in a dwelling unit. In 1940 this was the case for 16 per cent of the dwelling units in the study area and 17 per cent in the city. In 1950 it was the case for 14 per cent in the study area and 15 per cent in the city.

The changes that occurred in Hyde Park–Kenwood before the heavy influx of the 1950's can yield a base line for the measurement of the impact of the latter. All the indices of changes point to one conclusion: between 1940 and 1950 Hyde Park–Kenwood was becoming more like the rest of Chicago. The indices of dissimilarity show a fairly consistent tendency to decrease between 1940 and 1950.

Of course, these decreases can be brought about in two ways. First, the community may have declined from its high position. Secondly, Chicago as a whole may have risen more sharply than Hyde Park–Kenwood. Undoubtedly both these processes contributed to the declines in the values of the indices. Whatever the cause, relatively speaking, Hyde Park–Kenwood was not in 1950 as distinctively a high-status area as in 1940. For example, the index of dissimilarity for schooling dropped from 31 to 28, that for rent from 34 to 30, that for value of house from 40 to 34, and that for age structure from 8 to 7. Only the indices for occupation type do not show a drop, remaining the same for 1940 and 1950.

The changes since 1950 have pushed Hyde Park–Kenwood further in the direction of a loss in socio-economic distinctiveness. The most dramatic shift was, of course, in racial composition. As was mentioned, in 1950 the study area was 6.1 per cent nonwhite. In 1956, according to our best estimate,[11] the percentage of nonwhites increased to 36.7 per cent. In numbers, 23,162 nonwhites had entered the area, while 19,989 whites left. The total population increased from 71,689 to 74,862.[12]

---

11. Estimates from National Opinion Research Center, *op. cit.*

12. Estimates received from the Chicago Area Transportation Study differ somewhat, indicating 44.9 per cent nonwhite in 1956. This estimate is not as reliable as the N.O.R.C. Survey, being based on a sample one-fifth the size of the N.O.R.C. sample.

The distribution of nonwhites for areas within the neighborhood is shown in Table 2.2. Some areas have become virtually 100 per cent nonwhite, while others actually lost nonwhites between 1950 and 1956. Those tracts that are now over

Table 2.2—Nonwhite Population by Subcommunities and Tracts: Hyde Park–Kenwood, 1950 and 1956 *

Subcommunity	Tract	Percentage Nonwhite of Total Population 1950	1956
University Community	617	16%	61%
	618	4	12
	619	3	1
	620	9	3
East Hyde Park	611	1	2
	612	2	6
	621	1	5
	622	1	7
Kenwood	596	20	94
	597	3	70
	598	5	46
	599	5	32
Village Core	608	31	95
	609	3	73
	610	2	13
	613	4	7
	614	4	31
	615	1	52
	616	6	83
Border Zones	596	20	94
	597	3	70
	608	31	95
	616	6	83

* Source: U.S. Census 1950: National Opinion Research Center, *The Hyde Park–Kenwood Urban Renewal Study* (Mimeographed, Chicago, 1956).

50 per cent nonwhite are all located in the extreme west and north of the area—the parts adjacent to the Chicago Negro "ghetto." Those that lost nonwhites are at the other extreme geographically, located between the University and the lake.

Given this major shift in population type, one might expect large effects on the social and economic characteristics of the area. That there were some changes toward a downgrading of the area is clear from Table 2.3. *But these changes are in the same direction and of the same magnitude as the changes that were taking place in the area before the influx of the Negro newcomers.* In short, the in-migration of Negroes appears to have only accelerated changes which already were underway in the decade 1940–50. Note that the indices shown in Table 2.3

Table 2.3—Indices of Dissimilarity between 1940 and 1950, 1950 and 1956: Hyde Park–Kenwood

CHARACTERISTIC	INDEX OF DISSIMILARITY	
	1940–1950	1950–1956
Age	6.2	7.5
Type of Structure	.4	1.1
Number of persons per unit	9.9	3.6
Contract rent	22.0	28.0

compare Hyde Park–Kenwood with itself at two points in time—not the area with the city, as in the previous indices shown in this chapter.

In comparing the two sets of indices in Table 2.3, it is important to bear in mind that the two time periods are not equal. The index number for the earlier period covers a time span of ten years, while the index for the later period covers only six years. Hence the difference between the two periods are to some degree larger than they actually appear in this table.

In all cases the area shows some changes owing to, possibly, the nonwhite in-migration. Trends in age, type of structure, and contract rent are accelerated, while the trend toward less persons per unit is arrested. But the indices for 1950 to 1956 indicate that the area has not undergone changes much greater than a community of this sort might normally experience.

Despite the lack of comparability between the 1940 and 1950 census data and the 1956 Survey data with regard to measures of socio-economic class, we may gain some insight from Table 2.4. Data were collected for household heads only in the 1956 Survey, while the census tabulates occupations for all employed persons. Table 2.4 shows that there is a vast difference between white and nonwhite, but it must also be noted that Hyde Park–Kenwood nonwhites are of relatively high status: the percentage in the professional and technical group (8 per cent) exceeds the 1950 city nonwhite percentage (3.6 per cent) by a large enough margin to override problems arising from the data deficiencies mentioned above. Moreover, the similarity of the percentages of nonwhites in clerical and sales occupations (12 per cent for Hyde Park–Kenwood in 1956; 12 per cent for the city in 1950)—given that the inclusion of working wives and other nonfamily heads should increase this category—indicates higher socio-economic status for the nonwhites in Hyde Park–Kenwood than in the city as a whole.

Table 2.4—Occupational Distribution of Family Heads in Work Force: Hyde Park–Kenwood, 1956 *

	White	Nonwhite
Professional, technical and kindred	34%	8%
Managers, officials and proprietors	17	4
Clerical and sales	21	12
Other (operatives, manual, service)	27	76

* Source: National Opinion Research Center, op. cit.

We have strong grounds for assuming, as we show later on, that the whites who left the study area between the years 1950 and 1956 were not a random sample of the population. Indications are that the groups lower in socio-economic status tended to out-migrate. This means that, despite the wide gap between white and nonwhite occupational status shown in the above table, the real gap is reduced by the fact that the whites the Negroes replaced were not of as high status, and that the nonwhites entering are of a socio-economic status higher than the average Chicago nonwhite.

Further clues to recent changes in the Hyde Park–Kenwood area can be obtained by considering information on retail sales. Unfortunately, the only data available [13] compare the years 1948 and 1954, which bracket the period of heavy in-migration of the Negro newcomers. Retail sales in the area from 1948 to 1954 showed only a 14 per cent increase, as opposed to an increase of 17 per cent in the city as a whole. Presumably this is as expected, given the known slight drop in the socio-economic differential between the study area and the city.

There were also changes in types of establishments from 1948 to 1954. While the city increased in total number of outlets for apparel, furniture, automobiles, buildings, and drugs,

13. Chicago Community Inventory, *Chicagoland's Retail Sales* (Chicago: University of Chicago).

Hyde Park–Kenwood declined. The number of liquor stores in the city tended to decrease, but those in the study area increased; and, while the city changed little in number of eating and drinking places, the study area increased. The drop in the number of food stores in the city was more or less matched within the study area, but the gain for the city in the number of gasoline service stations and stores of the general merchandise group was not equaled in the study area. Finally, the group called the "other retail," including jewelry stores, increased in the study area more than in the city.[14]

In terms of type of retail sales outlets, then, the study area changed to become more like the rest of the city. The mean percentage difference by category between the study area and the city dropped from 9.3 per cent in 1948 to 8.2 per cent in 1954. Again, some of the distinctiveness of the neighborhood appears to have been lost.

For the residents of the area a striking indicator of its deterioration was a perceived increase in the crime rate. Indeed, the signal for one of the significant organizational efforts, the establishment of the South East Chicago Commission, was the robbery and attempted rape of the wife of a University of Chicago faculty member. Unfortunately, it is difficult to document the change in the Hyde Park–Kenwood area's crime rates that accompanied the shift in population composition. The crime data available are of doubtful validity [15] and can be clearly related to the Hyde Park–Kenwood community only for the period after 1952.[16]

According to Don Blackiston of the South East Chicago Commission staff, Hyde Park–Kenwood had fairly heavy crime

14. The figures compared in the above discussion are the percentage that one type is of the total number of outlets in the area. Thus, the actual number of eating and drinking places in the study area decreased, but the percentage of all outlets which fall in this category increased.

15. Recent articles in the Chicago *Sun-Times* (December, 1958) indicate that some fairly large proportion of offenses do not get reported as such from the precincts to the central statistical offices of the Chicago Police Department.

16. The 6th Police District includes the Hyde Park–Kenwood area plus a triangle to the north of the community, extending to 39th Street from Cottage Grove Avenue to the Lake. Since this additional area is one whose crime rates can be expected to be very heavy, the data for the total police district cannot be used.

rates for some time previous to 1950 because it was easily accessible to the criminal elements on the South Side. The community has been since the 1930's a "victim area" to which criminals come to find valuables to steal. The 6th Police District, which includes Hyde Park–Kenwood, has frequently been listed as having the second highest crime rate in the city, topped only by the Wabash police district on the South Side.

Since 1952 statistics have been available for various subsections of the Hyde Park–Kenwood area; they are shown in Table 2.5. The data document a substantial decline of 29 per cent in total offenses reported to the police in that period. Note

Table 2.5–Crimes Reported to the Police: Hyde Park–Kenwood, 1953–1957 *

	TOTAL OFFENSES (NOT INCLUDING RAPE OR HOMICIDE)					
	1953	1954	1955	1956	1957	Decline 1953–1957
Hyde Park–Kenwood	2,298	1,983	1,712	2,013	1,632	29%
Kenwood (47–51st: Cottage Grove to Lake Park)	588	543	508	600	460	22
Old Village (51st to 55th: Cottage Grove to Lake Park)	729	710	614	753	593	19
University Community (55th to 60th: Cottage Grove to the I.C. tracks)	591	453	377	366	339	43
East Hyde Park (area east of I.C. tracks)	390	277	213	294	240	38

* Source: Southeast Chicago Commission tabulations supplied by Don Blackiston.

that the largest declines are in East Hyde Park and the University Community—a tribute, perhaps, to the efforts of the South East Chicago Commission's law-enforcement activities.

Although the statistics on crime in Hyde Park–Kenwood leave the most pertinent questions unanswered, it is fairly clear that at the height of the influx of newcomers into the community its crime rates were very high. It also appears that crimes have declined since that time.

In sum it appears that Hyde Park–Kenwood slipped somewhat in its status as a desirable upper-middle-ciass neighborhood from 1950 to 1956. While the changes were not so great as to radically alter the character of the community, they were sufficient to cause considerable concern to the residents and to the institutions located therein.

Who Left?

Between 1950 and 1956 at least 20,000 residents left the area, to be replaced by others. Additional thousands have undoubtedly left the area in the last three years. Given the diversity of population types in Hyde Park–Kenwood and the concentration of the invasion in particular sections of the area, we may raise the question: Whom did the newcomers replace?

Only an oblique answer can be provided to this question, since it is no longer possible to observe directly those who have migrated. However, it is possible to characterize each of the nineteen census tracts in Hyde Park–Kenwood according to the increase in the nonwhite population of the tract which was experienced in the period 1950–1956. By contrasting the 1950 characteristics of low- and high-grain tracts, we may infer the population which was replaced by the newcomers. The specific technique we shall employ here is to correlate between the percentage gain in the Negro population 1950–1956 and social characteristics of the nineteen census tracts of Hyde Park–

Table 2.6—Correlations of Per Cent Increase in Nonwhites 1950–1956 with Social Characteristics of Tracts in 1950

Tract Social Characteristic	Correlation with per cent increase in nonwhite
Persons per regular household	+.72
Per cent in regular household	+.63
Per cent Jewish (1946)*	+.38
Sex ratio (males per 100 females)	+.35
Per cent dwellings with 1.51 or more persons per room	—.07
Median rent	—.14
Per cent owner occupied	—.16
Per cent dwelling units with no bath or dilapidated	—.27
Median income	—.36
Per cent professional or technical	—.42
Median years of schooling	—.46
Per cent widowed	—.54
Per cent over 25 years of age	—.58

* Per cent Jewish for 1946 was obtained from Eric Rosenthal, *Jewish Population of Chicago, Illinois* (Chicago: The College of Jewish Studies, 1952) reprinted in *Estimated Jewish Population of Chicago and Selected Characterstics, 1951* (Chicago Community Inventory, University of Chicago, 1954). Rosenthal's study is based on the distribution of Jewish surnames.

Kenwood. A high positive correlation between a characteristic and the percentage gain indicates that the nonwhite in-migrants were particularly likely to move into tracts with that characteristic; a negative correlation means the opposite.

Table 2.6 presents the correlation coefficients, from which several inferences may be drawn. First, migration has not been heavy to the tracts of highest socio-economic status. The tracts containing the highest median incomes and heaviest proportions of professional and technical workers, and with high levels of formal schooling, gained the least in proportion nonwhite in this period. Migration was heaviest to tracts with regular (i.e., full families) households, of fairly young age, and with large proportions of Jews.

In short, migration concentrated on the apartment house areas in Kenwood, the Village Core, and the border zones and made no appreciable inroads on East Hyde Park or the University Community.

Nor was the migrating primarily to those tracts with dilapidated units. It was to tracts with fairly good housing and rentals not much lower than average.

There are indications in the above data that the entering nonwhites replaced those elements in the population of Hyde Park–Kenwood that were neither at the top nor at the bottom of the local socio-economic pyramid. Furthermore, the invasion did not by 1956 make serious inroads on the population elements that set the tone for Hyde Park—the University Community and East Hyde Park.

Trends in the Location of
University of Chicago Personnel

The University of Chicago is the largest local employer in the Hyde Park–Kenwood area. Exclusive of nonacademic employees, some 1,200 persons are employed at present as either faculty or research workers on a professional level. More than 800 persons are employed as full-time faculty.

Despite all myths to the contrary, University personnel remained remarkably stable in their preference for Hyde Park–Kenwood as a residential area. For the faculty member or the researcher the community offered many advantages: location, relatively inexpensive housing, congenial society, and good schools.

Although faculty and administration became very much alarmed over the changes in the neighborhood that took place in the 1950's, they did not translate this alarm into a mass exodus, as Table 2.7 indicates. Of every category of academic employee distinguished in that table more than 70 per cent lived in Hyde Park–Kenwood or adjacent Woodlawn (a community

Table 2.7—Residential Dispersion of University of Chicago Personnel *

	University Community	Wood-lawn	Village Core	East Hyde Park	Ken-wood	Border Zones	Else-where	(N)
			PROPORTIONS LIVING IN					
A. All Faculty								
1939	57%	13%	10%	3%	0.3%	0.3%	16%	(294)
1947	49	13	11	3	3	2	19	(373)
1951	43	20	9	3	3	1	19	(401)
1957	45	11	12	4	5	0.2	22	(437)
B. Medical Faculty								
1939	55	15	5	8	0	2	15	(100)
1947	51	13	8	1	2	3	22	(91)
1951	44	15	10	5	2	1	24	(107)
1957	37	10	12	9	4	1	28	(125)
C. Deans & Department Chairmen								
1939	67	7	7	7	2	0	12	(44)
1947	65	4	8	4	6	0	14	(51)
1951	62	14	9	2	2	0	13	(57)
1957	60	7	11	3	5	0	13	(61)
D. Administrative Personnel								
1939	45	9	18	0	0	0	27	(11)
1947	38	15	8	0	0	0	31	(13)
1951	35	12	0	0	0	0	53	(17)
1957	29	10	10	0	0	5	47	(21)

* The data for this table are derived from the University of Chicago Telephone Directory for the years 1939, 1947, 1951 and 1957. A fifty per cent sample was taken of all faculty members who had appointments as instructor or higher ranks, and a hundred per cent sample was taken of deans, administrative personnel, and department chairmen. For every group, the requirement was made that the individual had to have an on-campus extension to be included in the study, thus eliminating personnel at the Argonne Laboratory and like installations off the campus.

Definitions of the residential areas follow the usage set down earlier in this chapter. "Administration" includes members of the Board of Trustees who are employed by the University and heads of Administrative units—e.g., Bursar, Comptroller, vice presidents of the University and the like. "Deans" includes only full Deans (i.e., not associate or assistant).

The medical faculty includes members of the following departments: Medicine, Psychiatry, Radiology, Pharmacology, Surgery, Obstetrics, Pathology, Pediatrics, and staff members affiliated with the Ben May Laboratory for Cancer Research.

The medical faculty are included in the tabulations for "all faculty."

directly to the south of the Midway). Only the administrative personnel showed any inclination to leave the area.

In 1939 more than four out of every five faculty members lived in Hyde Park–Kenwood and about three out of five lived in the University Community sector.[17] In 1957 these proportions had declined somewhat: four out of five still lived in Hyde Park–Kenwood or nearby Woodlawn and a little less than half lived in the University Community. Considering that the faculty had in the meantime increased by about a third and that the amount of housing available in the University Community is a fixed quantity, these figures represent an over-all stability in location that is quite remarkable.

Within the total group of University employees there are two subgroups that show trends away from the community. Medical personnel declined in residential attachment to the community from 85 per cent to 72 per cent. Although the numbers are very small, the sharpest drop in attachment to Hyde Park–Kenwood was seen among the administrative personnel, 27 per cent of whom lived out of the area in 1939, increasing to 47 per cent in 1957.

The findings of Table 2.7 are worth close scrutiny because myth has it that the faculty were leaving Hyde Park in considerable numbers during this period. Actually, it was the administration and the medical school faculty that showed mild signs of exodus, indicating the salience of these two groups to the University administration, whose movements were oversensitively reported as mass withdrawal.[18] Furthermore, whatever withdrawal has taken place of recent years seems primarily an extension of long-term trends that preceded the influx of Negroes in the postwar period. It should also be noted that few faculty members ever lived in the areas that experienced the greatest changes in population composition.

_____

17. Indeed, 46 per cent of the faculty lived in the area known as the "Golden Square."

18. Obviously, these data only pertain to net withdrawals from Hyde Park–Kenwood. If a professor left the University of Chicago to go elsewhere because of the change in the environment, this would not show in these net figures, especially if his replacement came to live in the Hyde Park–Kenwood area. The findings of Table 2.6, however, testify against any strong trend for the area having become so unattractive to the faculty that large proportions left for other parts of Chicago.

The statistics on residential stability shown in Table 2.7 are primarily net measures showing the location of faculty members at particular points in time. While the distribution of personnel may be fairly stable, the apparent stability may mask a great deal of change in particular persons. Indeed, one of the main reasons that the University of Chicago administration became particularly concerned with neighborhood conservation was that the deterioration of the neighborhood was a major factor in the loss of vital personnel.

In order to throw some light on this process, we computed the loss of faculty personnel through resignation, death, or dismissal for three periods of time. The resulting data are shown in Table 2.8. The data do not substantiate the idea of a

Table 2.8—Losses of University of Chicago Faculty Personnel 1939–1940 to 1940–1941, 1947–1948 to 1948–1949, and 1953–1954 to 1954–1955 *

Rank in the Earlier Period	PROPORTIONS LEAVING THE UNIVERSITY DURING					
	1939–1940 to 1940–1941		1947–1948 to 1948–1949		1953–1954 to 1954–1955	
	%	(N)	%	(N)	%	(N)
Instructor	15	(188)	27	(194)	22	(132)
Assistant Professors	7	(121)	15	(252)	15	(223)
Associate Professors	3	(110)	4	(158)	2	(184)
Professors	2	(157)	4	(218)	5	(260)
All Ranks	7	(576)	13	(822)	10	(799)

* The figures in this table were computed by comparing the two telephone directories issued by the University of Chicago for the periods in question. Names which appeared in the first directory but not in the second were assumed to have either resigned, been dismissed or died. Since most faculty members with ranks of associate or full professor have tenure rights, the losses of personnel in these two ranks are due only to death or resignation. Instructors and assistant professors do not have tenure and hence the losses of these categories also contain dismissals. Computations were made including only persons holding the titles shown above and having an on-campus telephone extension, thus eliminating personnel at the Argonne National Laboratory and similar attached research installations.

substantial exodus of faculty members during the height of the influx of Negroes into Hyde Park–Kenwood. In 1939–1940 to 1940–1941, 7 per cent of the faculty left the University. The corresponding figure for the period 1947–1948 to 1948–1949 is 13 per cent and for 1953–1954 to 1954–1955 it is 10 per cent. Although the rate is considerably higher for the last two periods as compared with the first, the highest rate is for the period *before* the heavy influx of the new population group.

There is some slight evidence that full professors were most likely to leave during the latest period under study, but the difference is hardly large enough to be free from idiosyncratic fluctuation.

It would have been best to compare these turnover rates with those from a comparable university which was not beset with the same neighborhood problems. Undoubtedly the increase in the rate of leaving the University of Chicago would have been larger in the later periods than in the earlier periods because of the generally greater mobility of the academic profession in the postwar period of great expansion in higher education. Unfortunately, similar figures for another university were not available.

Table 2.9—Losses of University of Chicago Faculty Personnel by Area of Residence: 1939–1940 to 1940–1941, 1947–1948 to 1948–1949, and 1953–1954 to 1954–1955 *

	PROPORTIONS LEAVING THE UNIVERSITY		
AREA OF RESIDENCE DURING EARLIER PERIOD	1939–1940 1940–1941 % (N)	1947–1948 1948–1949 % (N)	1953–1954 1954–1955 % (N)
University Community	7 (316)	13 (411)	9 (346)
Woodlawn	10 (80)	14 (122)	19 (137)
Village Core	7 (60)	13 (78)	13 (95)
Kenwood	17 (6)	18 (22)	0 (26)
Rest of Hyde Park–Kenwood	17 (29)	11 (35)	14 (28)
Elsewhere	13 (75)	16 (153)	11 (164)

* See note to Table 2.8 for data source.

A breakdown of rates of leaving by subareas of the Hyde Park–Kenwood community, as in Table 2.9, indicates that only residents of nearby Woodlawn show a consistent increase over time in the number of faculty residents leaving the University.[19] Woodlawn was experiencing at this time a heavy influx of non-whites and Puerto Ricans. The other areas in Table 2.9 show no consistent pattern of increase or decrease over time in the number of faculty members leaving the University of Chicago.

In short, although the University administration saw deterioration of the surrounding neighborhood as a threat to the

19. Most faculty living in this area occupied addresses in the 6000 blocks.

maintenance of the institution, through its effects on the faculty, the effects of neighborhood deterioration were not visible by 1954 either in the rate of leaving the University of Chicago or in the residential distribution of the faculty in 1957. How much of a subjectively perceived threat this was can be seen from the fact that all of our respondents connected with the University believed neighborhood deterioration had meant the loss of important personnel and had dispersed those remaining among the other neighborhoods of Chicago.

Organization and Political Characteristics

Given its institutions and the high socio-economic level of its residents, it is not surprising to find that Hyde Park–Kenwood has always supported a dense network of organizations. We would expect that any upper-middle-class neighborhood would be well organized. The presence in the area of the University of Chicago and other educational institutions strengthened this tendency by bringing to the area faculty families with more than usual interest in cultural and political affairs. In turn, the presence of this intellectually oriented component attracted to the area a population that shared these interests.

Although it is hard to judge whether Hyde Park–Kenwood is "organized" more than neighborhoods of comparable social-economic level, it is certainly the local consensus that this is so, as the following headlines and banner front, two-page advertisement appearing in the seventy-fifth-anniversary (1956) issue of the Hyde Park *Herald* would indicate:

31 ORGANIZATIONS—3,000 MEETINGS A YEAR!
AND WE ALL BELIEVE IN HYDE PARK

We've heard many Hyde Parkers say we are not only the world's most organized community, we are organized too much. That is why we want to pause a moment, review, and see just what our highly organized community has accomplished in the past.

Although the earliest settlers founded many organizations, those which survive to this day have been founded since the Columbian Exposition. In the periods from 1895 to 1920 the conventional organizations to be encountered in the usual up-

per-middle-class community were formed. The merchants of
Hyde Park–Kenwood founded the usual business associations
and "civic" clubs—Lions, Kiwanis, the 55th Street Businessmen's Association, and the like—which survive to this day in
somewhat reduced stature compared to their early importance.
The residents got together to maintain and improve their neighborhood. In 1901 the area we have called the University Community started the South Park Improvement Association to
maintain standards of neighborhood maintenance and to supplement municipal services by providing street sprinkling during the summer and snow removal in the winter, services which
are still provided today.

Other organizations founded during this early period seem
to express the peculiarities of a university neighborhood. Hyde
Park–Kenwood was a stronghold of the female suffrage movement and formed the first chapter of the League of Women
Voters immediately after World War I. The Hyde Park Council of Churches and Synagogues was one of the first ministerial
associations in Chicago, expressing the kind of liberal theolo-
gies that the residents were wont to hear in Saturday and
Sunday services.

The flavor of Hyde Park–Kenwood's organizational network in this early period was that of middle-class respectability
tinged somewhat with liberal "causes." A subdominant theme
was added by the art colony, some of the liberal members of
the University of Chicago faculty, and some of the student
body.

Until the Great Depression—in spite of strong liberal
minorities—on balance, Hyde Park–Kenwood endorsed the
Republican Party in national politics and strove for "good
government" on the local scene by occasionally shifting its vote
from one side to the other.

In the middle twenties and early thirties the subdominant
liberal and bohemian themes in Hyde Park–Kenwood began to
grow in strength, aided considerably by the change in the University of Chicago wrought by the new Chancellor Hutchins.
The most significant factor was the advent of the Great Depression. In the 1930's Hyde Park–Kenwood went liberal in
many areas of its life. From its annexation in 1889 to the De-

pression in 1931 no Democratic presidential candidate won a local victory. According to Alderman Leon Despres: [20]

Every Republican mayoralty candidate carried Hyde Park until 1927, when William Hale Thompson, who won in the fourth ward, could not carry the fifth (Hyde Park) . . . in 1931, Thompson carried the fifth and lost the fourth (Kenwood). Among aldermen, one Democrat won in 1899, but no other in the fifth ward won until 1933. In the fourth ward, Ulysses Schwartz (1923) was the only Democratic alderman until the election of Alderman Claude Holman in 1955.

In the 1931 primary Hyde Park and Kenwood contained ten voting Republicans to every voting Democrat. In the 1932 election the Democratic national ticket carried both wards, and in 1934 a Democratic alderman was elected, together with Professor T. V. Smith as Democratic State Senator. Senator Paul Douglas, then a professor at the University of Chicago, had his political start here. The Independent Voters of Illinois, a liberal organization now affiliated with ADA, met with sympathetic support in Hyde Park–Kenwood and has remained well entrenched locally, with a ward organization of a quasi-party character.

Hyde Park–Kenwood thus became a center of liberalism and radicalism in the Middle West. Labor leaders, some of whom were connected with the very militant industrial unions that sprang up in the early days of the New Deal, militants and leaders in the socialist movements and in the Communist Party of the thirties, all found their way into the community as residents. Liberalism in the nonpolitical sphere also made headway in Hyde Park–Kenwood during this period. The Hyde Park Cooperative Society was formed in 1933 and survives today as one of the largest supermarkets in the Midwest. The Unitarian Meadville Theological School had already affiliated to the University of Chicago in 1926. During the depression a meeting of the Society of Friends was started.

Without changing its socio-economic composition very greatly, the community came in this period to have a very liberal tone that was to affect profoundly its reaction to the

20. From feature article, "No Democrats Here—Then," a political history by Alderman Despres (*Herald,* October 3, 1956, p. 22).

threatened deterioration of the neighborhood some twenty years later. An excerpt from an interview with a long time resident of the area expresses the close connection between the University, the area and the liberal and socialist movements of the thirties:

Mr. X attended the University of Chicago in the late 1930's. Here, he developed a strong social consciousness. As a student, he became very active in the Socialist Club and in the Young People's Socialist League of Cook County. He feels that at that time he and his friends would rather have attended a caucus than eat. "We were definitely political animals." He left the socialist movement in 1941 because of its stand on the war.

The Hyde Park Cooperative Society, the Unitarians, the Reform Jews, and the Quakers, although liberalizing forces during the 1930 decade, were perhaps more likely to invest the energies of their members in the formation of the Hyde Park Nursery School (1939) than to participate in socialist politics. Taking on a more actively reformist role was the K.A.M. Temple, a very old Chicago Reform congregation which migrated from the old "ghetto" to Kenwood.

The social action wing of K.A.M. as early as 1939 studied Negro housing conditions in the areas near the temple (in a Border Zone near Cottage Grove and 50th Street) and called for open occupancy legislation, at a time when such a recommendation was a very radical move. Rabbi Jacob Weinstein, himself a well-known social reformer, believes that this activity of his congregation's Community Affairs Committee was the first step taken locally toward the resolution of Negro housing problems.

It is this *new* liberal Hyde Park, in a community organized first at the turn of the century that took on secondary layers of organization in the thirties, that constituted the social structure that confronted the problems of urban decay in the fifties.

Hyde Parkers in the 1940's defined themselves as living in "an unusual community." They were conscious of its relatively high income base, its atypically high proportion of professional and semiprofessional occupational groups, and its vocal political consciousness. They were also aware of its identity as an area with higher than average rates of political participation;

as the stronghold of an independent political organization (Independent Voters of Illinois), which maintained dues-paying memberships and ward organizations; and as having the unusual benefits of an expanding cooperative society,[21] and an outstandingly competent and articulate local newspaper. Of equal significance, Hyde Park and Kenwood residents were conscious of the fairly distinct differences between their social structure and styles of life and those of the immediate, surrounding residential locales. The internal sense of community, by 1940, was thus intensified by the "push" of the sense of difference,[22] and by the "pull" of common education, political activity, and the lingering memory of its being the first village in the South Side of Chicago.

The flavor of Hyde Park–Kenwood's organizational life is epitomized in the Hyde Park–Kenwood Community Conference, a civic organization started in 1949 by a group of liberals concerned with the then impending neighborhood changes and with establishing the community on an interracial basis. We shall consider the Conference in detail in Chapter 5.

Summary of the Community Setting

Most of the remainder of this study is concerned with how and why Hyde Park and Kenwood citizens, through their organizations and institutions, responded to the rapid changes taking place in their community during the 1950's. The purpose of this chapter has been to lay out the story of the objective underlying conditions characteristic of Hyde Park–Kenwood before and during this period of change.

Our analysis suggests that demographic and economic changes during the forties were not in fact the extreme upheavals that they are often reputed to have been; that, while

21. The Hyde Park Cooperative Society became, by the 1940's, far more than a cooperative grocery store. It included ever-growing associational extensions, a nursery school, a vacation camp, social clubs, a parent-educational center, and the like. The Cooperative has become a dominant functional substitute for the old Village.

22. At the scene of any of Chicago's frequent summer season race riots on the South Side in the 1940's, one could find Hyde Park Quakers seeking peaceful avoidance of violence and University students acting as anti-racist agitators and sympathizers.

the in-migration of Negroes during this period was rapid, the displacement of whites followed a patterned sequence. Negroes did not come to locate evenly throughout the community. Succession occurred along the border zones and in the Village Core. The out-migrating white families were predominantly from the middle and lower-middle-classes rather than from the upper-middle and upper-class professional and managerial populations residing in East Hyde Park, the University Community, and Kenwood. The fairly rapid out-migration of Jewish families, however, probably thinned dramatically the ranks of those oriented toward the cultural and intellectual and liberal resources of this community. The "cultural envelope" of University Community supporters and sympathizers had begun to deteriorate.

Apparently most important was the experience of relative community deterioration. The gap between the modal characteristics of Hyde Park–Kenwood and those of the city at large was swiftly narrowed during the forties and fifties, and this community always tended to emphasize its distinctiveness.

Our historical review suggests that this sense of uniqueness formed from the developments in two earlier periods. Between 1855 and 1926 the elements of a highly stable, prosperous, self-conscious community were laid steadily into place. During the thirties this foundation of stability and resourcefulness persisted. It was elaborated upon by the community's responses to the abrupt changes incurred during the Great Depression, however.

Few neighborhoods could be found in the urban North in which significant portions of the population were willing to achieve interracial or biracial neighborhood living. Of all upper-middle-class neighborhoods in the country, Hyde Park–Kenwood is perhaps the best equipped to tolerate and in some instances to encourage interracialism. The background of stability and prosperity, even growth, and the features of community organization and political liberalism underlie this capability. The special identity of this community as an arena for the world-famous University of Chicago has contributed to the same capable determination to cope with local problems.

The existence of ongoing organizations, particularly the Hyde Park–Kenwood Community Conference, through which broad discussions of means and ends in urban renewal could take place, was another precondition in community organization for renewal. One of the main tasks of this chapter has been to describe the many ways in which Hyde Park may be said to be uniquely hyperorganized, in political and community service organizations in particular. The relevant pre-existing organizations include the League of Women Voters, the Independent Voters of Illinois, the Hyde Park Neighborhood Club, the Cooperative Society, the South Park Improvement Association, and the Council of Churches and Synagogues. Other urban communities have such groups in abundance, of course. However, in very few of them have they flourished with great activity and vigor over a period of half a century in advance of neighborhood deterioration. Faced with impending deterioration, the community set up a vigorous community organization that represented a genuine innovation in voluntary organizations.

That certain neighborhoods in the community contain family dwellings rather than apartments helped to sustain sufficient continuity to traverse the long road to renewal. Hyde Park's particular type of seven-wave build-up from the original base of a suburban village was such as to include important home-ownership cores: the University Community, the central Kenwood area, and the older housing sections of the old Village Core amount to self-conscious, self-maintaining individual neighborhoods, with some likelihood of sustained socio-economic and ethnic homogeneity as well.

Many deteriorating urban areas, unlike Hyde Park and Kenwood, have been the arena for an endless succession of ecological changes—ethnic invasions and departures, socio-economic build-ups and declines, and alterations in land-use patterns from decade to decade—which do not permit the emergence of an enduring and organized community. The brief résumé of the historical phases through which Hyde Park and Kenwood have passed, listed below, shows telescopically what the isolated facts reveal in this social history: between 1855 and 1940 this community experienced only one period of social change and reorganization, and this phase came so late as to build upon rather than to eradicate the primary modes of social organization. The prosperous bohemians of the thirties, to be sure, replaced some railroad suburbanites. For the most part, however, the reorganization was incremental; it fused and blended with the continuing culture of the original village community.

Chronological Summary of Community Phases

1) 1855–1871 Origins of the Village Community as Railroad Suburb

2) 1872–1889 Population Growth, Physical Construction Initiated, Urban Absorption Begun

3) 1890–1925 Primary Organization of the Continuing Urban Community, Final Land Use Patterns Stabilized

4) 1926–1934 Phase of Abrupt Social Change, Basic Changes in Population Composition, Political and Social Characteristics

5) 1936–1948 Era of the Prosperous Bohemians Stabilized, Contemporary Organizational Structure Crystallized

6) 1949–1958 Abrupt Social Changes, Emergence of a Biracial Community

CHAPTER 3

Roads to Conservation
and Renewal

*T*he changes which we have described as taking place in Hyde Park–Kenwood in the post-World War II period were massive enough to be obvious to many, if not most, of the leaders of the community and to the institutions located there. However, the meanings of these trends for the future of the community were not clear. Nor was it clear what could be done about them, assuming that there was some degree of agreement on what was desirable to conserve in the community.

The task of this chapter is to project the reader back into the early 1950's and to explore the perspectives on community survival as they might have appeared at that time, given the knowledge we have today, and as they actually appeared to community leaders.

Properly to apprehend the spirit of those times, it is necessary to bear two things in mind. First, there was no precedent for the proposition that something could be done to preserve a community of the physical type and age of Hyde Park–Kenwood; all the precedents were in the direction of continuing decline. Secondly, longstanding interracial neighborhoods covering a wide area and with a dense population were nonexistent. In short, either to preserve Hyde Park–Kenwood as a white middle-class neighborhood or to stabilize it as an interracial neighborhood meant to attempt something entirely new in the way of community reorganization.

Specifically, we shall attempt three things in this chapter.

First, we will describe the problems that faced the community in the early fifties. Secondly, we will assess the resources that were present in the neighborhood to meet these problems. Thirdly, we will outline the alternatives to renewal which might have been employed to meet these problems on a short-run and on a long-run basis.

For convenience, we have classified the problems of conservation and renewal into three broad categories—inhabitants, physical plant, and mobilization of social powers. Within each of these we will show what were the problems faced by the community in the early fifties, the resources of the community which could be employed to meet these problems, and, finally, the solutions which were considered and those which were finally chosen.

The later chapters of this report will fill in the details of how the process of choosing among alternatives was actually carried through. Here we will be concerned primarily with the *solutions* themselves and the kinds of effects they had upon the goals in conservation and renewal.

Inhabitants: Problems and Resources

To conserve Hyde Park–Kenwood meant first of all to reduce the amount of turnover in the resident population. Thousands of families annually were leaving the area. In the period between 1950 and 1956 the nonwhite population was estimated to have increased about 500 per cent.[1]

There are two viewpoints from which one may consider turnover as a community problem. First, residents may emphasize their loss of established ties with long-term neighbors. In 1956, 48 per cent of the white residents had lived in Hyde Park–Kenwood for ten or more years, and 66 per cent of them for five or more. Only 4 per cent of the nonwhites had resided there for ten or more years, and only 17 per cent for five or more.[2] Thus, within a long-settled white residential population, many were bound to identify the exodus of their white neighbors as a great social problem.

1. Donald Bogue, *The Hyde Park–Kenwood Urban Renewal Survey* (N.O.R.C. Report No. 58, September, 1956), p. 100.
2. *Ibid.*, p. 131.

The other viewpoint identifies the major problem in the turnover as that of the nonwhite in-migration. This seemed a threat to many nonwhites who had prided themselves on having settled in a middle-class white neighborhood. To whites in the central portion of the community, where the in-migration was only beginning to occur, this turnover in the western sector seemed to pose a threat to the future stability of their own neighborhood.

The increasing rate of turnover became widely apparent by 1949. The goal of residential stabilization was soon embraced by most settled, long-term residents, regardless of their orientation toward nonwhites. Thus, while motives differed, population control or residential stability had become a common goal by 1952.

That the rate of population turnover was reduced is attributable to two major factors. First of all, we reported in Chapter 2 that the change began in portions of the community where the housing types were particularly suitable for the incoming population: the long blocks of apartment houses in North West Hyde Park with large three-decker flats. The movement of Negroes into smaller apartment houses and single-family homes would have been slower in any event. The second factor aiding the ability of the area was that large portions of the population had very strong motives for trying to conserve what they felt to be the desirable characteristics of the neighborhood. It is worthwhile to consider what these motives for staying were.

Some of the inhabitants of Hyde Park–Kenwood had considerable economic stakes in the area, which they could not very easily abandon except at cost to themselves. At one extreme the University of Chicago had over $200 million invested in its physical plant on the Midway—easily the greatest stake in the neighborhood. Other large institutions and businesses—for example, the apartment and transient hotels on the lake front—had considerable investments in the area as well. There is scarcely a market for a second-hand university campus like that of the University of Chicago, nor was it likely that the hotel owners would have been able to recoup their large investments in the physical plants of their properties. On a lesser scale, one must consider the economic stakes of those businesses and service establishments in the area that depended upon an upper-middle-class clientele.

Home ownership also can be considered as endowing a household with some economic stake in remaining in the neighborhood. However, as we saw in Chapter 2, few households in Hyde Park–Kenwood were home owners. The stakes of individual households in the neighborhood had to be of a less tangible sort. Many had sought to locate in the neighborhood because of its proximity to the downtown business section, and this provided a motive for some. But this too was not sufficiently strong a motive for locations with similar accessibility to the downtown business center in other areas of the city, particularly on the North Side.

The major strength of Hyde Park–Kenwood in retaining its population lay in its social "climate," the atmosphere of liberal intellectuality. This was a neighborhood quality not to be duplicated elsewhere in Chicago. It is hard to estimate how important such a motive may have been or how many individuals were touched strongly by it. However, it is clear that many were concerned to do something about the neighborhood because of this unique feature. Such persons were to form the backbone of the membership in the community organizations that were to take on the task of stabilization.

Another characteristic of the population of Hyde Park–Kenwood was a relatively unprejudiced or sympathetic view of the Negro newcomers. The large liberal contingent among the residents made it clear that few neighborhoods of its class composition anywhere have a population less prejudiced against Negroes.

The inhabitants of Hyde Park–Kenwood were important for the survival of the area in other ways as well. They represented a considerable reservoir of talents which were relevant to conservation and renewal. Several nationally known city planners made their homes in the community and were to give their services to the renewal effort. The University of Chicago has always been particularly strong in the social sciences, and social scientists were also to help by suggesting ways and means of organizing citizens into community organizations. Lawyers, real estate experts, race relations experts, public relations experts, and other professionals were available in numbers considerably beyond what one would expect to find in an ordinary middle-class urban neighborhood. Their dedication to the community led them to make their talents available without charge to community organizations. Similarly, the institutions of Hyde Park–Kenwood represented organizations with considerable administrative skills that were to be employed to great advantage in the years of planning and organizing for renewal.

The world-wide pre-eminence of the University of Chicago and its contributions to knowledge and scholarship also meant that it would have a ready and receptive audience for whatever suggestions it might make for renewal and conservation. An institution whose faculty had achieved such prominence, and whose former students had made such important contributions, could scarcely be ignored. Survival of the University of Chicago went beyond local interest to engage the attention of the national and even international scene. Influential citizens of the business community on the University Board of Trustees also attracted attention and aid far beyond that given most urban neighborhoods. Indeed, the presence of the University of Chicago in the area was to give the community's preservation an appearance of being in the national interest.

Inhabitants: The Conservation Task

A central goal of neighborhood conservation and renewal thus was to keep Hyde Park–Kenwood as a desirable middle-class residential neighborhood. There were others who would have preferred to have such a statement put in terms such as "a safe, clean, well-serviced community," qualifications that would avoid the mention of either race or class.

Whatever the qualifications placed on the goal, in practice the different statements all meant that roughly the same ends were to be sought. Conservation meant, first of all, bringing to a halt the white exodus. On this goal racial liberals and conservatives could agree. In effect, this meant stabilizing the numbers of Negroes at some minority proportion. The ratio—which had changed from less than one nonwhite in ten before 1950 to four nonwhites in ten by 1956—was defined as requiring firm control. There was also awareness of the necessity for removal of some portion of Hyde Park–Kenwood's population to lower its density. Some insisted that the removal be accomplished without regard to race, but the means to be employed inevitably implied that more Negroes were to be removed than whites.[3]

Whether one was a liberal or a conservative on the issue of racial integration in housing, the means available for population control were identical: control over Hyde Park–Kenwood's population had to be achieved by control over housing—removing deteriorated portions of the housing plant, rehabilitating structures that were not too dilapidated, and removing some structures in order to provide space for badly needed community facilities.

The physical plant of Hyde Park–Kenwood was to be the focus of efforts to conserve and renew the community. In practice, because the physical structures that were problematical were occupied by Negroes and lower-class whites, to conserve the area meant to propose extensive dislocation of these groups. Whether one liked it or not, neighborhood conservation and renewal meant the preservation of Hyde Park–Kenwood as a primarily *white* middle-class residential neighborhood.

The goal of conservation is, like any other social objective, modified by the means used to achieve it. To seek conservation through demolition, traffic-control arrangements, and obligatory rehabilitation means that residential stability can be achieved only within the limits of ability to pay and family size. Ability to pay means, among other things, the newly stabilized community must be restricted largely to a middle- and upper-class segment of the population; economic homogeneity will take precedence over racial integration. Although in abstract the two goals are not completely mutually exclusive, in practice they are. This is primarily characteristic of this neighborhood and others similar to it. Renewal of an old, established working-class area may have quite a different meaning.

Agreement on means between the racial liberals and the

3. More Negroes than whites occupied substandard housing: ". . . transition from white to nonwhite has occurred in areas having the highest proportion of dilapidated structures. But within each area, Negroes and other nonwhite populations occupy dilapidated structures in only moderately higher proportions than white residents." *Ibid.,* p. 45.

racial conservatives raised dilemmas for both. Liberals had to reconcile espousal of an interracial neighborhood with the goal of a reduction in the Negro population of Hyde Park–Kenwood. For the conservatives the goal of an all-white neighborhood had to be reconciled with the likelihood that any Negro who could pay the price would have access to housing in the area.

Inevitably the population goals of urban renewal and conservation were reformulated along class lines. Both liberals and conservatives came to agree that Hyde Park–Kenwood would have to be an interracial *middle-class* neighborhood. Negroes already in the area and living in structures meeting the physical standards, or who could pay the price for rehabilitated or new housing, would remain. In short, the liberals had to accept less racial integration and the conservatives had to accept more Negro neighbors than each group wanted.

The "working through" of these dilemmas brought the question of residential integration out into public discussion with a frankness rarely achieved in northern urban areas. In Hyde Park–Kenwood there was more direct confrontation of the problem of integrating lower-class Negroes into white middle-class society than perhaps in any other community in the nation. By and large, the local answer has been that integration cannot succeed unless the class level and customs of the two groups are approximately equal.

Physical Plant: Resources

The physical plant of Hyde Park–Kenwood impinged upon conservation goals in two ways. First, certain aspects of the plant were among the main causes for the decline in the neighborhood. Secondly, it was through transforming this physical plant that the conservation and renewal goals of the community were to be achieved.

By 1950, as Chapter 2 shows, Hyde Park–Kenwood was a "middle-aged" neighborhood. The apartment houses which contained the bulk of the dwelling units in the community were from thirty to fifty years old. Many contained large, spacious apartments, but these lacked the amenities now being built routinely into new apartments. Though much of the rental housing had been well maintained over the years, all suffered from the neglect of the war years.

The community's single family homes varied widely. In Kenwood there were showplaces designed by such famous architects as Frank Lloyd Wright, while in the old Village Core there were one-story wooden bungalows which predated the 1893 Columbian Exposition. Most of the single-family homes were of good quality, however, and had been well maintained over the years.

The physical plants of the institutions of the area were beginning to show the effects of reaching their middle years. With the increase in enrollment and the post-war burgeoning of research, the University of Chicago faced a period of replacement and expansion of its physical plant at the same time that available vacant space in the area was scarce. Other institutions, such as George Williams College and the Chicago College of Osteopathy, faced similar needs for expansion and replacement.

As Chapter 2 indicates, despite the fairly good over-all quality of the residential structures in the area, there were pockets of extreme blight—as for example, along 55th Street, Lake Park Avenue (which bordered the Illinois Central tracks) and Cottage Grove Avenue. In these border zones, apartments over stores, small flats, and old apartment houses were the first to show signs of deterioration. Later, some of the larger old single family homes in the streets off the business districts were converted into small flats and became the points of entry for a highly mobile population. Slums had their beginnings in these places and spread outward.

In addition, we have indicated there were undesirable features in the over-all physical layout of Hyde Park–Kenwood. For one thing, there was crowding of the land. The three-story apartment houses were built too close together. Parking space was at a premium. Little open space was left around parks, churches, schools, and institutions for their expansion. The grid street layout of the community made almost every other street a potential thoroughfare for heavy north- and southbound traffic.

The retail businesses and service establishments of the community were spread out in small stores along 55th and 53rd

Streets. Many of the stores were vacant as the modern trends in retailing acted against the viability of the neighborhood store. The efficient merchandising of the "shopping center" was not possible in a physical plant that was built to house retail stores serving primarily small neighborhoods.

In short, Hyde Park–Kenwood was built to serve the living patterns of an earlier era when there was little automobile ownership, when residents shopped daily for their needs in nearby stores, and when standards of living did not demand much in the way of open space.

Physical Plant: Rehabilitation

To conserve Hyde Park–Kenwood as it had been built would have meant preservation of an outmoded physical plant and design. In addition, for some portions of the physical plant rehabilitation to modern standards would have been financially impossible. It seems only natural that the concept of *renewal*, as opposed to demolition and reconstruction, was to be applied here. Renewal meant an attempt to modernize the plant and design without wholesale demolition and reconstruction. Slums were to be torn down, space created for necessary community facilities, expansion of institutional plant provided for, and the street pattern rearranged to meet modern traffic needs in a residential neighborhood.

The conception of renewal planning met with widespread enthusiasm in the community among all sectors—residents, businessmen, and institutions. It was clearly desirable to all that slums be torn down, that schools be allowed to expand, that parking spaces should be provided, and the like.

The happy unanimity over the general goal faded only when the particulars of renewal planning began to be spelled out. The problem is an old one of a general public interest clashing with the interests of particular individuals. For example, the planner's proposal of a modern shopping center appealed to the owners of retail businesses until it was realized that such a shopping center meant a sharp reduction in the number of businesses and that many small stores would be eliminated from the area. Everyone favored more play space for elementary school children, but when the play space proposed meant the elimination of particular houses, the residents of those houses tended to protest.

The concept of renewal of community facilities in practice means defining bit by bit what should be considered a community facility. It was fairly clear that a public elementary school comes under this classification. But is the University of Chicago—or a private welfare agency, or a church—a community facility? Do such institutions partake enough of the concept of public purpose to be given priority over adjacent property or special consideration in allocating newly vacated properties for expansion? Despite the national importance of an institution like the University of Chicago, individual residents began to demand equal rights.

Renewal planning was destined to involve much in the way of short-run overriding of individual interests in favor of a general public interest, loosely defined to include semipublic institutions.

Renewal planning focused on the refurbishing of the community's facilities, but residents were sensitive primarily to the housing implications of planning. Yet housing had to give way to provide community facilities. Particular residents who had worked hard to preserve the neighborhood found themselves "renewed out" of the community.

An additional dilemma accentuated this problem. The structures that were to be torn down could not easily be replaced by housing at any equivalent price level. New structures would have more modern amenities and be more expensive to build. The population and businesses displaced for renewal could return to their old locations only at some higher cost. Many were to be severely dismayed when they discovered that renewal meant being "priced out" of the community.

It is easier to see behind the proposals of a planner some malignant intent than to appreciate the constraints imposed by the economics of the building and construction industry and by the relatively firm limits of the existing plant itself. It is important to stress that any plan for extensive renewal of Hyde Park–Kenwood had to involve surmounting particular features dictated by the hard facts of the physical design of Hyde Park–Kenwood.

It is not necessary to consider any particular plan in detail in order to predict that some measure of opposition to it would inevitably arise. *Any plan that would attempt to remove slums, modernize community facilities, revamp the grid street pattern, and reduce total available housing would inevitably clash with individual interests.* Any plan would also alter the population composition. No plan for the renewal of Hyde Park–Kenwood could achieve the complete approval of all of the residents, businesses, and institutions in the area.

The Mobilization of Power and Resources

A declining urban neighborhood can be renewed only through the employment of broad governmental powers and considerable sums of money. The right of eminent domain is necessary to eliminate defects in neighborhood design, and large sums of money are needed to reimburse property owners for acquired properties.

In Chicago in the early 1950's public powers and public funds for these purposes had not yet been provided for in the creation of agencies charged with these tasks. Nor was the regular governmental machinery concerned with housing and zoning functioning as well as it might.

City agencies concerned with planning were weak and inexperienced, and it was only in 1956, sometime after renewal efforts had already started in Hyde Park–Kenwood, that the planning function was established in a Department of City Planning. Before that time a weak planning commission existed, with very inadequate staff and resources. Related municipal agencies designed to attend directly to the problems of conservation were also not established and in working condition until 1956.

The enforcement of housing and building codes, which had been allowed to slip during World War II, had not yet been brought up to prewar standards. Even when working well, their enforcement involved a cumbersome court procedure, with the penalties for violations so slight as to add only an additional small charge to the total cost of operating slum housing or else capriciously excessive.

At the same time little help was available from state and federal governments for the purposes of conservation and renewal. To be sure, the Federal Housing Act of 1949 provided funds for slum clearance, but only a very small portion of Hyde Park–Kenwood could be considered as an out-and-out slum. Furthermore, land clearance on a large scale in the community would defeat the goals of conserving the neighborhood. Aid was available for removing slums but not for preventing them.

A similar situation prevailed with regard to police protection. As was the case for other areas of the city at this time, the police district covering the community was undermanned and seemingly unable to provide adequate protection against criminals.

Anything that might be done to help preserve the community, then, would involve large sums of money. Mortgage money was needed to finance private rehabilitation of structures. Additional mortgage money was needed to finance home purchases for those who wished to settle in the area. Conventional mortgage houses were reluctant to lend money on structures in the area because of the anticipated neighborhood decline.

Thus two tasks faced Hyde Park–Kenwood. On a short-term, hold-the-line basis, it was necessary to obtain better utilization of existing governmental powers; Hyde Park–Kenwood needed enforcement of the local building and zoning codes, better municipal services, and more efficient police protection. Secondly, on a long-term basis, extensive governmental authority had to be obtained to remove expensive structures.

There are several ways to undertake the short-term stimulation of local government agencies. One possibly is what might be called a frontal attack on City Hall in the form of mass pressure—petitions, mass demonstrations, demands for the removal of police captains, and the like. As it turned out, pressure of this sort was not used extensively. A second way is to seek to reform government agencies through the creation of new legislation on building and zoning codes and the like. This approach was tried and was to some degree successful. Chicago now has a better code of laws covering these matters than it did at the outset of the fifties.

A third way is to attempt to supplement and aid municipal agencies in the pursuit of their objectives. This last approach was used with excellent success. Staff members of community organizations were assigned to inspection work and to liaison with governmental agencies. Effective pursuit of this last task required the growth of strong civic associations with full-time staffs.

The long-run rehabilitation planning for the community required greater efforts. Since the governmental machinery of the day bypassed almost completely the problems of deteriorating neighborhoods, it looked as if it would be necessary either to enlarge the scope of existing agencies or to create new ones specifically for the task. Work was quickly started in both directions, with the result that when the Federal Housing Act of 1954 was passed, set up under the Illinois Urban Community Conservation Act of 1953, machinery existed in Chicago to take immediate advantage of the Act.

The passage of the 1954 Housing Act, of course, presented a direct solution to the problem of obtaining power and funds for the conservation and renewal of declining neighborhoods. Had the Act not been available, local and state legislation placed on the books during the early fifties would at least have provided for the use of governmental powers, although the funds to be disbursed were not as extensive as those provided in the federal Act.

In sum, those who had strong stakes in remaining in the community viewed it as physically middle-aged, deteriorating and overcrowded. Its physical design was defined as outmoded —disruptive of optimum convenience, safety, and welfare. This image of the community's physical plant was by 1952 superimposed upon an excessive population turnover, interracial tension, and increasing social instability in general. Within the area crime, the declining quality of public schools, segregated housing, and overcrowding of illegally converted dwellings became indicators of this *perceived* instability. These were the problems as defined by vocal white leadership within Hyde Park–Kenwood.

Six proposed solutions received increasingly strong support during the fifties. Four were physical: to reduce land overcrowding, rehabilitate middle-aged housing, change street and traffic patterns, and centralize commercial facilities. Two were essentially social: to stabilize the rate of white out-migration and to strengthen the middle-class character of the resident population. Physical changes, of course, meant corresponding social changes. It was quickly seen that pursuit of these conservation goals would mean some transformation of the over-all character of the physical and social community; even if urban renewal was successful, Hyde Park–Kenwood would not be the same as it had been before World War II.

So much for the problems as defined by local leaders, the solutions proposed by them, and the resources and power they had to mobilize to apply the solutions. The story of how citizens participated in the process may be found in the total context of this study. The following section explains some of the *consequences* of their actions.

Urban Renewal as a Solution to Community Problems

Although urban renewal was the solution to community problems upon which community leaders finally converged, this was not the only solution proposed or even tried. However, the alternatives to urban renewal were found to be in one way or another unsatisfactory and were either discarded or used in a subordinate way.

One alternative was to do nothing but let "nature take its course." There is something to be said for this "solution." There is a limit to the amount of housing in Hyde Park–Kenwood that is suitable for conversion into the high-density living that usually characterizes a slum. The homes in Kenwood and in the University community are not as easily converted to the purposes of housing a lower-class population as are the three-decker apartment houses in North West Hyde Park. Yet the problems of deterioration cannot be contained within micro-neighborhoods. Crime particularly appeared to spread far beyond the entering wedges of deterioration, and while town houses do not make the "best slums," they still can be employed in that capacity. This alternative was discarded because there was too much at stake for the residents and the institutions to trust that the process of deterioration would be contained naturally within certain sectors.

Another alternative to conservation renewal was a program

which would rely on voluntary rehabilitation and on building-code enforcement. Indeed, this was the first approach tried, as we shall see in Chapter 4. The general consensus among community leaders in Hyde Park–Kenwood is that this approach works well up to a point but can only be a holding operation, slowing down and stopping the rate of deterioration but not reversing trends by rolling back the process of change.

A third alternative was some form of privately financed renewal. This too was suggested and has been tried in the form of private neighborhood redevelopment corporations. But the funds and powers that could be deployed by such organizations fell far short of what was conceived to be necessary. Furthermore, precisely in those areas of the community which needed the most extensive renewal private funds were least in evidence. A neighborhood redevelopment corporation could function for the purpose of acquiring land to be used for housing University of Chicago students, but the use of this corporate device for rearranging street patterns is impractical.

One by one the alternatives to extensive urban renewal were eliminated as major remedies. The leadership of the community, in seeking solutions to their community problems, was constrained to seek large-scale massive solutions. In large part, this occurred because the 1954 Federal Housing Act, with its new provisions for urban renewal, made such a massive program more feasible than any other. In turn, all the attempts tried up to 1954 made federal aid easier to obtain.

In other words, urban renewal on a large scale provided powers and funds to employ in "saving" the community that would not have been available if any other solution were attempted. Furthermore, to seek urban renewal made it possible to carry through other programs much more efficiently. For example, voluntary rehabilitation is much more feasible under an urban renewal program which guarantees financing for rehabilitation.

It should also be emphasized that no one group would be either a complete loser or a complete winner under a federally financed urban renewal program. Everyone would lose something and also gain something, and receipt of federal funds would generally offset losses. For example, an important consideration for the downtown political leaders was that it was not necessary for one part of the city to lose and another to gain by the renewal of Hyde Park–Kenwood.

Although demolition would affect nonwhites more than whites, there were also gains for the nonwhites. Federal assistance would provide strong guarantees of nondiscrimination in housing, for instance, and relocation of displaced residents by municipal agencies would supply some safeguard against being dumped into worse housing.

In short, none of the elements of a massive, diversified program would prove fully satisfactory to any of the participants; all would experience sacrifices and compromises in objectives. Liberals would find themselves obliged, if they wished to achieve renewal, to favor less racial integration than their principles would require. Conservatives on matters of race relations would find it necessary to endorse biracialism. Plan proponents would have to accept acquisition and clearance of their own homes or those of close friends. Businessmen would find themselves "planned out" of the community. Furthermore, the process of political participation would stimulate association between very strange bedfellows, who would be forced toward painful compromises before general goals were achieved.

Perhaps the best argument for extensive urban renewal was that its adoption made a large number of other solutions possible. Those community leaders who preferred voluntary rehabilitation would find that renewal made this an easier program to pursue. Even private redevelopment became easier when urban renewal appeared to be a real possibility: Chancellor Kimpton's appeal for funds for investment in the area on the basis that general federal renewal of the community would ultimately insure the wisdom of private capital investments was one thing; an appeal to the same sources when land values were declining and promised to decline further would be quite another matter.

In short, the approaches to community problems in an urban community like Hyde Park–Kenwood interlocked because action of one sort would not be forthcoming without promise of actions of other sorts from other sources.[4] Thus, healthy

4. According to Julia Abrahamson: "The task of stimulating government agencies to take action was begun by the Conference when in June 1953 it approached the Chicago Land Clearance Commission with the request

growth of the citizen movement fostered by the Hyde Park–Kenwood Community Conference from 1949 to 1952 became a signal to the great local institutions that local home owners could be counted upon to support problem solving programs. Efforts of the University of Chicago, in turn, encouraged investment by banks, hotel owners, and numerous smaller private institutions. The ensuing local consensus was presented to the municipal political leaders and to the banking and mortgage houses as strong evidence that a growing program of potential advantage was gathering momentum within Hyde Park. As each segment of the population swung into support, the scope of the action program increased proportionately, until it embraced self-help rehabilitation, code enforcement, slum clearance, private redevelopment, stimulation of welfare services, and, finally, planned renewal.

This set of interlocking programs, held together by the key of urban renewal, also coincided fortunately with the federal government's criteria of eligibility for urban renewal assistance, as embodied in the conception of a "workable program."

The seven essential requirements are: (1) adequate local codes and ordinances, (2) a comprehensive general plan, (3) an analysis of neighborhood characteristics, (4) adequate administrative organization for executing renewal, (5) assurance of the community's ability to meet financial requirements under the renewal program, (6) ability to rehouse the displaced, and (7) full-fledged citizen participation.[5] The road to conservation renewal in Hyde Park–Kenwood led straight toward fulfillment

---

to survey parts of the community for blight, on the basis of which it could undertake redevelopment. Harold Mayer, then chairman of the Conference Planning Committee, introduced the idea at a Planning Committee session to which I believe Julian Levi had been invited. The Conference Board approved the recommendation and promptly sent the request in, at the time urging SECC to support that request. Shortly thereafter Julian Levi went down to the Land Clearance Commission with Chancellor Kimpton and from then on took the initiative in pushing the project with city agencies. The Conference also kept pushing the University to undertake a planning operation." While this qualifies our statement that the task of stimulating government agencies into activity was taken on *primarily* by the University of Chicago and the South East Chicago Commission, it does not change the essence of the history.

5. Housing and Home Finance Agency, *How Localities Can Develop a Workable Program for Urban Renewal* (Washington, D.C.: U.S. Government Printing Office R-1, Revised, December, 1956).

of these requirements. It must be stressed that the road was followed long before the federal Act itself became public law. Once the new Housing Act was available, the already ongoing but uncoordinated projects in the community began to cohere around this means of greatest promise. Figuratively, the chassis for renewal was in creation when the federal legislation provided the wheels of implementation and the fuel of financial capital.

If our interpretations are correct—if few problems could have been resolved without continuing addition of new means for their solution, and if renewal hopes took on coherence under the new Housing Act—certain consequences follow.

The tactics of negotiation and opposition were shaped by certain limiting conditions. Proponents of solutions to Hyde Park's physical deterioration, changing racial balance, and threatened class homogeneity were forced to pursue what David Riesman has called the principle of "The more, the more." [6] As each new population element and organization boarded the band wagon to conservation renewal, veteran travelers had to strengthen their conviction of the total program's desirability. The appeals had to become *more* convincing, the variety of programs *more* extensive. The more support for the program as a whole increased, then, the more the scope of the program grew. The broader the support, the more the technics of changes were delegated to professional planners.

The same process may be viewed in a different way. Program proponents were, for example, encouraged toward certain political positions, as our study will demonstrate. Proponents had to identify their support with a need for *speed*, for the wider the support and scope of the program extended, the more urgent seemed the need for its execution. [7] The gloomy fantasy of a massive, global renewal program put to work too late to achieve its central objective came to plague some community leaders.

As support and scope grew, citizen participation became

6. Public lecture on the American economy, University of Chicago, 1958.

7. A central issue in the Aldermanic election campaign of 1959 became, for example, whether Alderman Leon Despres had secured renewal and redevelopment benefits *speedily enough* for his Fifth Ward! Numerous other examples of this effect appear in other chapters.

not merely a component in a "workable program" but a positive value in its own right. Its worth came to be measured more and more in terms of quantity and depth of citizen involvement and less and less in terms of degree of influence.[8]

The apparent urgency and importance of the urban renewal proposal brought together diverse groups in a "united front," which was broken by very few local residents. Several examples of the strong strain toward consensus will be given in detail in later chapters; here we can present one.

Public housing was the most controversial issue in the 1958 campaign to get the plan approved by the Chicago City Council. If we ask why the Preliminary Project Report in 1956 proposed eventual construction of more than 500 units of public housing, when the final Urban Renewal Plan as approved called for far less, we must answer that as proponents worked to build widespread support for the plan, the most controversial features of the program had to be eliminated. The program had to become big enough, but *bland* enough, to attract powerful supporters. Public housing in Chicago is controversial in several ways:[9] as a source of difficulty for anti-interracialists, as an investment dilemma for mortgage houses uncertain about investing in areas around public housing sites, and as a program of lower-class rather than middle-class housing. The absence of public housing in a governmentally financed plan was, for other groups, equally controversial.

The issue of racial discrimination, covert or manifest, had to be raised and worked through. For the community to reduce its density by demolition in its border zones, to increase land

8. That there were "second thoughts" on this matter that became evident about one month before final passage of the Urban Renewal Plan in City Council was reflected in the Hyde Park–Kenwood Community Conference Board meetings, where members directed the chair to prepare a memo accounting for the number of specific influences the Conference had to its credit in changing elements of the plan.

9. We should note that where to *locate* public housing, rather than number of units, type of housing, or the concept of public housing itself, often constituted the core of this issue. Many influential anti-interracialists were indifferent over the number of public units to be placed in a border zone location such as 47th Street and Cottage Grove Avenue, while they were militantly opposed to including units within the University Community. See Martin Meyerson & Edward Banfield, *Politics, Planning and the Public Interest*. (Glencoe: The Free Press, 1955) For an account of Chicago controversies over public housing.

values and rent levels, and to seek to build a "community of high standards" (meaning middle-class standards), most clearance would have to occur in nonwhite housing areas. A choice of emphasis had to be made. The emphasis would have to be on interracialism or on a middle-class neighborhood, as the two goals are in part contradictory. As comedian Mike Nichols expressed the dilemma: "This is Hyde Park, Whites and Blacks, shoulder to shoulder against the lower classes." Socio-economic class conflict often became more critical as an issue than did racial bias.

Underlying our interpretations is a view of the community leaders of Hyde Park–Kenwood as being constrained by the nature of the community problems they sought to meet and the solutions that were realistically available to them. In any such hindsight, there is communicated a sense of inevitability that may not be experienced by the participants themselves. In retrospect things hang together much better than they do at the time one makes single decision after single decision.

In addition, this chapter is written on a very general level. Things look very easy from this perspective. The day-to-day tribulations of community leaders seeking to form a consensus and searching for ways and means to meet community problems will be given better coverage in the chapters that follow.

CHAPTER 4

The Role of the University of Chicago in Neighborhood Conservation

The Midway, the southern border of Hyde Park, dominated the neighborhood during the Columbian Exposition. But along one edge of this temporary carnival promenade the first quadrangle of the University of Chicago began to rise, gray stone on gray stone, even as the concession booths and exhibits of the fair were being dismantled. By World War I the University had begun to tower physically and culturally above Hyde Park. Faculty homes and apartments by them surrounded the University on three sides for nearly a square mile. Only to the west was expansion limited by Washington Park.

To an extent greater than is true for most urban universities—for example, Columbia University in New York or the University of Pennsylvania in Philadelphia—the University of Chicago has been linked intimately with its neighborhood for more than fifty years. As we have shown, between three and four out of every five faculty members have always lived within a square-mile radius of the campus. In faculty circles proximity to Lake Michigan's beaches, the tree-studded streets surrounding the quadrangles, and the broad greensward of the Midway have long been pointed to as special benefits of positions at the University of Chicago. Hyde Park, from the 1930's on, also provided a social environment in which liberal intellectualism was a major theme rather than a minor accompaniment in civic groups and church circles. In such an enclave an academician could receive ready attention and respect.

After World War II the academic labor market became a scene for sharply competitive bidding as colleges and universities expanded greatly. The quality and character of a university's neighborhood was bound to become a factor affecting individual career decisions in this "teacher's market." Many University of Chicago faculty members who left the University since 1947 cited the decline in the caliber of Hyde Park as a source of disaffection.

By 1950 the avalanche of World War II veterans had subsided, and, like other schools, the University of Chicago began to find it harder to attract students, especially to its undergraduate college. In addition to its scholarly and scientific achievements, the University has run an excellent, although in some quarters controversial, undergraduate school. For a variety of complicated reasons, the undergraduate enrollment was beginning to drop alarmingly after 1950. University officials associated this decline with the decline in quality of local housing, which was then becoming visibly apparent.

When, in 1951, administrative control of the University shifted from Chancellor Robert Hutchins to his replacement, Lawrence Kimpton, three interrelated concerns were therefore given special saliency: strengthening of the declining undergraduate college, maintenance of the faculty strength and quality achieved during the thirties and forties, and community improvement. These were construed as interdependent objectives. They competed with the usual vast array of administrative goals, but only the related objective of endowment growth attained equal emphasis under the new Chancellor.

The interest of the University of Chicago in maintaining and improving its neighborhood is clearly unequivocal. Furthermore, the scope and pre-eminence of the institution, plus the motivation and power potential, make it a formidable machine for influencing community conservation. This combination of purpose and resources alone would prove sufficient to make the University the most important force for renewal on the metropolitan scene. There is more to the history of relationship than this, however, and we shall devote the bulk of this chapter to an account of conservation efforts in terms of the University and the many special devices its administrators put together to influence the course of conservation planning.

The viewpoint of this chapter is that the University's efforts lie behind much of what was accomplished in the process of renewal planning in Hyde Park and Kenwood. We know that other institutions and organizations played very important roles—but the University played the most important one. Nothing of the thesis of the "hidden hand" is intended in this approach, although some individuals have behaved in the course of conservation politics *as if* the University were some sort of secret and omnipotent power behind renewal.

There is a legend that about 1948 the late Louis Wirth, an eminent University of Chicago sociologist, wrote Chancellor Hutchins, urging him to turn his attention to the need for conservation of the University's neighborhood. Hutchins replied briefly, "You teach and I'll administer." This and other partly apocryphal stories have frequently been accepted as evidence that before 1952 University administrators and trustees were not concerned with the problems of the surrounding neighborhood.

This impression took even stronger hold in 1951 when leaders of the Hyde Park–Kenwood Community Conference arranged a meeting with Chancellor Hutchins to discuss local affairs. Hutchins is reported to have met the delegates cordially and then to have announced: "I am sorry to have to be abrupt but I have another meeting which I'm obliged to attend. All I can say is that I am personally strongly in favor of a University policy of racial non-discrimination." However, at the same meeting, after Hutchins' departure, University real estate officers questioned the aims and policies of the Conference and indicated clear disagreement with Conference's aims of maintaining an interracial community. Many informed respondents assert that Chancellor Hutchins' strong absorption in academic and national policy questions contributed to the institution's neglect of neighborhood problems of overcrowding and deterioration.

While these anecdotes may indicate shortcomings in the University's community relations, they do *not* fit historical fact. Although the University of Chicago first made a strong formal commitment to involvement in urban renewal in 1952, this decision was in line with a long tradition of concern and activity in the local community. As Harvey Perloff stated:[1]

The University of Chicago has been neither unaware of the need to protect itself against encroaching blight nor unwilling to take action to try to limit deterioration. The University has constructed and acquired housing for hundreds of faculty and staff members. It has assisted faculty members in the purchase of homes in the area and has pursued other real estate policies designed to control the nature of the use and occupancy of property in its vicinity. The University has helped to support, and its officials have held membership in, a number of community organizations, including Hyde Park Planning Association, Woodlawn Inc., the Hyde Park Community Council, and the South Side Planning Board. . . . The University was a prime instigator of the "Woodlawn Plan," a study of and proposal for community conservation undertaken in 1939 and published in part by the Chicago Plan Commission in 1946.

The principal forms of action before 1952 appear to have been subsidization of the Hyde Park Planning Association and Woodlawn, Incorporated, organizations concerned heavily with enforcement of zoning and housing codes, extensions of racially restrictive covenants, and, after 1948, the promotion of the inclusion of "conservation agreements" in contracts for real estate purchases. In addition, the University not only has a long history of land investments in the local area but has financed the construction of new housing (primarily for faculty use), purchased and renovated old residences, helped staff with the negotiation of mortgages, and furnished second mortgages to faculty purchasing homes in the neighborhood.

Like many large scale organizations, the University is hardly a monolithic structure whose authority lines all reach a peak in some single office. Rather, there is an extensive division of authority with many independent or semi-independent spheres. The physical plant of the University and its needs for expansion are under the control of a Vice-President in Charge of Business Affairs, who reports directly to the Chancellor. Real estate in the area held for investment purposes, however, is under the control of the Treasurer, who reports to the Fi-

---

1. *The University of Chicago and the Surrounding Community*, 1953, p. 7.

nance Committee of the Board of Trustees. Other agencies within the University handle local housing for students and faculty.

The Board of Trustees of the University is a "working board" of about thirty to forty members, many of whom have served for many years. Board committees most directly concerned with housing and conservation are the Area Committee and the Budget Committee, both of which have met very regularly during recent years. A long-standing policy position of the Board has been to make every effort to maintain the surrounding community as a residential area for faculty.

As one respondent put it, the University has long presented "many faces" to the community. This separation of powers accounts for the differences in policy and practice reflected in Hutchins' statements and the business office's use of restrictive covenants.

The faculty of the University of Chicago has played a role in urban renewal in a variety of ways. Its members with special knowledge or skills in planning, population, and urban studies have been called upon as expert consultants by municipal agencies. Many played leading parts in the Hyde Park–Kenwood Community Conference. Some have been consulted by the University administration for advice; for example, early in this period Chancellor Kimpton called upon Harvey Perloff, Philip M. Hauser, and Harold Mayer to suggest what steps might be taken to meet neighborhood problems. Out of this consultation grew the University's decision to undertake on its own initiative the preliminary steps toward urban renewal planning. While no enduring organization was set up to tap the wealth of talents available on the faculty, the administration has not been reluctant to use its faculty as a resource.[2] However, apart from the occasional use of experts, the major participa-

2. Under the traditional division of authority between a university administration and its faculty, the latter may feel quite free to turn down requests for aid on what might be conceived of as "housekeeping functions." Harvey Perloff, Chairman of the Committee on Planning, turned down the suggestion from Kimpton that he take the position of planner that later was taken by Jack Meltzer. Perloff's reason for rejecting the offer was that such a position was incompatible with his major commitments to teaching and research. Given this division of authority, an administration is understandably reluctant to call upon the faculty for help that involves a major commitment of time. Cf. footnote 12.

tion of the faculty at large has been as private citizens working primarily through the Hyde Park–Kenwood Community Conference.

Although the faculty members' role through the University administration has been slight, they have been an important factor in the University's actions in at least two respects. Assumptions made about the residential needs of faculty, students, and staff proved of importance in the trustee's decision to seek extensive conservation of the community. Secondly, the attitudes of faculty members concerning both conservation policies themselves and the relation of these to large institutional objectives as frequently and publicly expressed directly shaped policies pursued by University personnel in achieving urban renewal.

Hyde Park Planning Association

From 1947 until 1952 the University administration invested in the Hyde Park Planning Association as the organization most likely to solve local problems in a fashion favorable to the University. Before the Association was superseded by the South East Chicago Commission, it focused on efforts to enforce zoning, promoted building-code inspections as a means of preventing illegal conversions, and emphasized neighborhood cleanup and traffic control projects and extension of restrictive covenants. The Planning Association—which never planned, in the professional sense—drew its chief support from the large hotels east of the Illinois Central tracks, from realtors, and from the University of Chicago; in 1952 it had a membership of about 600. Dues were based on a percentage of the value of the property held by individual members—meaning, of course, that the University was the ranking member.

With a one-man staff, the Association accomplished little more than the cementing of relations between the large institutional and business interests in the area. The Association's commitment to residential segregation was instrumental, incidentally, in generating the forces that combined in 1949 to form the Hyde Park–Kenwood Community Conference. The Association stood between the Conference, with its strong emphasis on the possibilities of interracial living, and the University of Chicago. When the University's new Chancellor decided to involve himself actively in conservation in 1952, two difficulties confronted him. As the University's organizational "agent" in community affairs, the Planning Association was too weak to handle the new mission of Kimpton's administration, and publicly it was too divorced from the local citizenry.

A broadly based community organization, the Hyde Park–Kenwood Community Conference, already existed in the area. Conceivably it might have been the local vehicle for the expression of the University's concern with renewal. But the Conference at that time, as we shall see in the next chapter, was too divorced ideologically from the institutional and business interests of the area to fill this role. Instead, a new organization was built.

The Committee of Five

In 1952, following a series of crimes which had attracted widespread local attention, a mass meeting was called jointly by several organizations to protest the rising incidence of crime in the area. The meeting held on March 17 in Mandel Hall on the University of Chicago campus, was attended by an estimated 2,000 Hyde Park–Kenwood residents. For the first time, University officials met with the general public on matters of mutual interest and concern. Law enforcement and crime prevention were the immediate issues which brought together University officials, community leaders, and the general public. Crime in the area had reached proportions that seemed threatening to residents and institutions alike. Crime prevention was an issue on which the divergent interests in the area could readily converge. At the mass meeting a Committee of Five was established with Kimpton as chairman and composed of prominent civic leaders. This committee undertook to form a new organization to work for increased police protection, to enforce housing and zoning codes, and to "represent" the community.

Out of a wide array of local problems, the Committee of Five selected for primary emphasis crime prevention and the attack against illegal conversions of old houses and apartments. In the Committee's own words:

To meet these and other community problems, the committee recommends the following program: First we propose the establishment of a permanent organization to be known . . . as the South
East Chicago Commission. We recommend the establishment of an
office in the Hyde Park YMCA Building . . . with a full time professional staff. One of the functions of this office will be to act as a
listening post for our entire community. Anyone within the community can call or visit the office at any hour and report anything that he or she regards as an irregularity. . . If the committee's
program is adopted tonight, this office is ready to start functioning
with a skeleton staff tomorrow morning, and its telephone number
will be FAirfax 4-4008.

The Commission was created, complete with specification of
functions, a skeleton professional staff, an office, and a telephone number.

The public report of the committee also recommended to the
Board of Directors of the new organization at least eleven other
projects for the Commission, including conservation and rehabilitation:

One of the most challenging suggestions made to the committee was
the possibility of an effective conservation and rehabilitation program for specific buildings or even whole blocks or sections of the
area. In this connection, I should like to mention the need for planning within our community. There are those who have a deep suspicion of planners, and this is understandable. It is meaningless to
build up a big chart or mock-up if the net result is only to sit
around and admire it. On the other hand it is hard to know what
you are going to do until there is some over-all plan for what ought
to be done. We need new and improved housing in the area. We
must try to interest insurance companies and other sources of capital in a program of rehabilitation or orderly conservation . . . and
the erection of new housing units.

While a ballot was distributed at this public meeting to enable those attending to make their recommendations, obviously
the central objectives of the Commission had been thoroughly
spelled out in advance by the Committee of Five. Its machinery
was also thoroughly "pre-structured" by the committee. In the
same public report, Chancellor Kimpton, as Chairman, announced:

If the Committee's report is adopted this evening, we are prepared
to recommend the names of sixty distinguished and representative

members of the community who have agreed to serve, and we propose that the additional fifteen members be appointed by the provisional board of directors from suggestions made by members of the community. The ballot provides space to enable you to make *your* recommendations for these additional board members.

This and all similar arrangements suggested by Chancellor Kimpton were accepted by majority vote at the May meeting, including the provisions that no fixed fee should be charged for memberships and that membership should be kept open "to every resident, business, institution and community organization subscribing to the purposes and program of the Commission," with the exception of political organizations. In the same presentation, Kimpton announced the University's intention to contribute $15,000 at once to the Commission's first annual budget and pledged at least $10,000 for each of four succeeding years.

Few of the leaders within the Community Conference most active at that time were included on the slate of sixty prospective board members; but the Reverend Leslie Pennington, a founder of the Conference, was elected as one of the fifteen write-in nominees. Moreover, Hubert Will of the Committee of Five—who also was active in the Conference—became Secretary of the Commission Board.

The Commission promptly established headquarters in the Hyde Park YMCA Building, as a location where local residents could enter and leave without being "marked" as complaint carriers. According to the Commission's first executive Director, Dr. Ursula Stone (a temporary appointee), also a member of the Committee of Five, the Commission immediately became absorbed in receiving reports on misdemeanors, crimes, and building-code violations.

Julian Levi was appointed Executive Director of the South East Chicago Commission in the Fall of 1952. A corporation lawyer with experience in industrial management and the son of a prominent rabbi, Mr. Levi had been raised in Hyde Park and was well known as an aggressively competent administrator with strong personal attachments to the community and the University of Chicago.[3] Upon his appointment, he promptly

---

3. His brother, Edward H. Levi, was Dean of the University of Chicago Law School.

established a staff of two full-time workers, a community organization representative, and a University-trained sociologist charged with law enforcement.

Every mode of organization carries with it special gains and losses. The gains implicit in the model on which the Commission was founded were apparent to most community leaders from the outset. This creation of a community organization from "the top down" guaranteed strong financial support, unambiguous goals, and, most characteristically, great speed in action. The groundwork for the Commission was laid within seven weeks by the Committee of Five, and on the morning after a public mandate had been obtained the structure emerged intact and in operation.

The losses or costs are less apparent but no less inevitable. The Board of Directors, meeting after the Commission's temporary staff was already at work, was destined to become little more than a source of financial support, a provider of sanctions, and a sympathetic audience for the Commission staff, in spite of its explicit embodiment of policy-making responsibilities. The Executive Committee meetings became a place for relatively confidential reports on special problems confronting the Executive Director, without becoming a group within which solutions to these problems were devised. The larger Board of Directors tended increasingly to become an assembly through which the accomplishments of the staff could be disseminated and a vehicle for the solicitation of funds. Most of the Commission Board members, when interviewed, echoed the view of this businessman who had served since 1956: "Most of our actions are rubber stamps. It's mostly because Julian Levi is such an aggressive, hard-working director. We haven't voted him down on anything all year." ·

Clear evidence was obtained in interviews that membership on the Commission Board was early defined as a token of community status, particularly as a share in the aura of prestige that flowed from the close participation of University officials and trustees in the activities of the Commission. It became more important to belong to and to support the organization than to shape its goals and techniques. As one veteran Board member expressed it:

The most important thing about the success of the Committee of Five was that Kimpton himself took on the assignment of working as a Committee member. . . . this meant the committee was able to command large resources by way of personnel and consultation, and when it came time to set up the Commission it was possible to get very influential local figures into it from the start. From then on, there was no alternative to working with the Commission if you wanted to be in on the exciting events and decisions being made about renewal. Many persons since have fought to get on the Board because of the prestige one gets from proximity to Larry Kimpton. There's a real pleasure in being on a close first-name basis with Larry.

A few of the inevitable consequences of this type of organization might be explored briefly. The nominating committee of the Commissions' Board of Directors selects candidates from what they consider to be the "power groups" in the community, including the hotel owners, the white and nonwhite real estate firms, the business and professional men's associations, and the several institutions. The full membership of the Commission is convened only once each year, to hear a progress report from the Executive Director. The result is that, in spite of the intentions of the Committee of Five, the South East Chicago Commission has come to be defined from without as an agency representing the University of Chicago, other local private institutions, and business enterprises. As one sympathetic respondent expressed it:

. . . the members of the Commission Board are very interested and responsive individuals. It is unfortunate that they have been characterized as rubber stamps for the actions of the Executive Director. Actually, it would be better to think of them as a group of men who are acting the way men act on the Board of Trustees of some charitable agency—they have to act with sharply limited knowledge of day-to-day operations.

The "Downtown" Road to Renewal

Although the South East Chicago Commission had received a directive to prepare plans for community conservation and renewal, there was little in the way of available organizational machinery. The Federal Housing Act of 1949 provided machinery and funds for the redevelopment of areas which had become hopeless slums, but such neighborhoods as Hyde Park–Kenwood which were as yet only threatened with deterioration, were not covered in existing legislation and funds on either national or local levels.

The facilitating governmental action was not long in coming. Two series of events that began in 1952 were to culminate in legislation making community conservation a real possibility.

First, the City Council of Chicago passed a resolution calling for establishment of an Interim Commission on Neighborhood Conservation. In July, 1952, in response to Council action, Mayor Kennelly appointed James Downs, Jr., then his Housing and Planning Coordinator, as chairman of the Interim Commission, which was provided with a budget of $50,000. Downs—President of the nationally known Real Estate Research Corporation and a member of the prominent real estate firm of Downs and Mohl—had made a study of conservation in West Kenwood as Housing and Planning Coordinator in 1951. More important, according to his own account, he had been active in attempting to interest University of Chicago administrators in local neighborhood redevelopment as early as 1948. It was Downs' Interim Commission which delivered a report in November, 1952, calling for the creation of a permanent Community Conservation Board. The permanent Board was the municipal agency through which urban renewal in Hyde Park–Kenwood was to be accomplished.

From another direction, work also began in early 1952 to outline ways in which conservation and renewal could be accomplished. The Metropolitan Housing and Planning Council —a civic association concerned with planning in the Chicago metropolitan area—set up a committee to study how declining neighborhoods could be shored up through government and private planning efforts. The Conservation Committee eventually produced a massive report which significantly affected legislation by the state government.

Most important for Hyde Park–Kenwood was the Conservation Committee's decision to use that community as its major example. Undoubtedly this selection was only partly fortuitous; many of the Council's members had close connections with the community and the University. On the Conservation Committee of the Council in 1952 were Reginald Isaacs, head of the planning unit of Michael Reese Hospital, and Harvey Perloff, Professor of Planning at the University of Chicago. The Council Director, Mrs. Frederick H. Rubel, had long been a resident of Hyde Park. The Conservation Committee was chaired by Remick McDowell, a business executive who was working toward a Master's Degree in Business Administration at the University. Also on the Committee, and extremely active in its leadership, were Sydney Stein, Jr., then Chairman of the Hyde Park–Kenwood Community Conference, and Ferd Kramer, a University of Chicago graduate and a senior member of Draper and Kramer, a prominent real estate firm with extensive business on the South Side. (In 1952 more than one-third of the Board members of the Metropolitan Housing and Planning Council either lived in Hyde Park or Kenwood or were graduates of the University of Chicago.)

Furthermore, a grant to the Conservation Committee was made by Glen Lloyd, a member of the Board of Trustees of the University, who saw the Committee's work as contributing directly to the solution of the University's neighborhood problems.

Reginald Isaacs, who became the Conservation Committee's Research Director, had also been associated with an earlier effort to provide a plan for conservation of Hyde Park–Kenwood. In 1950 he participated in a community appraisal study of the South East Side (including Hyde Park), the staff for which had been drawn from the Department of Architecture and City Planning at the Illinois Institute of Technology and the School of Design at Harvard University. This survey investigated physical conditions in the area from 31st to 59th Streets and State Street to the Lake. A model plan suggesting ways of conserving the area was developed and published.

Later in 1952 Albert Svoboda, Assistant Treasurer of the University of Chicago, joined the Conservation Committee of the Metropolitan Housing and Planning Council. The city government's Interim Commission on Neighborhood Conservation worked actively with the Conservation Committee's privately paid staff of planners and researchers.

When the Conservation Committee of the Council first convened in March, 1952, its members readily accepted Isaacs' suggestion that Hyde Park–Kenwood would make the best pilot area for the study. Relations between the Council and the University illuminate the means by which the latter proceeded to mobilize a series of influential groups for local reconstruction. The Council's inquiries were self-initiated. The University simply invested in the Council Committee's work at the tactical moment.

The Objectives of the South East Chicago Commission

Four major objectives have been pursued by the South East Chicago Commission. First, the Commission sought with some success to obtain enforcement of building and coding regulations and to obtain proper police protection in the area. Secondly, the Commission sought to work out a program of action that culminated in the urban renewal plan for the community. Thirdly, it tried to encourage residential stability and community identification among the upper-middle-class residents. Finally, it tried to build support among leadership groups in the area and in the city as a whole for a program of amelioration of neighborhood conditions.

These major objectives have not met with uniform success. The Commission's day-to-day housekeeping activities have been most successful, and the decline in crimes reported to the police and the undoubtedly superior enforcement of housing and zoning regulations in the area are at least partially due to the activities of its staff. The Commission must also be considered successful in working out an action program and in getting the program accepted among "power groups" in Hyde Park–Kenwood. In contrast, the organization was unable to maintain effective public relations or to represent itself as a citizen's community organization.

In the words of an extremely well-informed, long-term Board member of the Commission:

The SECC has never built a program of public education or public information. This is its greatest failure. The mess surrounding the South West Hyde Park Redevelopment Corporation was not at all necessary, for example. . . . The University, with the help of the Commission, has continued to make enemies through the kinds of land purchase and building purchase practices they have engaged in. Even old, established residents of the community have discovered recently that the University has been quietly buying up every available middle-income house. People who would have remained here have simply been forced to leave or to squeeze into small apartments. None of this has been carried on with any awareness of the consequences it leads to—hostility toward the University and the Commission.

The Commission's inability to establish itself as a citizens' organization in the eyes of residents and the metropolitan area is in part the result of its organizational structure. This was designed as a "top-down" structure within which authority would be centered heavily in a small group of people. Beyond making contributions and giving help when called upon by the staff, there was little a member of the Commission was ever asked to do. With its expenses guaranteed by the University and other institutions, there was no necessity to spread membership throughout the area and develop a program which would involve members in the Commission's activity. In part, its image as a special-interest organization developed from its activities in the community that, as we shall show, involved the heavy use of University prestige and power to accomplish its objectives.

The failure in public relations has often been ascribed to Julian Levi. Although Levi's aggressiveness cannot be denied, it is also the case that the direct assault kind of operation engaged in by the Commission would make any Director of the organization a somewhat unpopular man in many quarters. To exploit fully the advantages in speed and power implied in the Commission's make-up and organization meant moving without much regard for public relations.

The prestige of the University affected not only the willingness of residents to become Commission members, but the ability of the Commission staff to accomplish its goals. Levi's earliest efforts were concentrated on restricting the operations of real estate speculators in Hyde Park, who since 1949 had been strongly attracted by the profits in racial succession. Racial succession has always meant an opportunity for gaining great profits through illegal conversions and higher rents to Negro tenants.

The South East Chicago Commission tried to cut down on

profit making from racial turnover in several ways. First, Levi was able to obtain tighter controls on the issuance of building permits, which include conversion construction. In this effort, Levi effectively brought to bear his own legal skills and executive abilities. Identical efforts had been made with less success by the Hyde Park Planning Association earlier, and by the volunteer legal panel of the Community Conference. Levi gained his crucial additional leverage from the sponsorship of the University and similar local institutions. He could in effect represent the most powerful community interests in demanding protection from the Chicago Department of Buildings and the Mayor's Housing and Redevelopment Coordinator.

Pressure on real estate speculators was also channeled through the University's strong connections with the business community. Banks and insurance companies were warned that their funds were in jeopardy when invested as mortgages on illegally converted property. Insurance companies were persuaded to suspend policies written on badly maintained properties. Publicity about the ownership of notorious slum properties was given to the press, which published unflattering accounts of the abuse of housing decency. The files of the Commission contain sets of correspondence with slum owners and operators directly pressuring for the raising of standards of maintenance.

The Commission's activity was strongly supported by the University's extension of its real estate holdings [4] in Hyde Park, Kenwood, and Woodlawn—eloquent testimony, as far as downtown political authorities and local realtors were concerned, of the clear intent to resist conversion. In expanding its holdings, the University commissioned the largest real estate management firm in Chicago, Baird and Warner, to manage the newly purchased properties; this firm was obliged, therefore, to coordinate its activities with the director of the Commission. As a result of this liaison and because realtors were heavily represented in the Commission as a whole, a majority of the real estate firms in Hyde Park and Kenwood also established coordinating liaisons with the Commission. By 1955 this system had been perfected by the Commission to the point where applicants

---

4. The University raised a special fund of $4 million from its alumni and friends to be used in neighborhood activities.

for housing in selected sectors of Hyde Park and Kenwood were being screened by the Commission staff. Many realtors explained that this included control over Negro movement into these areas.

The power of the University of Chicago working through the program of the Commission is shown equally well in the area of crime prevention. An incident early in the history of the South East Chicago Commission is suggestive of this leverage. The Commission hired two full-time private policemen to investigate a lake-front hotel that had become known in the community as the locale of various criminal activities, and the information collected was then given by Julian Levi to the insurance company that insured the hotel. The company disclaimed all knowledge of the criminal activities and swiftly canceled its coverage. When the hotel's mortgage holder was informed that insurance on the property had been canceled, he demanded immediate repayment of his loan. Foreclosure forced out the operators of the hotel, and, understandably, the new managers took pains to remove the criminal elements.

Similar tactics were successfully employed against tavern keepers identified by the Commission staff as maintaining undesirable bars. It is doubtful whether the same approach would prove equally effective if the Commission had lacked substantial financial resources and a ready access to the worlds of insurers and mortgagors.

Another example that demonstrates the close working relationship among the University, the Commission, and other groups in the community involved conversions in a local apartment dwelling. When a real estate speculator purchased a six-family apartment house and promptly moved in nine Negro families, the local block group of the Hyde Park–Kenwood Community Conference spotted the move and reported it to the Conference. The block group also shared its problem with the Commission. The day after the nine families moved in, Julian Levi visited the speculator, threatened him with legal action for violating the housing code, and confronted him with evidence of overcrowding; at the same time a generous offer to buy was made by the University real estate office. The speculator sold the apartment dwelling to the University on the next day, and one day later the nine Negro families were moved out by the University's real estate managers. Had this purchase and eviction not been possible, legal action through municipal channels would at best have achieved the levying of fines against the speculators—months and possibly even years after the conversion occurred.[5] Thus, it is one matter to threaten prosecution via the courts and another to be able to buy up properties which are in violation of the law.

The story as reported is based on information received from individuals in close contact with the South East Chicago Commission. The conflicts between the Commission and the Conference may be seen in the difference between the story as reported above and the following description obtained from a knowledgeable staff member of the Conference:

Yours is not a true account. . . . After one or two Negro families had moved into the building, the block group, at the suggestion of the Conference, arranged a meeting because of incipient panic in the block. I was invited to the meeting and so was Levi. The owner of the building had been violating building laws for some time . . . and one resident of the block, acting hastily, had persuaded some of his neighbors to join him in taking out an injunction to stop the owner from further conversions. It was believed that the owner had retaliated by renting to Negroes. At the block meeting the group was assured that action would be taken to prevent overcrowding and was advised by the Conference to invite the Negroes to its next meeting, which the group did. It was later that other Negro families were moved in. The action taken by Levi was independent. He did not even inform the Conference of it, nor about the University's purchase of the building—which we learned of indirectly.

5. As evidence that legal action alone never proved an adequate or efficient tool in code enforcement in Hyde Park, we would note that the Community Conference has enjoyed the benefits of an outstanding, well-qualified legal panel (volunteers) from 1952 through the present. This group was largely responsible for achieving comprehensive revision of the housing ordinances, as these were codified in new city ordinances in 1956 and again in 1957. One of these legal experts explained that the local and state statutes, however, have always been fairly adequate, and that the real dilemma was municipal administrative "incompetence," and that after great expenditures of skilled effort the possibilities for improved code enforcement in Chicago were extremely weak. This expert asserts that a climate has not been created to date in which administrative enforcement of codes is possible. He said that the penalties for housing code violations were either insignificant or whimsically arbitrary and that many speculators make calculated risks in accord with this custom.

During 1952 and 1953 the South East Chicago Commission specialized in securing better enforcement locally of the housing and building regulations. In addition, the primary job of Don Blackiston, staff criminologist, was to press for adequate police protection for the community. While the techniques employed to obtain these ends were often effective innovations in community organization, the goal was essentially that of obtaining the best kind of community protection available under local law.

The Commission and Planning

The report entitled *Conservation,* written by the Metropolitan Housing and Planning Council's commissioned staff, appeared in February, 1953. This three-volume document contained evaluations of a large number of devices that existed or could be created through legislation to accomplish planned conservation. The tools favored most strongly for this task were embodied in The Urban Community Conservation Act, which was submitted as a bill in the Illinois State House of Representatives.

The Conservation Committee also considered the use of private redevelopment corporations, a device which was later to be used in Hyde Park–Kenwood. It was noted that, although no activity had ever been carried out under its authority, a Redevelopment Commission for Chicago had existed since 1941 and, further, that "It might be possible to amend the Act so that its field of operations would include conservation areas, retaining the administrative mechanism and the neighborhood corporation idea (p. 254)." The study concluded, however, that the redevelopment corporation had serious shortcomings —namely, too great a dependence on local initiative, neglect of a comprehensive organizational framework within which to proceed, and the finding that "The granting of eminent domain to private corporations may be unwise from a public policy standpoint if not from a legal one (p. 255)."

Although the Conservation Committee's strongly endorsed conservation through over-all community planning, heavily subsidized by public funds, the South East Chicago Commission initially preferred private (as opposed to public) renewal. This was in part a division of political arenas, with "downtown actors" working toward public financing for conservation and the Commission concentrating on release of private resources for redevelopment. Given the University's strong backing of the Conservation Committee's activities, the early emphasis in the South East Chicago Commission on private means of renewal illustrates again the multifaceted quality of the University's policies.

Julian Levi devoted great energy to the task of making the private redevelopment corporation a usable renewal tool. He successfully persuaded the state legislature to amend the Neighborhood Redevelopment Corporation Act.[6] Originally the law permitted a redevelopment corporation to be organized only for the purpose of eliminating slums; under the amendments that Levi personally presented before the legislature in 1953, the public purposes for which redevelopment corporations might be used were broadened to include conservation of deteriorating housing and commercial sites. Most important, the 1953 amendments specified that if a redevelopment corporation obtained the consent of the owners of 60 per cent or more of the property within a given area, the corporation would thereby gain the right of eminent domain over the locale, subject to the supervision of a municipal commission.

Despite the fact that each had strong support from the University, the activities of the downtown Council and the local Commission were *not* coordinated. Julian Levi was promoting a modified Redevelopment Corporation Act in the state capitol at the same session in which the head of a Metropolitan Council Committee appeared to urge passage of a Conservation Act. Sufficient misunderstanding resulted to damage somewhat the

---

6. The original Act, held constitutional by the Illinois Supreme Court, permitted any three residents and citizens to organize a private corporation with a capital of not less than $1,000 and then—under the supervision of the Neighborhood Redevelopment Commission, appointed by the Mayor —to carry out a redevelopment plan. The local corporation was to get its financing from the sale of stock. It was authorized to make mortgages and property loans, propose street closings, propose new constructions, call for demolition of old buildings—in brief, to undertake a great variety of redevelopment operations. The original law required, however, that 60 per cent of the land in an area need already be purchased or under option by the corporation.

relations between the Commission and the Council. Both laws were passed in 1953.

The Urban Community Conservation Act, largely a product of the efforts of Reginald Isaacs' staff (outlined in their report), and brought through the legislature by the efforts of the Metropolitan Housing and Planning Council, was approved in July, 1953, a year prior to its federal equivalent.[7] The City Council (stimulated by the report of the Interim Commission) created a Community Conservation Board for Chicago in September, 1953. While this Board was organized early in 1954, it did not begin operating until the appointment of the late General Richard Smykal as full-time Commissioner in October, 1955. Thus, state and municipal machinery for urban renewal were created by 1954, some months in advance of the federal Urban Renewal Act.[8]

The rhythm of University and Commission activities paralleled the tides of the school year. The school year of 1952–1953, for example, was devoted to creating the Commission and building the policing program, and to University support of the preparation of the *Conservation* study. By the close of that academic year the means for securing revisions in the Redevelopment Corporation Act, or for obtaining a state Conservation Act, had been established.

The school year 1953–1954 opened on several new notes. The curriculum of neighborhood renewal underwent expansion, naturally without elimination of any "old courses." In October, 1953, the Maryland–Drexel Redevelopment Corporation presented pictures of its plans in the *Herald* and announced its

7. Illinois municipalities derive their housing powers from the State. The Conservation Act gave full authority to cities to initiate and to administer conservation renewal, but all municipal acts were defined as subject to the approval of the Illinois State Housing Authority. Incidentally, it was this Act which formally defined the meaning of conservation: "An area of not less than 160 acres in which the structures of 50% or more of the area are residential, having an average age of thirty-five years or more. Such an area is not yet a slum or blighted area." This Act also established the functions and structures for a community conservation board and for neighborhood conservation community councils.

8. Title I of the Housing Act of 1949 authorized federal assistance toward slum clearance. The Housing Act of 1954, however, broadened the provisions of the 1949 law to authorize federal assistance toward the *prevention* of the spread of slums and urban blight through rehabilitation and conservation of deteriorating areas.

intention of becoming the first to use the new redevelopment laws. At the same time, the University applied for a grant from the Field Foundation to set up a planning unit.

During the Summer of 1953 the Chicago Land Clearance Commission was persuaded to survey the most noticeably blighted section of Hyde Park, and in the Fall the Commission held joint public meetings with the Hyde Park–Kenwood Community Conference to discuss plans for slum clearance in this surveyed section. In other words, this school year became the "year of planning," following as it did on the year in which organizations were created and legislation enabled. The Kenwood Redevelopment Corporation, although not subsidized by University investments, as was the Maryland-Drexel Corporation, was also formed in November, 1953.[9]

Organization ties were in no sense neglected during this "year of planning," of course. For example, Lawrence Kimpton and Julian Levi met with the Hyde Park and Kenwood Council of Synagogues and Churches in December, 1953, to encourage these institutions to lay plans for future individual space requirements.

By 1954 these efforts resulted in the creation of machinery for neighborhood redevelopment and renewal, but no specific method of planned renewal had yet been devised for Hyde Park or Kenwood. The next step was to see to it that municipal political leaders were committed to conservation in the area. First, an understanding between Mayor Kennelly and the University of Chicago, mediated by James Downs, Jr., was reached in about January; it was agreed that the University would take a part in the planned renewal of Hyde Park and Kenwood. In March, 1954, Mayor Kennelly announced:

A bold plan for large scale urban redevelopment of the four and one half square miles southeast of Chicago, intended to reverse the trend towards deterioration. The area from 39th to 67th Street, Cottage Grove to the Lake, will serve as an official model planning project to develop a pilot plan for conservation efforts in other areas of the city. (*Herald,* March 24, 1954) The Chicago Plan Commission, the University of Chicago, and the South East Chicago Commission, working closely with the Hyde Park–Kenwood Com-

9. Officially incorporated, after months of paper work and capitalization efforts, in April, 1954.

munity Conference, will be jointly responsible for the drafting of this plan. The plan will be prepared in stages which will meet the urgent necessity for the immediate initiation of various projects in the area.

Hyde Park–Kenwood became the first "stage" in the program and, to date, the only stage. The focus on this segment, however, left unattended what planners call a "gap area" between 36th Street, north of which is located the Lake Meadows Development, a large-scale slum clearance project, and 47th Street, where Kenwood begins, an area that had exhibited more rapid deterioration than Hyde Park–Kenwood.

Planning Operations

In March, 1954, the Marshall Field Foundation gave a grant of $100,000 to the University of Chicago to be used for planning. That same month Jack Meltzer was appointed as Director of the Planning Unit of the South East Chicago Commission, with offices on the University campus.[10] Activities of the new Planning Unit exhibited the same swift decision-making, technical and administrative proficiency, and use of political leverage "downtown" as marked Commission and University action.

As much as possible, technical and administrative work ordinarily the province of municipal agencies was taken over by the University, the Commission, and the Planning Unit. They functioned increasingly from 1954 through 1957 as semipublic organizations performing tasks that might have been undertaken eventually by the Community Conservation Board, the Land Clearance Commission, and the City Planning Department.

This assumption was a consequence in large measure of the embryonic stage of the municipal agencies in question. The Community Conservation Board, for example, did not have the funds and other resources required to maintatin a staff of technically competent planners and housing experts until late in

---

10. A professional planner who had already served as private consultant to Lawrence Kimpton was approached for the job. He indicated that if he accepted it, he would want Mr. Meltzer as his assistant. When these negotiations deteriorated, Meltzer was offered the directorship.

1957. This arrangement stemmed, too, from a belief that an outside organization could move faster than a municipal agency —a view for which there certainly was much support. There was also the feeling that the municipal authorities lacked the competence to handle conservation, that if city agencies had to be involved under the law, one could still take on and execute important portions of their work for them.

This approach was applied by the University and the Commission in a number of other ways. The Commission staff supplemented the actions of the building department and the police department by conducting intelligence reconnaissance on law violations and by developing extralegal (but not illegal) ways of insuring compliance. The Board of Trustees swung the weight of civic organizations and the important business community. Some University resources were also used to implement the renewal plans through real estate purchases—$4 million having been employed in this fashion, mostly to purchase buildings close to the campus.

The pattern of University action reached its full expression in the handling of the Urban Renewal Plan. Despairing of the ability of the Community Conservation Board to move rapidly enough toward renewal, the University undertook to do the technical planning itself.[11] The University of Chicago contracted with the city (in 1955) to produce an Urban Renewal Plan, including both preliminary and final versions. Its planning unit, of course, would do the actual work. The federal government had to approve the preliminary plan before releasing funds for the final plan, and this was accomplished by 1957.

The placement of the Planning Unit in the community itself made the planner sensitive to local requests. Private citizens, staff members of the local institutions, and community organizations enjoyed throughout the planning process an unusual degree of access to the technical staff. Planner Jack Meltzer was receptive to all, carrying through on his statement on taking over the position that planning would be done in consultation with the community.

---

11. It is important to stress that at the time this report was written the municipal agencies concerned are very much better equipped to undertake these functions. Urban renewal in Chicago in the future can be handled by these agencies—perhaps not as swiftly, but with some dispatch.

The technique of undertaking the work of municipal agencies was further employed after the final plan had been announced. The meetings of the Conservation Community Council—a board of local citizens appointed by the Mayor to review the plan and give its approval—were attended by the staff of the South East Chicago Commission, who acted as the staff of the Council. Public hearings held by the City Council were also attended by Commission staff members, who functioned to marshal evidence and assemble documents in support of the plan.

Penalties of the Arrangement

We have described the pattern of University participation in the renewal endeavor. The advantages of this style, clearly enough, are efficiency, speed, and strong control. The disadvantages that became most apparent by 1956 were a weakening of public good will toward the University and the Commission and an increasing discrepancy between what University representatives considered effective renewal activity and what municipal agencies considered good work. In this section we want to illustrate how these disadvantages imposed limitations on the University's performance of its role.

Our first example is drawn from the record of small businessmen and their reactions to "Hyde Park A and B."

Three months after his appointment, Planner Jack Meltzer had completed his first plan, "Hyde Park A and B," a proposal for clearance of a sector of semiblighted residential and commercial properties along 55th Street and the Illinois Central tracks. The plan was officially designated as "Hyde Park Redevelopment Project Number One." The "A and B area" contained 1,750 dwelling units and included twenty-two bars and taverns. "Hyde Park A and B" consisted of forty-seven acres that contained 40 per cent of the blighted buildings in Hyde Park, although it covered only 6 per cent of Hyde Park's land. The area presented a seedy, run-down appearance in keeping with its traditional function as the historic center of the area's literary and artistic Bohemia. By 1954, however, most of the Bohemians had left 55th Street, and there remained only the unattractive shell of what had been, as a unique locale, a vital contributor to American culture. One building, once the temporary address of several nationally known writers, was in 1954 known as "misery mansion."

When planning for Redevelopment Project Number One began, the 1954 Federal Urban Renewal Act had not yet been passed, much less tested in the courts. It was therefore necessary to proceed under the Housing Act of 1949, which provided that the federal government would give two-thirds of the cost of land acquisition and razing in areas officially defined as slums.

The general area covered by "Hyde Park A and B" had been considered earlier as appropriate for redevelopment by the Conservation Committee report of the Metropolitan Housing and Planning Council. In fact, plans of a very general nature for the area had been included in the report. Drawn up by Harry Weese, an architect on the Conservation Committee, the plans called for a large shopping center to be built along 55th Street, replacing many existing retail outlets. This plan had been presented by the South East Chicago Commission to the Business and Professional Men's Association of 55th Street, and these merchants reportedly favored the Weese plan strongly. Although resembling in general the earlier plan drawn by Harry Weese, Meltzer's proposal called for a much smaller shopping center. He also introduced a small park and expanded the space reserved for the Philip Murray Public School.[12] His reduction in the shopping center was made on the basis of estimates of the amount of facilities needed in the area.

The merchants, bankers, and other businessmen of Hyde Park were poorly organized in 1954. A 55th Street Businessmen's Association existed alongside a comparable 53rd Street Association; these groups did not merge until 1956. Furthermore, the 55th Street businessmen were repeatedly characterized by well-informed respondents as composed mainly of conservative owners of small shops, barbers, dentists, and service and goods retailers. While many had been located on 55th Street

---

12. Meltzer had concrete reasons for reducing the size of the shopping center. He realized that large, well-known retailers would attract heavier capitalization by investors and, secondly, that retail purchasing practices in Hyde Park had been changing for years, to the disadvantage of numerous small local retail outlets, because of changing transportation facilities and differentiating clienteles.

for more than ten years and had witnessed the deterioration of the locale, they had done little, individually or collectively, to combat the process or to strengthen their own business position through advertising, community service, or mutual efforts.

The earlier Weese plan, as we said, was discussed with the businessmen. The later plan, drawn by Meltzer, was announced before consultation with these merchants. When their Associations were informed of the proposals, the merchants did not understand fully that they would be relocated out of their existing sites. They did grasp readily the point that successful redevelopment would attract new money and increased trade into the 55th Street locale. The Associations were therefore among the first groups to endorse the "A and B" proposals. Their feelings were summed up at the time by a 55th Street druggist who told a *Herald* reporter:

I'm not interested in having my business interrupted, but I realize I can't stop progress. . . . I don't think it is fair to put out people who have been here and then when the center is built, let in businesses which were never here before. If we must be moved aside to preserve the community, it seems only fair to give us first chance to relocate here. (*Herald,* July 14, 1954)

The Chicago Land Clearance Commission approved the Meltzer proposal on July 6, and the City Council held public hearings on July 20. At the hearings spokesmen for the businessmen sought guarantees of rights to be relocated in the new commercial structures which would be built on the cleared land. At the hearings Julian Levi testified that the plan had "the full measure of citizen support and participation so often sought and so seldom achieved" (*Herald,* July 21, 1954). Numerous organizations, including the Hyde Park–Kenwood Community Conference, announced their support for the proposal, and individual citizens within the proposed clearance area testified in favor of the plan at a hearing by the Housing and Planning Committee of the City Council.

In order to speed matters further by obtaining a sympathetic hearing from the federal government, a delegation of twelve prominent citizens, most of them connected directly or indirectly with the University of Chicago, and four representatives of the municipal government traveled to Washington. The delegation met with President Eisenhower and Administrator Albert Cole. Within a very short period after this meeting, Commissioner Cole announced an allocation of $6,800,000 for "Hyde Park A and B."

The Land Clearance Commission had swiftly accepted Meltzer's proposal, changing it only slightly. Using this plan as a guide, the Commission advertised for redevelopers. The redeveloper who would buy the land was not required to follow Meltzer's plan in every detail but needed only to guarantee that the land would be used for the purposes set forth in that plan.

Five bids were submitted on the plan, although, in the speed that pervaded the entire procedure, none were given fully detailed information about the restrictions on land uses and community practices. After the first-choice bidder had withdrawn, Webb and Knapp of New York City secured the contract on the basis of a second set of plans drawn up with the assistance (again) of architect Harry Weese. The Webb and Knapp Plan contained a shopping center even smaller than the one shown in the Meltzer Plan. The Webb and Knapp Plan was approved by the City Council, the Illinois State Housing Board, and the Urban Renewal Administration in February, 1957, more than two and a half years after Redevelopment Project Number One had been approved in outline!

Demolition began in May of 1955, however, less than a year after Meltzer announced his proposal. Between late 1954 and 1957 local merchants became increasingly dissatisfied. In 1955 David Sutton—owner of one of the largest businesses in Hyde Park, a former city alderman, and a long-time associate of Mayor Daley [13]—assumed active leadership of the 55th Street Businessmen's Association. He announced firmly the policy position of the association in an open letter to the Land Clearance Commission and the *Herald* editor:

To summarize, we feel that many of the merchants now on 55th Street . . . would prove to be excellent tenants for the shopping center; and they should have first consideration for stores in the new center; and they should have first consideration for stores in the new center. We consider it imperative that the shopping center be Stage 1 and that whenever possible, existing business facilities

---

13. Sutton became Conservation Community Council chairman in 1957.

be allowed to remain in operation until the new center is ready for occupancy. . . . (*Herald,* April 13, 1955)

In May Ira Bach, then Land Clearance Commissioner, and his Deputy, Phil Doyle, met with representatives of the 55th Street Association. They reported hopes of finding a "friendly redeveloper" who would give priorities to the businesses already located in the clearance area, including careful staging of demolition and a guarantee to leave part of the north side of 55th Street standing so that portions of the business community could continue operations during redevelopment. Bach and Doyle also promised speedy construction and relocation assistance.

It became increasingly evident during 1956 that critical decisions bearing on the fate of local businessmen and on precisely how the "A and B" sites should be redeveloped rested with neither the Land Clearance Commission nor the South East Chicago Commission, but with the private redevelopers bidding for the job. Moreover, their bids had to be considered principally in terms of costs, quality of plans, and ability to carry out plans, rather than in terms of "friendliness" to 55th Street merchants.

Demoralization among the merchants—chiefly a conviction that businessmen had been "sold a bill of goods," or, among others, "that we had no voice"—deepened into bitterness. In December, 1956, David Sutton, speaking for the Association, demanded publicly that Mayor Daley seek the resignations of Ira Bach and Phil Doyle. As one informed businessman located on 55th Street commented:

The businessmen on 55th Street feel double crossed and taken for a ride on the "Hyde Park A and B" plan. We were promised stores on the north side of 55th and homes on the south side. This plan was approved by the Conference, by the Commission and by the City Council—but then Webb and Knapp changed it. One lesson I've learned from all this is that final plans are determined by the developer. The city and civic organizations have very little to say when the plan is financed by private money. . . . Under the old plan we would have had a larger shopping center and displaced merchants would have had a chance to re-establish themselves here. Now the center covers a much smaller area and the merchants are out of luck. Don't get me wrong—I'm one hundred per cent for redevelopment. All the business people were for it. But after we got it, many of us faced displacement.

Another informed respondent stated that these merchants had never fully understood that they were going to have to leave the locale. Their initial approval was based on their conviction that they would not have to leave or to relocate nearby *until* the new center had been erected. A second well-informed respondent remarked that the first *Weese* plan had seemed to provide sufficient space for immediate and direct location of long-term resident businesses into a huge new shopping center.

Faulty public relations also characterized the South East Chicago Commission's launching of what we shall call "The Park Plan." In 1954, two weeks after the City Council first approved Redevelopment Project Number One, the South East Chicago Commission proposed publicly that the Chicago Park District build a six-and-one-half-acre neighborhood park in a residential block immediately adjacent to and partly overlapping Project Number One. The proposal, called "Renewal Project Number Two," suggested that the Land Clearance Commission sell some of its property acquired from Hyde Park A to the Park District and that the latter acquire and clear the remainder of the proposed park site. The proposal, nearly identical with a plan prepared by the Park District in 1948 but never enacted, envisioned a $100,000 park connecting three bordering institutions—a Catholic Church and parochial school, a public school, and a youth service agency. The Commission statement said:

This second proposal is like the slum clearance proposal—a move to seize an opportunity while it exists. As such, it is not a paper plan; it is a program which is designed to go ahead immediately.

Persuasive reasons for the proposal were set forth in the Commission report. The Commission, however, neglected to "sound out" in advance residents in the neighborhood concerned, and the park plan was announced "cold." When it learned that 132 families would have faced relocation in connection with Project Number Two, the block group in the locale organized resistance immediately, prepared petitions to delay consideration of the plan, and chastised its parent organization, the Conference, "for neglecting to inform or initiate discussion with either of the two active block organizations affected prior to the presentation of the plan to the Park District."

The block groups promptly engaged in a series of meetings with the Community Conference Planning Committee and simultaneously published letters in the *Herald* explaining that, while the residents favored the concept of a recreation park and were not objecting solely on the basis of private interests, they also felt no relocation procedures existed to insure that any of them would ever gain the future benefits of the park. Furthermore, the amount of blight in the proposed site was extremely negligible and better clearance sites for park use could be found in the area, they asserted.

The Conference staff and Board of Directors—which could hardly have protected the interests of their block groups, since they were not informed in advance about Project Number Two —reviewed the proposal with its Planning Committee and confronted the controversy in a policy statement in November, 1954. The Conference approved the park proposal and attached a series of recommendations intended to protect the residents in getting fair sale prices and effective relocation.

The plan was quietly dropped, apparently on two counts. The Park District took the position that it could not approve the proposal at that time, and the strong opposition to the proposal induced the Commission staff to stop promoting the plan. These pressures, incidentally, stemmed not only from the block groups but from the 55th Street businessmen as well. One of the influential leaders of the Businessmen's Association labeled the proposed park, a "likely loafing place for bums."

We believe this case demonstrates the penalties for neglect of public relations. As an instance of community conflict, it also serves as a measure of the latent but ever-present limits within which power to renew can be exercised—limits established on the one side by municipal agencies, with their precedents and techniques, and on the other by organized citizens.[14]

---

14. The experience of success in affecting policy gained by block groups in the case of the park proposal conflict also stimulated the later formation of the Tenants and Home Owners Association, a group which splintered from the Conference; on the basis of leadership and members drawn

The same hasty and ill-considered style of action also characterized the real estate purchasing practices of the University. For instance, on the same day in January, 1956, 300 residents in seven newly purchased South West Hyde Park apartment buildings received eviction notices from Baird and Warner, real estate managers for the University. The University gave no advance warnings, and there were no block-group discussions. No announcement of this plan was made to the Committee of Six (the body composed of two representatives apiece from the University, the Commission, and the Conference). After much hostile publicity about the eviction notices, University real estate director Charles Gibson announced:

Just two months ago we emptied a building on Maryland Avenue, and there was no fuss about that. This time eviction happens to be going on in a more highly organized area. (*Herald,* January 18, 1956)

Despite the impatience and rapid pace typical of the University attack, it was forced to compromise in the carrying out of renewal with the time-consuming nature of governmental machinery. The timing of the several phases of Redevelopment Project Number One represents the limitations the renewal process imposes on energetic actors. The first "year of planning" of the University and the Commission closed in July, 1954, with the City Council approval of "Hyde Park A and B" and with the delegation's trip to Washington. But acquisition, relocation and demolition were the bottlenecks which brought the breakneck schedule of the University to a halt. Demolition did not begin until May 18, 1955, a year later. Construction by Webb and Knapp has still to be completed at this writing (1959).

Apparently, the long delay ahead was not anticipated by University and Commission leadership. They were not sufficiently aware of the political necessities surrounding participation of governmental agencies in Chicago. In other words, acquisition and relocation are time-consuming and the munici-

from the two block groups that had fought the park issues, this Association became a source of real opposition to the larger renewal plan developed by the Commission and the Planning Unit. See Chapter 8 for fuller treatment of this opposition group.

pal machinery ponderously slow. For instance, the Land Clearance Commission did not complete appraisals on Project A properties until nine months after the City Council approved the Project.

By July, 1955, one year after initial Council approval, delays of city agencies (at least as perceived by local interests) had produced a state of urgent dismay within the University and the Commission. University officials and others met with Mayor Daley to press him to activate the Community Conservation Board, strengthen the City Building Department, and speed the Land Clearance Project. The same delegation met with Housing Coordinator James Downs and urged his cooperation in expediting clearance. In particular, the delegation criticized the Land Clearance Commission for not hiring outside appraisors to speed acquisition in Projects A and B and for delays in preparing a prospectus to interest developers.

To city officials these impatient complaints seemed ill deserved. A Land Clearance Commission spokesman stated that the time schedule for land clearance, "far from lagging, is going on at such a rapid pace compared to similar projects in the city and elsewhere in the country that it might actually be considered alarming in some quarters." The total amount of public money involved in Projects A and B was close to $7 million, he said—an amount which the federal government insisted be spent wisely. He charged that the speed desired by the neighborhood leaders would put the Land Clearance Commission in the position of "being a panic buyer," paying unwarranted prices in order to speed renewal by perhaps a month.

Conflict between the South East Chicago Commission and city agencies over the pace of renewal characterized relations between the city government and the Commission all through the process of achieving renewal in Hyde Park–Kenwood. In part, this conflict is common to all local neighborhood-municipal government relationships. The municipal officials have to schedule their activities according to the needs of many projects and at the same time accomplish their day-to-day housekeeping functions. No one project can for long preoccupy a municipal agency without some degree of dissatisfaction arising elsewhere in the city.

But Hyde Park–Kenwood was no ordinary neighborhood.

The resources of great wealth, prestige, and legal and administrative skills, plus the political leverages which the University
of Chicago could command, put more than ordinary pressure
upon city officials. What appeared to the Commission and the
University officials as unwarranted delays were perceived by
city officials as breakneck speed on high-priority goals. Undoubtedly, conservation moved faster in Hyde Park–Kenwood
than in other parts of Chicago.

Final Comment

We have been able to discern a consistent pattern to the
University's actions in urban renewal. It shied away from the
local scene and its inhabitants and concentrated mainly on
moving the power centers in municipal government. But this
does not mean that there was no citizen participation in the
urban renewal planning process; on the contrary, there were
many points at which University goals had to be modified as
a direct result of citizen participation through local organizations. The story of these changes has been reserved for later
chapters. Most of these instances, however, took place from
1956 through 1958–subsequent to the publication of the first
Preliminary Plan for Urban Renewal—although several are
cases where University goals were rejected successfully by citizens in pursuit of competing objectives.

Despite the maladroitness with which public relations were
handled by the South East Chicago Commission and the University, there is no doubt that their policies have been accepted
both within the community itself and within the larger city.
Two factors combined to produce, as an end result, better public relations than were deserved.

To begin with, there was the urgency of the neighborhood
situation itself. Some action was necessary if Hyde Park–Kenwood was not to deteriorate seriously. This goal united the
University, business interests, home owners, and residents. The
likely consequences of inaction were so visible that any action
on the part of a great institution (as the University of Chicago
was regarded) would have been well received. Further, the University's use of a wide variety of different kinds of action on a
number of extremely popular issues—crime control, illegal

conversions, and building maintenance—and its long-term remedies as embodied in slum clearance and urban renewal stimulated even greater acceptance. The largest institution in the
area took its "proper" place in the view of residents and city
leaders as the initiator and developer of remedies for the
threatened "disaster."

Widespread public acceptance of the University actions
also resulted from the division of labor that arose between the
South East Chicago Commission and the Hyde Park–Kenwood
Community Conference. For a variety of reasons (treated in
detail in Chapter 5) the Conference functioned to provide the
public relations that the University was apparently unable to
develop itself. Information about the various plans and devices was disseminated widely through the community by the
Conference, whose set-up as a membership organization tied
into a fairly extensive network of block groups made it uniquely
suitable as a device for reaching the concerned and articulate
members of the community.

In a way, the Conference's strengths were the Commission's
weaknesses and vice versa. The Conference's difficulties in taking on planning functions made the Commission's leadership in
providing remedies easier. Similarly, the Conference's ability to
reach the "grass roots" made the Commission's difficulty in so-
doing less of a deficiency. Although no formal agreement was
ever made between the two organizations, a symbiotic relationship arose, which made for relatively even progress toward
neighborhood conservation.

In what sense may we conclude that a University program
underlay and buttressed the entire range of renewal efforts in
Hyde Park and Kenwood? The interpretive narrative has
shown, we believe, that the University of Chicago, by making the
following decisions and taking the following steps, established
the goals and devised the means through which conservation
became a viable probability for its surrounding neighborhoods:

1. (1948–1951) Progressive abandonment of efforts to
protect the area through restrictive covenants and conservation agreements (Efforts to use unwritten agreements may
persist.)

2. (1952) Decision to create the South East Chicago Commission

3. (1952) Support for and direct involvement in the program of the Metropolitan Housing and Planning Council

4. (1953) Development of liaisons and agreements with city agencies (Housing Coordinator and Office of the Mayor and Alderman Merriam) concerning renewal programming

5. (1954) Arrangement of the Field Foundation Grant to provide for the establishment of a local Planning Unit, and support of the Unit's Redevelopment Project Number One ("A and B")

6. (1955) Subsidization of the South West Hyde Park Redevelopment Corporation, creation of corporate structures for systematic purchase of local real estate, and development of the Saarinen Campus Plan in relation to the Redevelopment Corporation plans for South West Hyde Park

CHAPTER 5

The Community Conference
and Urban Renewal

*I*n the conservation of Hyde Park–Kenwood the citizenry had two important roles to play. The first was to remain settled in the area while the process of altering and repairing the physical structure was going on. Had the mass exodus begun in the early 1950's continued at the same rate throughout this decade, Hyde Park–Kenwood would have been profoundly changed. Building popular confidence in a future whose content was highly ambiguous was one of the important tasks attempted by the Community Conference.

Its second major role was to provide mass support and understanding for the renewal plan itself. The public officials whose approval was necessary for the use of government powers and funds could not have been insensitive to strong signs of mass local distrust or disapproval of the various projects devised by the University and its Planning Unit. Attaining widespread positive support from residents was thus a key function performed by the Hyde Park–Kenwood Community Conference.

It is this second role of insuring wide sympathetic understanding for the planning projects that will occupy the bulk of this chapter on the Community Conference. This emphasis is not meant to underrate the importance of maintaining community morale. Without residential stability Hyde Park–Kenwood may well have gone the way of neighboring areas to the north. Nor shall we put forth the thesis that the role of the Conference was entirely a passive one of acting as a transmission belt between the Planning Unit and the citizenry it could reach. There have been many points at which the Conference not only mediated but influenced the conservation planning process.

Other organizations that participated in the planning process will be considered in subsequent chapters. We chose to study the Community Conference first and in greatest detail for several compelling reasons. The Conference was the first organization in the local community to initiate and promote planned renewal as a solution to the problems of Hyde Park–Kenwood. Since 1949 it has been the largest local civic association and has been widely recognized as the spokesman for the public on issues requiring decisions by planners and city officials.

The chapter recounts the story of how the Conference originated, grew, and came to define its goals. As mentioned in Chapter 2, we shall not duplicate the excellent history to be found in Mrs. Julia Abrahamson's book, *A Neighborhood Finds Itself* (New York: Harper & Brothers, 1959), on which we have relied and which presents a more richly detailed description of the human side of Conference services. Instead, we shall center upon the relation of the Conference to renewal planning. This involves giving closest attention to the work of the Planning Committee of the Conference, as well as some consideration to the efforts of the Conference staff to mediate between citizens and the official Planning Unit.

The Founding Period—The Evolution of Conference Philosophy and Tactics

The Hyde Park–Kenwood Community Conference was founded in 1949. Hyde Park–Kenwood, as Chapter 2 shows, had long had a rich organizational life, and civic associations had existed almost from its beginnings as an urban neighborhood. However, from the outset the Conference differed sharply from its immediate predecessors in two respects: first, it was the outlet for the liberal intellectual elements of the community; secondly, it developed radically new mechanisms for connecting itself with a wide range of community residents. In fact, the emergence of the Conference can be ascribed to the obvious deficiencies of its predecessors in these two important respects.

The most immediate predecessor of the Conference was the

Hyde Park Community Council, created in 1946 to act chiefly as a coordinating council for the existing organizations in the area. Its relations with the citizenry were indirect, and it had no authority from its member organizations to make binding decisions.

A more powerful group, the Hyde Park Planning Association (dealt with briefly in Chapter 4), represented chiefly the University and the hotel owners of East Hyde Park. The Planning Association was active in devising and maintaining racially restrictive covenants.[1] In its philosophy and program the Planning Association was far removed from the liberal intellectual element in the community.

Attempts on the part of the liberal elements of the community to bring the Hyde Park Community Council into some sort of program of improving race relations failed. For example, in 1946, the local chapter of the American Veterans' Committee, with the help of Dr. Leslie Pennington and Rabbi Jacob Weinstein, formed a Council Committee on Race Relations. This Committee, vigorously opposed by the Hyde Park Planning Association, was unable to formulate any plan of study or action.

At the same time events on the national scene strengthened the interracial ideology of the liberals in Hyde Park–Kenwood. The United States Supreme Court ruling on restrictive covenants pertaining to race made the interracial neighborhoods of the liberals' long-standing plea not only a desirable but an inevitable occurrence. Added to the usual moral appeal was the new argument that interracial neighborhood living was on its way and that neighborhoods like Hyde Park–Kenwood would have to face a new pattern of existence very shortly.

The feeling of the inevitability of interracialism spread quickly to other areas of life. For example, discussion was started in the Hyde Park Council of Churches and Synagogues on the desirability of integration within local churches. The First Unitarian Church, under Dr. Pennington, soon announced a policy of open membership and began to receive a small num-

---

1. For a detailed description of restriction efforts, see Zorita W. Mikva, *The Neighborhood Improvement Association: A Counter-Force to the Expansion of Chicago's Negro Population* (M.A. Thesis, University of Chicago, 1951).

ber of Negroes. Soon thereafter the 57th Street Meeting of the Society of Friends and the KAM Temple also announced policies of open membership. A slight tide of sentiment seemed to be favoring closer ties between whites and Negroes. At the same time there was no organizational form within which this new sentiment could find an expression.

By 1949 it was equally clear that racially restrictive housing policies had seen their day and that Hyde Park–Kenwood would soon undergo an infusion of Negroes. No existing community organization seemed able to adjust to this new situation or to provide ways of preserving the essential flavor of the community and at the same time incorporating the newcomers. These then were the background conditions under which the Conference was organized.

The immediate impetus for the founding of the Conference was a meeting in the First Unitarian Church of persons nominated by local rabbis and ministers as individuals interested in civic affairs and race relations. The leadership at this meeting and in the earliest part of the Conference's history came from among Hyde Park–Kenwood's religious congregations and particularly from three liberal religious groups—Unitarians, Reform Jews, and Quakers. It was at this meeting that the decision to form the organization was made.

Among the policies established at the first meeting, three remained of determining significance throughout the life of the Community Conference. The charter members decided (1) to form a citizens' organization with as wide an individual membership base as could be recruited; (2) to avoid both left-wing interracial utopianism [2] and right-wing racial restrictionism; and (3) to work toward the goal of community improvement, conceived of at the outset as a matter of stimulating self-help rehabilitation and enforcing housing and zoning codes in the

---

2. Fragments of the Communist Party were located in Hyde Park during the immediate postwar period, and these were naturally eager to join forces with any suitable citizens' movement. Avoidance of this potential stigma was agreed upon from the outset. The perceived existence of "enemies" to the left and to the right (principally the Hyde Park Planning Association and related restrictive-covenant promoters) doubtless gave Conference leaders an early opportunity to achieve a differentiated identity and group unity.

battle against overcrowding and illegal conversion and as exploratory discussion of planning.

The first funds in support of the Conference came from $100 subscriptions solicited from sympathetic local residents and some churches and temples. This $1,000 was sufficient to start the Conference off—to pay for paper, stamps, and telephone service to reach toward the future membership of the organization.

Mrs. Julia Abrahamson became the first secretary to the newly formed Board of Directors and was shortly appointed Executive Director, a post she held until June, 1956. Mrs. Abrahamson had much to do with founding the Conference and has influenced its development more than perhaps any other individual.

Mrs. Abrahamson's activities before she became the "prime minister" of the Conference give some hint of the style of activity which she was to bring to her new office. She and her husband spent 1945–1947 in India working on relief and rehabilitation after the Bengal Famine. An author and publicist by profession, Mrs. Abrahamson had previously worked for the Julius Rosenwald Fund in the field of race relations. She was thus equipped with very special skills in community organization, social service projects, publicity, and philanthropic enterprise. In 1948, on their return from India, the Abrahamsons were appointed cochairmen of the Social Order Committee of the 57th Street Meeting of the Society of Friends in Hyde Park, a group which interested itself in stimulating social action to alter the pattern of residential flight and to improve interracial understanding.

Other persons present at the founding meeting were also to give the Conference much of its distinctive style. For example, Professor Herbert Thelen, head of the University of Chicago Human Dynamics Laboratory, was present.[3] Thelen's group had become interested in stimulating "grass-roots" citizen action in 1947, before the Conference was formed, and had con-

---

3. For the full description of the Laboratory's role, see Herbert A. Thelen and Bettie B. Sarchet, *Neighbors in Action* (University of Chicago, Human Dynamics Laboratory, 1954); Herbert A. Thelen, *The Dynamics of Groups at Work,* (University of Chicago Press, 1954), chs. I and XII; and Bettie B. Sarchet, *Block Groups and Community Change* (University of Chicago, Human Dynamics Laboratory, 1955).

ducted a research seminar to develop a program for involving groups in social action. The same seminar in 1949 worked with the Conference to set up large group meetings designed to present citizens with some of the social problems facing them and to encourage problem-solving efforts.

The involvement of the Human Dynamics Laboratory in the work of the Conference at this early stage had important repercussions on its program. Very early the Laboratory staff, aided by Conference volunteers, was able to make a number of surveys yielding valuable information on how residents were reacting to neighborhood problems. For instance, the early interviews conducted by Laboratory students indicated to Thelen that there existed an immediate need to "take steps to halt panic and to stabilize the area." Although everyone on the Conference Board knew that some people were moving out of the community, knowledge of the extent and the intensity of the motivation to leave was given substance by Thelen's research.

As important a contribution to the Conference was the set of social-action techniques and accompanying ideology that Thelen and his group could offer. The group-dynamics techniques for reducing interpersonal tension and individual anxiety by working with small face-to-face groups became the standard procedure for organizing and maintaining block groups. The ideology of the group-dynamics "movement" contained certain premises which were also shared by the religious groups which led the Conference at this early date: (1) When ordinary people participate with others in working through their collective problems, the solutions arrived at will be soundly conceived and capable of being put into practice by the people themselves. (2) Social problems can best be solved by the avoidance of conflict and the pursuit of cooperation. (3) Cooperation can be achieved when full communication exists between individuals and groups. (4) Conflict means the absence of effective communication.

This orientation to social action became a hallmark of the Conference, especially in its earliest years. The emphasis on "grass-roots" democracy undoubtedly proved to the Quakers, Unitarians, Reform Jews, believers in consumers' cooperatives, and liberal intellectuals that the Conference was an organization in which they would feel at home. In this sense, the Conference can be said to have been an expression of the neighborhood.

There exist in many neighborhoods throughout the country groups that would be profoundly attracted to the orientation to social action represented by the Conference in this early period. But it is not likely that they would represent nearly so large a proportion of the neighborhood's residents as was the case in Hyde Park–Kenwood in this period. Nor is every neighborhood likely to have at hand such skilled practitioners in group dynamics as Thelen and his associates.

During 1949 and 1950, for example, the Human Dynamics Laboratory staff assisted the Conference in conducting a series of public meetings. This could perhaps be achieved by any citizen's organization, but the distinguishing feature was the quality of the public meetings. These included a formidable battery of devices designed both to entertain and stimulate group action, including dramatic skits of local problems, role-playing experiments, "buzz sessions," and problem censuses—instruments we shall not pause to define, since they are adequately described elsewhere. Later, when the techniques of effective block-group organization had been clarified through practice and research, Thelen's group produced a manual on how to establish and maintain block groups.

In 1950, the Conference, with the aid of the Laboratory, began to locate and train leaders to start groups on their own blocks. These new leaders, moreover, attended biweekly seminars held in the University Laboratory, where their skills in group management, recruitment, and problem solving were sharpened through practice and discussion. By 1952 the Conference and the Laboratory had set up a Community Clinic, which met every three weeks. Anyone who wanted to start a new group was welcome to attend for training and consultation. We shall assess some of the consequences of these block organizations later in this chapter.

The work of the Conference and the Human Dynamics Laboratory provided a set of block groups throughout the community, each organized around block problems and related, albeit somewhat loosely, to the Conference. These block groups were not necessarily composed of Conference members, nor were the block groups bound to respect Conference policies.

Conference members were often among the more active members of the block groups, and members of the Conference were urged to join block groups. The Conference staff made itself available to the block groups as a source of advice and guidance, and as a channel of communication to the community at large, and to such power groups as the University and the municipal government. In turn, the block groups were the Conference's ties to the publics of Hyde Park–Kenwood. They also served as an important recruiting ground for membership in the Conference.

In the first year of the Conference's existence, and before the block groups were firmly established throughout the community, the recruitment of membership to the Conference was aided greatly by the organization's participation in research designed to gather data on the Hyde Park–Kenwood area. In 1950 the Michael Reese Hospital Planning Staff began a Community Appraisal Study in cooperation with the Chicago South Side Planning Board and other groups. Faculty members and graduate students of the University of Chicago Committee on Planning, many of whom were early members of the Conference, also were involved in the planning of the study.

The aim of the Community Appraisal was to collect a wealth of population, economic, and institutional information to provide a basis for first-stage planning. By strong and enthusiastic commitment to this enterprise, the Conference leadership availed itself of far more than the indirect services of a variety of planning professionals. By assuming the burden of local field work required for the self-survey, the Conference seized upon a direct means of involving citizens in Planning, and, by implication, in the operations and goals of the Conference. This move worked to strengthen the Conference in a fashion similar to its collaboration with the Human Dynamics Laboratory—but, significantly, in a different social field. At the same time that Thelen and his associates were at work helping the Conference erect a substructure of local block organizations, Martin Myerson, Richard Meier and Reginald Isaacs and other planners and their planning students (from Harvard, the University of Chicago, and the Illinois Institute of Technology) were at work exploiting the volunteer services of the Conference membership. The Conference Board and its staff worker, Julia Abrahamson, needed only to give these enterprises some degree of coordination and identification with Conference goals. Over 200 volunteers donated thousands of man-hours to the enterprise of the Community Appraisal, becoming Conference members, not by the payment of dues, but through involvement and participation.[4]

From its very beginning, then, the Community Conference put forth a coherent philosophy of social action. It mustered the personnel most capable of putting that philosophy into action through their mastery of the techniques of group organization. It was a movement designed to attract political and religious liberals and to reach others through the formation of block groups. A roster of the leadership of the Conference was like a local edition of *Who's Who*, drawing heavily on the faculty of the University and the other institutions in the area, plus the considerable talents of other residents.

The philosophy and techniques of the Conference were admirably suited to recruiting heavily from among the residents of Hyde Park–Kenwood. They appeared to be quite appropriate for solving the major immediate problem of stemming the panicked exodus from the neighborhood. The block groups provided a kind of therapeutic context in which individuals could air their fears, establish or reaffirm a sense of community and neighborliness, and take some specific action toward the reduction of immediate local problems. Mrs. Abrahamson's book *A Neighborhood Finds Itself* contains instance after instance of how block groups performed the important function of stabilizing the neighborhood in this early period.

The growth of the Conference in this early period was heavily dependent on these techniques of group organization, in part because it could not rely on sufficient coverage in the local paper, the Hyde Park *Herald*. The *Herald* from 1949 until August, 1953, was under a management that did not emphasize reporting on the activities of civic associations. Moreover, the editor and publisher—who was not a liberal Democrat, as was his successor, Bruce Sagan, interested in promoting improvement and reforms—often did not print the stories about Con-

4. The tangible result of this involvement was publication by the Conference in June, 1951, of *A Report to the Community: A Preliminary Review of Area Problems and Possibilities*.

ference actions which were sent him, even though Conference officials took pains to avoid promotional stories and submitted only reports of significant events. Eventually, Conference leaders discovered that when they felt it essential to have something published as news, they had to visit the editor in person.

Inspection of back issues of the *Herald*, from 1952 through 1958, shows a radical difference in the extent of coverage given Conference events and policies. The evidence is clear that it was not until June 30, 1954, that the *Herald* began to give full coverage to the Conference; for the period from 1949 through 1953, the formative years for the Conference, it would be difficult for a historian of ten years hence, relying on press coverage alone, to conclude that the Conference was anything but one among dozens of small civic voluntary associations in Hyde Park–Kenwood.

However, the Conference's philosophy and tactics had their drawbacks, which were to manifest themselves in stronger measure at a later period. For one thing, a grass-roots philosophy also contains a definition of who is *not* of the people. As one charter member of the Conference put it:

The first leaders of the Conference were thoroughly convinced that they were the voice of the community's "grass roots." But the way these people defined the "grass roots" always tended to exclude small businessmen, realtors, and the big leadership for the institutions.

To be fair, one must admit that these groups were not particularly friendly to the Conference. Indeed, Chancellor Hutchins' abrupt and almost discourteous treatment of the Conference leaders (cited in Chapter 4) who sought to establish contact with the University certainly did much to establish the University administration as an outgroup.[5] Nor did the East Hyde Park hotel owners who were organized into the anti-integrationist Chicago Hotel Owners' Association seem to the Conference to be a part of the community whose support it would be appropriate to seek. The hotel owners pursued a policy of boycotting the Conference, and none were members until after 1952

---

5. A definition much in line with usual faculty distrust and suspicion of administrative officials.

when Sydney Stein, a businessman, became chairman of the Board of the Conference.

To illustrate how easily the Conference abandoned attempts to reach this group of hotel owners, we may draw upon the description of a luncheon meeting between hotel owners and a Conference representative. The Conference delegate, according to his own recollection, came to this meeting with no strategy for strengthening relations other than improved communication. On hearing the hotel owners' assertion to the effect that "We will never write, 'Welcome Negroes' on our doormats," he became disabused of the possibility of improving communications, and the matter was dropped at that point.

Another group excluded from the definition of "grass roots" were the local businessmen. Although some businessmen were members of the Conference, the *local* shopkeepers, realtors, bankers, and professional men organized in the local businessmen's associations were not as assiduously cultivated as were the residents and other types of organizations.

This early definition of "grass roots" excluded from Conference membership and support the most powerful and prosperous members of the Hyde Park–Kenwood community.

Another consequence of the Conference's orientation to social action is that it tended to center on self-help measures that could be carried out by groups of individuals using their own resources. Conference tactics did not include the mobilization of large-scale resources. In particular, the kind of urban renewal on the scale presently authorized was outside the vision of early Conference leadership.

The federal, state, and municipal legislation that now makes possible such action had not, of course, been enacted as yet in 1949 (with the exception of the 1949 National Housing Act, which allocated funds for total clearance and redevelopment of slum neighborhoods). This contrasts with the actions of the South East Chicago Commission, which relied so heavily on existing governmental machinery and on creating new mechanisms.

To illustrate this orientation to social action through governmental machinery, we paraphrase part of an interview with a leader of the human-dynamics groups. He related how each spring the members of his block group would get together and have a "block cleanup day." After sweeping the street and the sidewalks, the residents would have an informal party, sometimes with music and dancing. They were about to hold their block party two years ago when the municipal street department reached their block with a mechanized sweeper and took care of the spring cleaning. There was a tone of resentment in the leader's account: it was somehow better that the residents do it themselves than have it done for them by the city government. We do not insist this orientation was common among *all* Conference members.

The "grass-roots" orientation of the Conference was a political asset in one respect, however. The emphasis on self-help meant that the Conference did not make frontal assaults on municipal government, a blundering tactic often associated with popular social movements. The Conference made no "demands" on the city government for special consideration; they did not present long petitions; nor did they seek to "throw the rascals out" or "reorganize the police department." During the first years the Conference leadership established contacts "downtown," and its requests for municipal help were voiced softly and in face-to-face interviews rather than through the newspapers. In dealing with public officials, Conference members acted neither like protesting radicals nor with the moral indignation so aptly described by David Riesman as characteristic of middle-class participation in politics. The style was more in the tradition of Quakerism, with its emphasis on moral suasion through personal contact. While these tactics were not likely to produce flurries of activity "downtown," they were also not likely to cut the Conference off from access to government officials.

Acting out the philosophy of social action it inherited from its environment and leaders, the Conference grew rapidly from 1949 to 1952, as Table 5.1 documents. This first phase represents a period in which the Conference philosophy had its fullest flowering. The Chairmanship of the Board was held by Dr. Leslie Pennington, minister of the First Unitarian Church. Mrs. Julia Abrahamson was Executive Director during this period, in which the post developed into a full-time position.

This was also the period in which the Group Dynamics Laboratory was most involved in the work of the Conference.

Conference Organization

The Community Conference began to assume its present form of organization around 1953. The machinery described here is characteristic of the Conference from 1953 through 1958. Although new committees were created and old ones dissolved, and new policy goals were formulated and old staff routines revised, for the most part the Conference has retained the broad outlines of the organization it had created by 1954. The most important change since 1954 has been an increase in the number of components at work on every echelon—additions made possible when more funds became available.

Figure 5.1 presents the table of organization of the Conference as it appeared in 1958. The governing body of the Conference is a thirty-six-member Board of Directors, elected on

Table 5.1—Summary of Hyde Park–Kenwood Community Conference Growth, 1949–1958

Year	Size of Membership		Budget	Board Chairman
1949–50	1200	(No Dues)	$ 1,700	The Reverend Leslie T.
1950–51	1200	(No Dues)	11,500	Pennington, Minister,
1951–52	800	(Estimate)	12,200	First Unitarian Church
1952–53	1000	(Estimate)	15,000	Sydney Stein, Jr.,
1953–54	1200	(Estimate)	30,000	Investment Counsel
1954–55	2100	(Estimate)	39,500	Elmer W. Donahue,
1955–56	3000	(Estimate)	48,000	President, Wabash
1956–57	3798		59,700	Screen Door Company
1957–58	3897		64,800	
1958–59				Harry Gottlieb, Mortgage Specialist, Draper and Kramer

Executive Directors

Mrs. Julia Abrahamson	1950–1956
James V. Cunningham	1956–1959

Size of Professional Staff *

1949–50	none	1953–54	three and a half
1950–51	one	1954–55	four and a half
1951–52	one	1955–56	five
1952–53	one and a half	1956–57	six and a half

* Excludes paid clerical workers.

Figure 5.1—Table of Organization, Hyde Park–Kenwood Community Conference

MEMBERSHIP   BLOCK GROUPS

BOARD OF DIRECTORS

Standing Committees
1. Nominating
2. Membership
3. Finance
4. Planning
5. Schools
6. Parks and Recreation
7. Maintaining an Inter-racial Community
8. Legal Panel
9. Real Estate
10. Advisory
11. Public Relations
12. Budget
13. Personnel

BOARD EXECUTIVE COMMITTEE

BLOCK STEERING COMMITTEE

EXECUTIVE DIRECTOR

Professional Staff:
Block Directors
Administration Assistant
Clerks
Renewal Information Officer
Code Enforcement Officer
Tenant Referral Officer
Real Estate Officer

a staggered-term basis by the membership for three-year terms. Board member candidates are nominated by a Nominating Committee [6] appointed by the Board,[7] and the Board also appoints an Executive Director. The officers of the Board constitute an Executive Committee, which handles decisions between Board meetings. The Executive Director attends meetings of both the

6. In most years the Nominating Committee has prepared slates with only enough names to fill the vacancies then open, although petitioners usually extend the list and introduce competition. A recent amendment to the bylaws requires future slates to contain more candidates than offices.

7. Additional nominations may be made by Conference members by presenting to the Nominating Committee a written petition signed by twenty-six members.

Board and the Executive Committee and often prepares the agenda for such meetings, but he is a member of neither.

Board members tend to be drawn from the Conference membership stronghold in the University community area. Given the concentration of Conference support in this area, and the criteria for selecting Board members, this distribution is to be expected. The criteria used by the Nominating Committee in selecting candidates stress heavily Conference and other civic activity, experience in community or professional leadership, and the capacity to devote time to Conference work.

In contrast to the Board of the South East Chicago Commission, the Board of Directors of the Conference has always been a very active force in directing the organization. The Board meets at least once a month, and meetings last on the average three to three and a half hours, during which members attend to all Conference programs in close detail. In addition, a majority of the members serve on at least one of the ten to fifteen standing committees of the Conference as officers, primarily responsible for communicating committee recommendations to the Board. Other committee chairmen are ex-officio Board members.

The Executive Director is a salaried employee, a professional community organizer who is responsible for the day-to-day direction of every phase of Conference activity. The core of his responsibility is to direct the Conference staff, represent the Conference publicly, and coordinate work at all echelons. Maintenance of the membership base and management of the budget are his two most demanding responsibilities. High dedication to the job is assumed to be a prerequisite to employment. During some weeks in 1958, for example, Executive Director James Cunningham worked from 8:30 to 5:30 daily, using his lunch hour to conduct business. In the evenings he was back at work from 8:00 p.m. until 10:30 four nights out of seven, leading meetings, giving speeches, or transacting business. Some Saturdays and Sundays were given over to working with block-group projects and to preparing for the week ahead.

The full-time paid professional staff has varied from two employees in 1953 to seven in 1958. Staff offices, which serve for meeting the public by day and to house committee meetings by night, are located in a large store-front office on the ground floor of a commercial building in the heart of Hyde Park.

In 1958 the seven employees performed the following specialized tasks. An administrative assistant and her staff of clerks did the bookkeeping, kept the voluminous records of meetings and special reports, and ran the headquarters office. The two Block Directors were responsible for stimulating new block-group organizations and maintaining the quality of the old. Other staff members served as Code Enforcement Officer and Real Estate Director.

Most unique were the functions of Tenant Referral and Urban Renewal Information. The Tenant Referral Officer kept a list of rental vacancies in Hyde Park and Kenwood and supplied this information to prospective residents in search of quarters. The goals of this program were to help stabilize occupancy by locating potentially stable residents in favorable vacancies, to help preserve the racial balance of residents in biracial apartment dwellings, and indirectly to increase the cooperation of building managers with improvement goals of the Conference.[8]

The Urban Renewal Information Center was opened in April, 1958, supported by a grant from the Sears Roebuck Foundation. Staff members provided detailed and authoritative information on renewal planning in response to all inquiries. Maps of plans, special information sheets about requirements, and the details of acquisition, demolition, and relocation schedules were made available upon inquiry. Providing such information was not a new function for the Conference, but with foundation funds a formal program could be started.

Since 1953 the number of standing committees of the Conference has expanded from ten to thirteen. These committees are appointed by the Board and are manned by Conference members willing to volunteer their services for one or two years. Committee chairmen are often Board members.

Standing committees make policy recommendations to the Board of Directors, thus playing a direct role in policy forma-

---

8. Particular attention was paid to maintaining a biracial balance in particular blocks or structures to prevent them from becoming all Negro. The Conference soon learned that to keep an apartment house biracial, it was necessary to continually replenish the supply of white tenants.

tion. Although subordinate to the Board, these committees are free to define their immediate goals and determine means for their achievement. Committees vary in size from ten to twenty-five members and take their tasks very seriously; the most active have regulations that members who fail to appear at three successive meetings may be dropped from the committee and a replacement obtained from the Board.

The functions of the committees listed in Figure 5.1 are mostly evident from their titles. Among the most unique in function are the Planning Committee, the Committee on Maintaining an Interracial Community, the Parks and Recreation Committee, and the Legal Panel. Since 1954 the Committee on Maintaining an Interracial Community, for example, has worked to secure city-wide support for an enforced program of open occupancy in housing. The Parks and Recreation Committee publishes annually a Recreation Directory that lists all Hyde Park–Kenwood facilities, works with various city agencies to maintain and improve parks in Hyde Park–Kenwood, and formulates policy recommendations on planning for parks and recreation in the community. One of its recent achievements, that of designing a new kind of play lot to be constructed in North West Hyde Park as part of the renewal plan, is described in Chapter 7.

The Legal Panel is composed of experienced lawyers who provide consultant services for any Conference program, as requested. The Panel was also very active prior to renewal planning in securing prosecution of zoning and code violators downtown. Its members helped write the basic legislation that led to a new housing code for the city.

The Community Setting and Committee Work

Before considering the remaining elements of Conference organization, it is well to review how the relatively unique community context affects Conference operations, particularly the volunteer committees. For the most part, a voluntary civic association is as good as its volunteers are able to make it. Hyde Park–Kenwood is able to provide an unusually skilled cadre for the Conference.

Most Conference committee members are recruited primarily from professional and managerial strata: architects, lawyers, professors, doctors, and ministers; labor relations and personnel experts, business managers, and contractors. As a consequence, the Conference volunteer comes to his committee meetings experienced in the craft of group discussion and decision. Accustomed to demonstrating initiative, and conditioned toward assuming responsibility, Conference committee members are observably oriented to the value of "doing a good job" in preference to merely "giving some time to the community."

Conference volunteers by and large strongly identify with the community. This identification—itself a feature of the social structure of this community—intensifies the readiness of Conference volunteers to pursue seriously their assumed responsibilities. Living in an area that is dense with civic organizations, Hyde Parkers generally take strong pride in the number and frequency of meetings which they manage to attend.[9] The result is a social climate in which it is assumed that one is a joiner and a volunteer.

Conference volunteers tend to be drawn from a background of memberships in a series of interrelated organizations. The archetypal male committee member, for instance, might be a member of the K.A.M. Reform Temple, a member of the Independent Voters of Illinois or the Democratic Federation of Illinois or both, a labor relations advisor to the United Automobile Workers Union (local), a subscriber to the Chicago *WFMT Listener's Guide,* and an employee of the Metropolitan Welfare Council. A woman volunteer is, archetypally, a member of the Hyde Park Consumers Cooperative and the Unitarian Church, a leader in the Parent Teacher's Association, and a committee worker for the Hyde Park Neighborhood Club.

These committee volunteers are for the most part upper-middle-class residents of eastern sectors of Hyde Park. They are politically inexperienced, in the sense of direct relations with the political "regulars," but they are supported by a matrix of progress—and education-oriented associations, all of

9. For example, in the 1959 aldermanic election campaign, Democratic Party candidate Allen Dropkin was repeatedly criticized as inactive because he was not on the record as having attended any of the 500 meetings conducted to discuss urban renewal, while Alderman Leon Despres was listed as having attended more than seventy-five. This comparison was asserted by *Herald* publisher Bruce Sagan in several campaign speeches.

which tend to embrace an identical ideology. This setting happily provides a kind of common universe of discourse among committee members. Repeatedly exposed to the same goals, the same issues, and the same means for their attainment, committee volunteers are often able to communicate tersely and precisely in the full confidence that they will be understood. This common universe of discourse reduces the distance that must be traveled to reach group consensus.

Other incentives stimulate effective performance by Conference volunteers. Board members are customarily nominated from within the ranks of the most active committee members. Insofar as Board membership is a well-publicized honor in this community, many volunteers invest additional energies in their committee work in hope of special recognition. A similar incentive is intramural committee competition. In an improvement-oriented, problem-solving community, such as Hyde Park–Kenwood, the identification and definition of new problems and the mobilization of resources to resolve them has become a culturally valued activity. Insofar as the community is also extremely fluid, and the variety of events ever changing, every committee confronts an opportunity to locate new tasks, to redefine old ones, and to demonstrate achievement through innovation and success. Boundaries among tasks thus remain indeterminate, and competition for the highest rating of accomplishments tends to be stimulated.

The Block-Group Organization

Few community organizations are as widely acclaimed as the Conference. The city-wide and nation-wide prestige of the organization is based largely upon the use of block groups as devices for reaching a mass audience and stimulating self-help community improvement. The block groups, which are organizationally separate from the dues-paying membership of the Conference, are composed of the residents of a block drawn together on the basis of geography and common neighborhood concerns.

Between 1949 and 1953 the most vital source of Conference strength was the block-group network. The program of building block groups grew from the two trial groups established by the Conference and the University of Chicago Human Dynamics Laboratory, each covering a six-block strip, into forty groups covering 190 block strips. (A block strip is one side of a residential city block.) Some groups extended to both sides of one residential street; others extended for two and even three block strips in a line; and in East Hyde Park an Area Council emerged that represented about twelve square blocks in a luxury apartment zone where individual block groups were impossible to organize.

In 1954, reviewing the activities of block groups, Bettie Sarchet concluded:

These groups have an impressive record of activities carried out, including . . . turning vacant lots into tot-lots; repairing broken sidewalks; improving property; installing lights in alleys; removing abandoned cars; quieting fears and rumors about changes in the neighborhood. In addition to individual block action, groups have united in setting up community-wide cleanup projects that involve local business men, property owners, tenants, and the ward superintendent's office; working with the Alderman's office to get broken sidewalks and curbs repaired; improving youth services; working on problems of overcrowding and multiple occupancy.[10]

The block groups have always been independent of the Conference. Residents may belong to block groups without becoming members of the Conference, as we have noted, although most Conference members are themselves active in their neighborhood block groups. Some block groups require payment of dues for membership; in others funds are obtained by voluntary contributions and membership is a matter of simple participation. Some block groups include a membership roughly representative of the block-strip population. In others home owners tend to exclude tenants, or some other criterion for membership flourishes.

The block groups are autonomous, but their activities are coordinated through two channels. Most important is the Block Steering Committee, composed of neighborhood block-group leaders and the block directors on the Conference staff. The block directors serve as the other channel; they are group-work professionals responsible for organizing new block strips, stimulating activity in old groups, and maintaining close neigh-

10. Sarchet, *op. cit.*, pp. 10-11.

borhood liaison between the Conference Executive Director and community residents.

As the quotation from Bettie Sarchet reveals, most block groups were at first concerned chiefly with stabilizing and improving their neighborhoods through self-help efforts, zoning and housing code enforcement, and maintaining morale. After 1955 block groups turned their attention increasingly toward renewal planning. The importance to the organization of the Conference of this shift from improvement activity (called "housekeeping functions" by block directors) to renewal planning rests in its consequences for citizen participation as a whole. In 1954 forty block groups were active, covering about 190 block strips. During 1955 the Conference stepped up its block-directing efforts, and as planning became the watchword in neighborhood after neighborhood, block director Irving Horwitz extended the number of organized blocks to about forty-four in 1956. When a second block director was added to the staff in 1957, the number of reported organized blocks jumped to fifty-two.

Block-group activity reached its peak during 1957, but as renewal plans became firm, these neighborhood units had more to think about and less to do. Housekeeping functions somehow dwindled in salience as responsibility for transforming the community began to shift from residents to public agencies and professional staffs. By 1958 fifty-two block groups were listed on Conference rosters, but the actual number of groups active in any sense at all was estimated by block directors to be thirty-three. By the time the Urban Renewal Plan was enacted, Conference leadership had to review completely the question of the future functions of block groups.

The Block Steering Committee nominates two of its members to the Conference Board of Directors, in this way linking the autonomous "grass-roots" of the organization with its highest echelon of leadership. This arrangement guarantees that block-group representatives on the Board are intimately in touch with other block-group leaders. This has always carried certain costs with it as well. The two Steering Committee representatives to the Board tend to speak for a specific constituency. They bring to the Board concrete proposals for action from the Block Steering Committee, their own Executive Committee, and even from individual block groups on special occasions. This constituency differs from the electorate, which votes for election of other members of the Board of Directors. These differences sometimes produce strains within the Board.

There remains in describing the organization of the Conference only the task of noting at what points its structure departs significantly from the structure of thousands of similar voluntary associations found anywhere. These points may give clues to the relatively unique achievements and to the operating difficulties of the Conference. Perhaps most significant is the feature of community penetration. Community residents are drawn into the life of the Conference at all three of its volunteer echelons: board members are elected directly from the membership; committee members, although appointed by the board, are recruited from the membership at large as people identified as potential leaders; and block groups are autonomous yet closely tied to the committee structure, the staff, and the board of directors. Of nearly equal significance is organizational flexibility of leadership roles. The Executive Director, although not a member of the Board of Directors, is free to participate directly in committee work; and he has ready access to block groups through the block directors. Board members serve on the standing committees, and many double as leaders in their neighborhood block groups.

The Conference grew organically out of the context of a special community setting. It was not grafted on, and its interlocking character gives it a framework for continuing recruitment of members and leadership. Its mandate as an organ of community improvement is a natural product of its close bonds with religious, educational, cultural, and civic associations of a complementary kind.

Present Conference Membership

The claims of the Conference to wide representation of the local populace are based, in large part, on the direct coverage of the community through membership in the organization and on the indirect coverage attained through the block groups. Although there is some overlap between these two bases, with many members of the Conference also participating in block groups, it can nevertheless be said that the organization extends to an impressive extent into every portion of the Hyde Park–Kenwood community.

The extent of the success of the Conference in obtaining the support of the population of the community can best be appreciated by comparing it with other community organizations and evaluating it in the light of what we know in general about participation in urban voluntary organizations. Outside of churches and labor unions, there are very few organizations serving an area which can claim a coverage of roughly one in every ten families, as the Conference could claim in 1958. This figure means that at least one person in over 2,400 households was a dues-paying member, and in about 1,500 of these households there were two or more members. How many additional families were reached through the block groups or were close supporters (but not dues payers) can not be ascertained, but it is only conservative to estimate that this group of "Conference sympathizers" must be at least as large as the dues-paying membership.

In sum, we can estimate that at least one in five Hyde Park–Kenwood households was a member of the organization, enrolled in one of the area block groups, or close enough to the Conference to be sensitive to its public statements and to support its position. If we accept this estimate, then the claims of the Conference to be a "grass-roots" organization have greater validity than the claims put forth by any other community organization of its type.

To present the evidence substantiating this assessment of the representative character of the Conference, we have analyzed the membership lists of the Conference for the year 1958. Unfortunately, it is not possible to make a similar analysis of the membership of the block groups with which the Conference was working.[11]

In 1958 Conference membership numbered 3,897 individuals representing 2,424 households.[12] As Table 5.2 indicates, Con-

11. Some clues as to participation in block groups can be obtained from Bettie Sarchet, *op. cit.*

12. Conference membership rules allowed several members of the same family to become members at reduced rates per person. Mailings of Conference publications and memoranda are made to households rather than to individuals.

Table 5.2—Areal Distribution of Conference Membership in 1958 *

| SUBCOMMUNITY | CONFERENCE FAMILIES | |
	Number	Per cent
University Community	851	35%
A. "Golden Square"	723	30
B. Remainder of University Community	128	5
Kenwood	280	12
Old Village Core	557	23
Border Zones	200	8
East Hyde Park	442	18
Remainder	94	4
Total	(2,424)	(100%)

* Based on a count of membership lists of the Hyde Park–Kenwood Community Conference as of late 1958. Member of the same family residing at the same address are not counted as separate individuals in this tabulation. Thus the 2,424 families used in this analysis represents approximately 3,897 separate individual memberships.
  See Chapter 2 for definitions of the subcommunity boundaries used in this table and in Tables 5.3 and 5.4.

ference membership covered every one of the subcommunities within Hyde Park–Kenwood that we distinguished in Chapter 2.

The density of Conference membership, however, was not uniform throughout the community. As one might expect from the general nature of participation in voluntary associations and the particular attractions of the Conference ideology and program, the density [13] of membership is particularly high in the University Community and East Hyde Park. While the over-all density of membership is 9 per cent, indicating the proportion of Hyde Park–Kenwood families with membership in the Conference, the density for the University Community is 21 per cent and that for the Old Village Core is 5 per cent.

In short, the density figures indicate that where the liberal, intellectual element is strongest, so is the Conference. One out of three Conference members lives in the University Community, although only one out of six residents of the area lives in that subcommunity.[14]

13. Every study of participation in voluntary organizations indicates that membership in any organization (save labor unions) is more likely the higher the occupational and educational level.

14. Conference membership was also heaviest in those areas in which demolition under urban renewal plans was to the lightest.

Table 5.3—Density of Conference Membership in Hyde Park–Kenwood in 1958

Subcommunity	Membership	Number of Families (1956) *	Proportion of Families Who Are Members
University Community	851	3,982	21%
Kenwood	280	4,988	6
Old Village Core	557	10,360	5
Border Zones	200	3,393	6
East Hyde Park	442	3,891	11
Total Area	2,330	26,614	9

* Source: National Opinion Research Center, *The Hyde Park–Kenwood Urban Renewal Study* (Mimeographed, Chicago, 1956).

Table 5.4—Stability of Conference Membership by Subcommunities in 1958

SUBCOMMUNITY	Median Year When First Paid Dues	1951 or earlier	1952	1953	1954	1955	1956	1957	(N)
				PROPORTION OF 1958 MEMBERSHIP WHO WERE MEMBERS IN					
Golden Square	1954	.10	.28	.41	.49	.59	.65	.92	(720)
Rest of University Community	1957	.09	.14	.23	.35	.38	.41	.77	(128)
Kenwood	1955	.09	.19	.26	.34	.46	.58	.87	(280)
Old Village Core	1957	.04	.09	.19	.27	.35	.42	.81	(556)
Border Zones	1957	.05	.10	.17	.22	.33	.41	.67	(199)
East Hyde Park	1955	.05	.18	.28	.38	.51	.64	.88	(440)
Remainder	1957	.02	.07	.10	.12	.16	.24	.86	(94)
Total Membership	1956	.07	.18	.28	.36	.46	.54	.85	(2,414)

Not only is the Conference best established in the University Community and East Hyde Park, but members from those areas are more likely to have participated longer in the organization, documenting further the historical origins of the organization among the liberal, intellectual population elements. Table 5.4 presents data on when the present membership first started to pay dues, presumably the year in which they first became members.[15]

15. Actually the figures in Table 5.4 refer to the year in which members first paid dues from their present addresses; hence, the figures understate the longevity of the membership.

Half of the present membership of the Conference had become members by 1956. However, half the members from the Golden Square had already joined by 1954, and the members from East Hyde Park and Kenwood had reached the half-way point by 1955. The border zones, Old Village Core, and the remainder of the University Community did not reach the half-way mark until 1957.

The Conference Planning Committee

In assessing the Conference's part in the redevelopment and renewal of Hyde Park–Kenwood, central attention must be given to the Planning Committee. This Committee's function has been to bring to bear on problems of planning those talents available among the Conference membership. Only the Board of Directors itself has played a more crucial role in the formation of Conference policy and in providing machinery for citizen participation in the planning process. It is primarily for these reasons that we devote so large a portion of this chapter to the Committee. However, this extended discussion can serve another purpose as well, for the experience of the Planning Committee epitomized Conference style of policy formation during the period when planning for urban redevelopment and renewal was underway.

From its beginning in 1949, the Planning Committee has been able to muster an impressive array of professional talent. A roster of Committee members includes many persons known nationally as among the best in the fields of planning, geography, real estate, and public administration.[16] The first chairman was Harvey Perloff—with Martin Myerson as second in

16. Including Martin Myerson, now Vice President of ACTION and Professor of Urban Studies at Harvard; Reginald Isaacs, now Professor of Planning at Harvard University; William Frederick, now Director of the New York office of the Council on State Governments; William Keck, national award-winning architect; Gilbert White, Chairman of the Department of Geography at the University of Chicago; Maynard Kreuger, Chairman of the University of Chicago Undergraduate Social Science Program; Philip Hauser, Chairman of the University of Chicago Sociology Department; James Cassels, pioneer in cooperative-housing planning; Robert Stierer, City Manager of Louisville, Kentucky; the late A. C. Shire, nationally known planner; Walker Sandbach, General Manager of the Hyde Park Cooperative; and Harold Mayer, Professor of Geography.

command—a city planner by profession, who enjoyed the cooperation of other experienced planning professionals, including Harold Mayer and Reginald Isaacs.

The Committee proceeded promptly to assume responsibility, with cooperating organizations, for preparation of the Community Appraisal study. By 1951 the Conference Planning Committee in its report on the study had already offered to the city a comprehensive series of suggestions for renewal planning in Hyde Park–Kenwood.

It should be noted that the report appeared at a time when the University of Chicago administration was indifferent to planning and only indirectly involved in conservation efforts. This endeavor of the Planning Committee was the first systematic attempt to consider ways of renewing the community; it may be viewed as laying the groundwork for the Metropolitan Housing and Planning Council Conservation Committee in 1952. Reginald Isaacs [17] directed the Community Appraisal study as Director of Planning at Michael Reese Hospital and as a member of the Conference Planning Committee. Much of the survey data used, we may recall, was collected by Conference volunteers.

From a formal viewpoint, the structure of the Planning Committee has remained fairly constant throughout the life of the Conference. Its members, their number varying from year to year from fifteen to roughly thirty, are appointed for two-year terms by the Conference Board of Directors. The chairman is appointed by the Board Chairman. The Committee is responsible directly to the Board in the case of policy decisions but has always been left comparatively free to define its functions.

The Dilemma of the Committee— Strategy or Tactics?

The primary dilemma of the Conference Planning Committee was that it was not given a clear mandate to make policy, although it was obliged to make more than technical decisions. As long as the Committee was making assessments of the fa-

---

17. Isaacs was also to be the planner on the research staff of the Metropolitan Housing and Planning Council Conservation Committee.

cilities and population of the area or making general suggestions concerning renewal and redevelopment (as in the
Community Appraisal Study), this dilemma did not become
obviously manifest. But as soon as the University set up its
Planning Unit and the job of maintaining Conference contact
with the unit fell to the Planning Committee, it became apparent that the Conference had placed the Committee in an impossible position.

The dilemma first became obvious when the Committee of
Six was formed, and the Conference sent as its representatives
two Planning Committee leaders. Because the Committee of
Six was set up at the same time as the Planning Unit of the
University, the Conference (following Levi's announced views)
defined this body as a technical advisory group. The University
and the South East Chicago Commission sent to the Committee
of Six their highest-level policymakers—Newton Farr and Julian Levi (South East Chicago Commission) and William B.
Harrell and Lawrence Kimpton (University of Chicago).
While the Planning Committee leaders who were sent to represent the Conference were undoubtedly competent men, they
were hopelessly outclassed in terms of their authority [18] to
make policy commitments on behalf of the Conference. Perhaps
as an expression of its mixed-status membership, the Committee
of Six met less and less frequently as its first year (1954) drew
to a close.

The Conference delegates to the Committee of Six were
quick to recognize that they had been placed in an awkward
position. At the close of 1954 they recommended to the Conference that they be replaced by persons from a higher policy
level, the Chairman of the Board and the Executive Director.
The recommendation recognized that if the Committee of Six
was going to function as a policy and information clearing
house, Conference delegates would have to be coordinate in authority to the delegates from the Commission and the University. They also recommended that a technical advisory
committee be set up to work directly with the professional personnel of the Planning Unit; this recommendation was not

---

18. Indeed, one of the Conference representatives to the Committee of
Six was at the time a very junior member of the University of Chicago
faculty.

taken up. From 1955 on, however, Conference representatives to the Committee of Six were the Chairman of the Board and the Executive Director.

From the point of view of the Conference, the important outcome of this series of events was to center broad policy questions about planning in the hands of the Board of Directors and the Executive Director. Naturally, the Board continued to rely heavily on Planning Committee recommendations.

The Dilemma of Volunteerism

There was no dearth of technical talent among the members of the Planning Committee. At least one of its members had been offered the job of University Planning Unit Director, and several others might easily have qualified for the job. From 1949 to 1954 these talents were put to use exploring different kinds of solutions to the problems of renewal and conservation in Hyde Park–Kenwood.

There are serious limitations on what men can do—no matter how great their talents—when those talents can be employed only outside of their regular occupational commitments. The Planning Committee could not draw up a plan; it could only offer general solutions.

From 1949 to 1954 the Committee chose to concern itself with a wide number of renewal problems. Subcommittees were set up to look into and report on problems deemed most hopeful of solution. One subcommittee, for instance, worked with the volunteer legal staff of the Conference to revise existing zoning and housing and building codes. Another subcommittee explored the possibilities of erecting low- and middle-income housing in Hyde Park. After the Community Appraisal was completed late in 1951, the Planning Committee met regularly during the next two years to receive the special reports of its subgroups and to discuss fairly general questions of policy, recommendations on which were then forwarded to the Board of Directors.

The essential characteristics of the work engaged in by the Committee were twofold. First, conservation in the area was conceived of as primarily a matter of housing. The Committee took the viewpoint of its constituents that the neighborhood problems were primarily those of the renewal, conservation, and reconstruction of housing units. Secondly, the solutions offered were necessarily general rather than specific; to work out the specific details required more than part-time contributions, no matter how devoted these part-time efforts were.

Until 1954 the work of the Planning Committee along these lines seemed useful and plausible. However, after the Planning Unit of the University began to produce specific proposals concerning the solution of Hyde Park–Kenwood problems, the work of the Committee became more and more difficult to achieve. It made little sense to continue seeking general solutions when the specific details were being worked out by a Planning Unit that had an authoritative place in the decision-making process. It made more sense that the Planning Committee should serve as the technical arm of the Conference, evaluating Planning Unit proposals.

But this decision had two major consequences. First, the work of the Committee was determined by the flow of Planning Unit production. Secondly, the Planning Unit became the chief determiner of the kinds of renewal problems that would be tackled. The Unit was more concerned with the facilities of the neighborhood, parking, shopping, etc., than with housing. In place of the general question of whether new middle-income housing was feasible, for example, the University and its Planning Unit gave first consideration to locating pockets of blight, analyzing traffic patterns, and relocating the commercial units.

The shift from matters of general policy exploration— from the question of what kind of community do we want and how can we achieve it?—to matters of technical analysis and decisions, block by block and building by building, and the severely increased pace of decision making was a rigorous challenge to the Planning Committee. From the fall of 1954 through 1955 the Planning Committee met more and more frequently; its subcommittees struggled valiantly to keep abreast of virtually every detail of the planning process. Planning Committee members met often with the official Planner, Jack Meltzer, during this period. Yet a group of appointed volunteers, however dedicated and skilled, acting in the absence of a clear mandate for participation and involvement, *cannot* decide, step by step, precisely what constitutes the local public interest in a rapid-fire chain of technical decisions.

In brief, the Conference Planning Committee foundered in the new flood of communications and decisions. Factions formed within the Committee, and some members, facing the uncertainty, became relatively inactive. Dissatisfaction with the organization of the Committee grew, and by late 1955 the Conference's most important link to participation in renewal planning was threatened with internal disorganization.

The Evolution of the "Transmission-Belt Function"

The proposal made by the Planning Unit to build a park next to "Hyde Park A and B," described in Chapter 4, started a series of events which transformed the Planning Committee's conception of its function in urban renewal. As the Planning Committee was the Conference's mechanism for such participation, these events also changed considerably the role of the Conference in urban renewal.

When the Planning Unit announced the proposal for the recreation park, the Planning Committee began its evaluation of the proposal. A committee made up of three members of the Planning Committee and four representatives of the block groups was formed. Committee opinions remained divided after weeks of study, and two reports were submitted to the Conference Board, which accepted the minority report. The stress that resulted was deepened by the manner in which the South East Chicago Commission, which took the leadership initially in proposing the park, did not fully include the Conference in its deliberations. The block groups directly concerned charged the Board of Directors and the Planning Committee with hasty and ill-considered action. The objections of the block groups and the ensuing public clamor forced the Conference and the Planning Committee to reconsider what role the Committee would take in the preparation of the urban renewal plan.

In consequence, the Committee resolved to specialize in two essential public services: first, reporting to the community on the plans and intentions of the Planning Unit and related municipal agencies; and, second, the transmission of citizen concerns about the content of the plans to officials within the Planning Unit. Note that both functions were limited to the exchange of information—down to the citizenry and up to the planners. Of course, the Committee never ceased reviewing the technical features of the plan, nor did it stop evaluating proposals. The change was in emphasis.

These decisions greatly simplified the tasks of the Planning Committee. Stripped of ambiguous responsibilities and removed from the peripheral arenas of code formulation and enforcement, the Committee created for itself a workable program. The long-term consequences for the Community Conference, however, were at that time difficult to assess. Among other effects, these decisions "passed the buck" of endorsing or withholding approval on renewal plans to the Board of Directors and the employed staff. For, at one level or another, someone had to decide whether the Conference intended to endorse, and in turn to promote, the specific features of the forthcoming renewal plans.

The Board had, of course, always assumed ultimate responsibility for forming policy. Under the post-1955 Planning Committee "reorganization," moreover, the Board and the Planning Committee together agreed that the Committee would continue to make judgmental recommendations to the Board. But the decision to operate as a channel for the exchange of information had the effect of reducing the potential of the Hyde Park–Kenwood Community Conference as a source of policy influence on the planning process. The *locus* of internal responsibility for decisions about endorsement, support, opposition, and withdrawal in issues underlying the content of the plans became more diffuse and less effectively defined.

It is important to consider how it was possible for block groups that were only indirectly related to the Conference to make so strong an impact on its policy, as in the case cited above. In large part, this is a function on Conference ideology and self-image. An organization which sees itself as representing the interests of the population at large, and particularly those of the small property owner or tenant, can hardly fail to be embarrassed if some significant segment of this group objects to its policies, at the same time claiming not to have been represented in the relevant decision making. This sensitivity amounts to a widely distributed veto power; any block group or significant portion of Conference membership, if it succeeds in obtaining an audience, can bring the Conference machinery to a halt.

In order to prevent conflict with its constituents, the Conference has been forced to spend a great deal of its efforts on building consensus beforehand so that its policies and recommendations have the least possible chance of encountering popular opposition. This has meant a very slow decision-making process within the Conference, giving an appearance of fence straddling.

Relations with the Planning Unit and the Commission

The University of Chicago, the South East Chicago Commission staff, and their Planning Unit were, as described, committed to swift execution of renewal. Given their board support from institutional, economic, and political sources, they could afford to neglect local public relations in developing their plans. Besides, the Community Conference, prior to 1954, had worked unstintingly to prepare the public for renewal—to build a citizenry receptive to the demands, opportunities, and sacrifices implicit in reconstruction. The staff of the Commission could easily consider the creation of favorable community support a job already underway.

What remained for the Conference to undertake, therefore, was creation of an efficient program for transmitting information about planning decisions to the local public. This was a necessary activity, it had not been attempted by official municipal agencies or the South East Chicago Commission, and it represented merely an extension of the Conference tradition. Thus the Conference Planning Committee, lacking a role in the planning activity itself, assumed the unglamorous function of mediating between the planners and the public.

The new program was formulated by late 1955. Conference block directors would meet regularly with active block groups to report on current planning activities of the Planning Unit. In turn, block group members would express opinions about the plans as these affected their particular blocks, including

points of view on specific buildings that should and should not
be demolished and on ways of handling traffic-pattern changes.
Each staff member would then write a report on his meeting and
send copies to the Executive Director of the Conference, to
Jack Meltzer in the Planning Unit, and to the Chairman of the
Conference Planning Committee. The same block-group opinions were often transmitted to Julian Levi at the Commission
via Jack Meltzer or through the Committee of Six.

The Planning Committee would then discuss the block-level
suggestions as a matter of course at each of its regular meetings. The Conference Block Director met frequently with the
Planning Unit to discuss these recommendations, and delegates
from the Planning Committee also participated periodically in
this exchange.

These procedures constituted the function of communicating public needs to the planners jointly by the Conference staff
and the Planning Committee. Jack Meltzer's own testimony,
private and public, and the record of his Planning Unit's operations, both support the statement that the receipt of this
"grass-roots" information was of the highest value to the work
of the planners. The intelligence thus transmitted was used to
test, qualify, and supplement the data already on hand from
surveys and other analyses. It also placed limits around the
range of physical solutions to the renewal problems in dozens
of subsections of the community. When the planners designed
intended changes that contradicted citizen recommendations,
their knowledge that this was the case introduced greater care
into the decision-making process and provided ways for explaining the need for changes in terms that residents had employed in the first place.

As director of the Planning Unit, Jack Meltzer, of course,
discussed planning questions with hundreds of local residents.
From his first day in office, he made himself readily accessible
to all citizens. As far as the process of exchange was coherently
organized, however, it functioned in such a way that the Conference staff and the Planning Committee were placed between
the Planning Unit and the public.

This process was neither political bargaining nor direct
consultation with those being affected by the decisions of the
Planners. It was not bargaining because the Conference and its

Planning Committee did not take positions for or against the desirability of policy suggestions expressed by block group members. It was not consultation because, for the most part, the Conference machinery performed as a buffer between officials within the Planning Unit and the public.

The Conference's Public-Information Campaign

The new conception of the function of the Conference was that of an active mediator between the planner and the public. It was an "active" program in that the Conference sought out both parties, urging the planners to make their proposals public and exhorting the public to consider the plan's details and react to them. It was "mediation" in the sense that the Conference was to transmit information between the public and the planners without adding its own evaluations.

The first event of the new program was a meeting of block-group leaders held in October, 1955, in which they were informed for the first time of the broad outlines of the Preliminary Plan for urban renewal. The meeting was held despite the great reluctance of the Planning Unit and the South East Chicago Commission to release any information about the Preliminary Plan at that time. Thus only the broad outlines of the work were discussed. Indeed, it was not until a second meeting in March and a third in June, 1956, to which block group leaders and selected members of the Conference were invited, that some of the details of the Preliminary Plan were revealed.

These meetings were the beginnings of a large-scale public education campaign that absorbed much of the energies of the Conference during 1957 and 1958. James V. Cunningham, who replaced Mrs. Abrahamson as Executive Director of the Conference, has divided this program of public education into three phases in his article on the subject.[19] The first stage lasted until the spring of 1956 and consisted of meetings between individual block groups, Conference Block Director, and representatives from the Planning Committee. The second stage, initiated by the meetings described above, at which the

19. "Citizens' Role in Planning for Urban Renewal Related," *Journal of Housing*, Vol. 14, No. 10 (November, 1957), pp. 382-385.

Preliminary Plan was unveiled to selected persons, reached a peak of activity in the winter of 1956–1957. That winter Planning Committee members utilized the special August 22 issue of the *Herald*, which contained most of the text of the preliminary report and an excellent array of simplified but accurate maps. Thousands of copies of this issue were distributed by Planning Committee members at block group meetings. Cunningham's article describes these meetings:

A copy of every meeting report was sent immediately to the planners. Fifty-seven block groups held one or more meetings on the preliminary report . . . 21 churches institutions and organizations. (Reached at these 21 meetings were many hundreds of non-residents with a stake in Hyde Park–Kenwood.) Attendance at block meetings ran from six to 250, with 30 about average.

In January, 1957, the Planning Committee reorganized on an area basis, dissolving its functional subcommittees. The Hyde Park–Kenwood community was divided into seven sectors, and the subcommittee appointed for each sector undertook the responsibility for holding public meetings in its subarea.

Officials from the municipal government (including the Building Department, Community Conservation Board, Land Clearance Commission, and the Office of the Housing and Planning Coordinator), representatives of the Planning Unit and the South East Chicago Commission, and Conference officials attended these meetings to explain the Preliminary Plan and to answer questions.

The plan of each meeting was to present the general outlines of the Preliminary Plan and to give the details as it applied to the area in question. Through the block groups, the Hyde Park *Herald*, and by means of leaflets, these area meetings were given wide publicity.

The area meetings enabled the Conference staff and Planning Committee to introduce the Conference point of view to those officially involved in the drawing up of the Final Plan. For some of the meetings agendas were carefully prepared in advance to cover topics of particular concern to the Conference. This was particularly the case with the issues of public housing and middle-income housing should be included in the plan. These issues were inserted into the agenda of the public meetings, and participants from the block groups and Conference membership were urged to bring them up in area meetings.

Although the public clamor for middle- and lower-income housing that appeared in these meetings was not sufficient to insert strong provisions along these lines into either the Preliminary or Final Plans, the issues were kept alive, and much of the public discussion of the plans centered around these points. It is, however, important to point out that agreement sufficient to make these housing provisions a central concern was never achieved within the Conference itself, nor was there entire agreement within the Planning Committee. Ultimately, the Conference made a formal public stand in favor of public housing to be built on sites scattered throughout the community in testimony at the public hearings on the Final Plan, and there is still some possibility that such housing may be built in Hyde Park–Kenwood.

During the second stage, in addition to the large subarea meetings, the Planning Subcommittees sponsored smaller public sessions, at which block leaders would convene to discuss limited problems together with planning representatives. On occasion, when the questions were especially pressing or problematic, Jack Meltzer or one of his assistants from the Planning Unit would attend.

Procedurally, this Planning Committee program during the second stage established a precedent for the Conservation Community Council—the nine- to fifteen-man group required under state law to be appointed by the Mayor with the task of passing on the Final Renewal Plan before its submission to City Council. The Conservation Community Council, formed late in 1956, decided to hold a series of public hearings on the Preliminary Plan. They employed the seven subareas already devised by the Conference Planning Committee, which cooperated with the Council in arranging these hearings and also participated in presenting testimony. The Council decided to hold these hearings, although they were not required by law. The procedures used were closely similar to those set up by the Planning Committee, and to a large extent participants were drawn from the ranks of Conference membership.

The Conference and the Block Groups
in the Planning Process

Block Steering Committee representatives to the Conference Board are nominated by a constituency composed partly of citizens who are not members of the Conference. Other Board members are elected by the Conference membership from a slate prepared by the Nominating Committee of the Board and have no specific constituency to represent. These differences in source of authority and manner of elected have stimulated persistent strains within the Board of Directors. Block Steering Committee members also favor direct political action, seeking political solutions to community problems and speaking from a position of implicit threat (i.e., "If you want the support of the block groups, then . . ."). In contrast, as the Conference program was clarified, the other Board members behaved more and more as if they were serving as trustees to a welfare or philanthropic organization, as one Board member put it in an interview. Many of these men and women, in fact, were increasingly anxious to "avoid the taint" of political action.

Two examples of the sensitivity of the Conference to the block groups have already been treated but deserve repetition at this point: First, in 1954 the Board of Directors endorsed the recreation park proposal made by the Planning Unit. The two block groups threatened by the proposal complained strongly, within the organization, that the Board had not given full enough consideration to their objections to the proposal. There developed increasing strain within the Board between the Steering Committee representatives and the other Board members. Secondly, in 1956 the Board endorsed the University-sponsored clearance of four square blocks within southwest Hyde Park, again without attending closely to the sentiments of the block groups within this site. On this occasion, as Chapter 6 traces in detail, the fissure between the block groups from the acquisition site and the Conference became public knowledge and accounted for much internal stress before harmony was partially restored.

On both these occasions the block groups involved were more than merely disaffected. They became eventual sources of opposition to the total renewal plan. The groups opposed to the recreation park became the nucleus for the formation of the Tenant and Home Owners Association, described in Chapter 8. The South West Hyde Park block groups became the membership base of an *ad-hoc* neighborhood organization in a strong, long-drawn-out battle to prevent clearance in the area. Where disaffection and defection did not occur, general disorganization or, at the very least, severe weakening of the affected block groups took place.

Indeed, as the Conference grew in size and came to claim more and more to be *the* guardian of *the* commonweal of Hyde Park–Kenwood, it was inevitable that it would come into conflict with the specific interests of block groups concerned with maintaining the positions of particular persons in limited areas. While the Conference could well afford to take a stand in favor of a proposal involving the widespread demolition of houses in a particular block, the block group in question would often be unable to take a stand in favor of such a broad viewpoint.

The question of what was the constituency represented by the Conference has never been clarified. Part of the difficulty lay in the Conference's goal of representing the public at large. But a great source of difficulty also lay in its relationship to its members on the one hand and to the block groups on the other. As we saw earlier, Conference membership was widely distributed throughout the area, although the heaviest concentrations were in the University Community and East Hyde Park.

The active members, however, were also active Hyde Park–Kenwood residents in general. They were active not only in the Conference but in the block groups, the PTA's, the churches, other civic associations, and even the South East Chicago Commission. For the Conference to take a stand often meant to go against the expressed wishes of some part of its membership or closely connected organizations. Increasingly, the activities of the staff were involved in prefabricating consensus among closely related groups and organizations in order to prevent conflict after policy stands were announced. The Conference Board and staff began to rely more frequently on policy pronouncements made jointly with interrelated groups and organizations.

This tendency was heightened by the overlapping leadership between the Board membership of the South East Chicago Commission and the Conference. It could be resolved by depicting the Conference as a leavener of solutions. Conference staff members, particularly under the direction of James Cunningham, came to define themselves as mediators of differences between the conflicting interests of community groups. This took on the appearance of a gain in prestige for the Conference, but in fact it introduced the penalties of loss of clarity in policy deliberation and reduction in the levels of consensus that could be achieved.

For example, before the Final Plan received the formal approval of the Conservation Community Council, in mid-1958, Cunningham proposed to the Conference Board that it vote in favor of a joint statement to be made by the Conference, the United Packinghouse Workers, the Urban League, the National Association for the Advancement of Colored People, and several other organizations. The joint statement was read, in preliminary draft, to the Board at its May, 1958, meeting. It announced that the signers supported the Final Renewal Plan and listed a number of ways in which the Plan should be revised before execution. Cunningham explained that this statement, as a compromise, would enlist the other organizations in fuller support of the Plan that they would otherwise announce. Tactically, it would soften their opposition to the Plan. In turn, it means the Conference would share in specifying criticisms of the Final Plan.

Among the Board members responding to the proposed statement, the strongest endorsement came from the Block Steering Committee member present. A majority of Board members, however, favored elimination of criticisms from the joint statement—in effect, rejection of the proposed statement itself. Among the majority arguments were the following questions: Should the Conference engage in such politics? Would the South East Chicago Commission be among the signers? (The obvious answer was, No.) Was this not a matter to bring before the Committee of Six? Would this statement really represent the points of view of all block groups? Would the statement represent the Conference position (which had not yet been drafted)?

Our review of the structure and functions of the Conference Planning Committee indicated the Conference was very weakly connected to the sources of economic and institutional power in the community and to the official channels authorized by the city government for planning.

Conference lines of communication with the "grass-roots" were ambiguous in that the organization could never clarify whether it should lead or follow the block groups. A different organizational form would not have removed these difficulties; indeed, given the ideology of the Conference, and its voluntary character, it is probable that tight and effective links for communications "up" and communications "down" could not have been forged in any event.

Furthermore, there were instances in which the Conference took bolder, politically more "liberal" stands than its block group affiliates. The Conference Director testified at the City Council Public Hearings in favor of scattered public housing, a component not included in the Plan as approved by the Conservation Community Council. This testimony included specified locations where block groups would "welcome" placement of such public housing. In fact, the Conference testimony supported public housing somewhat against the individual preferences of a majority of block group members and possibly against the private preferences of a majority of Conference Board members. As more than one experienced participant put it, Conference members will be "collectively pleased and individually disappointed" if public housing is included in the renewal program. Thus, at times Conference ideology prevailed over every variety of structural ambiguity. Indeed, it may have been this very ambiguity which facilitated a policy stand on this unpopular issue.

The same ambiguity of relationship between block groups and the Conference freed block groups to pursue special interests of their own, when it came to efforts to influence the planning process. In Chapter 7, a case study of North West Hyde Park, we shall review the successes of one block group leader and his members in pressing for recognition of their renewal wishes.

Internal Organization and External Relations

In a voluntary organization, such as the Conference, much of the day-to-day negotiating with outside agencies is carried on by the paid staff. In the Conference the crucial figure in this respect was that of the Executive Director. As in so many voluntary organizations conducted by a paid staff, the Director and his staff increasingly accrued authority to act independently of the Board. The Board, responding to the same influence of routine, became increasingly responsive to the policy recommendations of the Executive Director.

Unlike many similar groups, however, Conference employees exhibited long-term stability in office. When James Cunningham assumed the directorship in 1956, his staff included four professional members retained from the staff directed by Mrs. Abrahamson; two of them were personally strongly identified with the policies and procedures adopted under Mrs. Abrahamson, which included a tradition of managing consensus in Board meetings. Cunningham came to his new position fresh from the experience of directing the Independent Voters of Illinois (I.V.I.)—a political group with a vigorous, tactically oriented Board of Directors, to whom he was accustomed, apparently, to serving as executor.

Internal frictions inevitably ensued. By the standards of some staff members, the new director did not adequately "direct" the Board of Directors. By the standards of some Board members, the new director was "too politically oriented." In spite of great overlaps in membership, the I.V.I. was essentially different from the Conference in organizational form and function, and Cunningham's career experience was for a period a source of some stress. His accommodation to the new position had the double strains of resolving staff tensions and redefining through practice the relationship between Conference Board and Executive Director.

Within his staff, which was larger than that maintained by Mrs. Abrahamson, Cunningham gave employees relatively autonomous functions by decentralizing responsibility and by sharpening the specialization of each employee. One would not say that under his management the Conference offices were possessed by lower morale than under Mrs. Abrahamson; but his approach did mean office operations were comparatively "routinized," sociability reduced, and interaction centered around day-to-day tasks in preference to policy discussion.

In his relations with the Board Cunningham made two revisions of older practices. He assumed a less outspoken and directive role than had Mrs. Abrahamson and became deliberately deferential to the wishes of the Board. When issues were left hanging, he declined to resolve them, except on rare occasions, preferring to reserve his potential authority. He prepared the advance agendas for Board meetings in greater detail, conferring with committee chairmen, preparing discussion strategies with selected members, and, in general, emphasizing preliminary structuring of the meeting.

As his special province, Cunningham reserved the difficult task of negotiating Conference objectives with other groups, institutions, and agencies, and the related task of mediating differences between a diversity of parallel organizations. During 1957 and 1958, then, the work of the Conference in interacting with other groups devolved principally upon James Cunningham and those volunteer committees who shared this work on instruction from the Board.

Although the University of Chicago Administration announced on several occasions approval of the work of the Conference and expressed the conviction that renewal depended upon support of the Conference, the Conference never gained dependable and tangible cooperation from the administration.

The Committee of Six eventually came to be defined by Conference members as crucial to successful coordination of efforts between Conference and University. This coordination was more a hopeful myth for the Conference, however, than a matter of practice; for, while the Committee of Six met more or less bimonthly during the renewal planning phase (1957–1958), its deliberations were rarely productive of policy decisions or agreements. Rather, the Committee of Six—the only visible link between University and Conference—served as a platform from which University and Commission intentions were announced, Conference suggestions entertained, and points of disagreement clarified. Its two vital contributions to Conference success were its operation as an apparent medium for policy negotiation and its provision of limited advance information to the Conference representatives. Even these limited contributions were diminished by the fact that the Conference was firmly outmanned in the Committee (four to two), and on a few occasions Conference delegates felt constrained to hold the

Conference Board to agreements even when the delegates had both opposed the decision. Although a united front was not obligatory under the *modus operandi* of the Committee of Six, action in the Committee tended to be interpreted by some Conference delegates as binding on the Conference.

In 1957 the Conference Board undertook the delicate task of probing the University administration and members of the Board of Trustees for financial contributions. Although the University administration appeared to endorse as "essential" the work of the Conference, making the request for funds reasonable enough, the effort netted no funds. By this date, as we shall demonstrate in Chapter 6, University administrators realized that they could count on Conference support for the Final Renewal Plan, whether they supported the Conference or not.

The Conference was similarly unsuccessful in its efforts to create influential bonds with the South East Chicago Commission. Though Mrs. Abrahamson and Julian Levi represented diametrical opposites temperamentally and ideologically, these two experienced organizers weathered the storms of competition, overlapping programs, and the struggle for self-definitions. Thanks to the Quaker principles of Mrs. Abrahamson, these clashes were seldom made public, but they placed barriers between the two agencies between 1953 and 1955. Cunningham had achieved an uninfluential yet satisfying rapproachement with the South East Chicago Commission by 1957. The basis was simple: the Conference—as our analysis of the Planning Committee suggests—assumed primary responsibility for informing the public and maintaining local morale during the planning period, while the Commission staff continued its functions of crime control, code enforcement, and direction of the Planning Unit with the University of Chicago. Of course, the Conference never ceased its vigilance over code violations.

The ascendance of the Commission in this *modus vivendi* is easy to comprehend. As Chapter 4 revealed, it had the direct backing of the prime interests in the community and direct access to the Planning Unit. Furthermore, its internal structure gave the Commission director much greater autonomy and authority than that enjoyed by the Conference director. Cunningham's assumption of a subsidiary role was grounded in an accurate, realistic appraisal of this difference between the two organizations. Although he probably underestimated the implicit, potential power of the Conference (which lay in withholding support from the renewal program), this was a threat he could not have carried out in most instances. Without a true constituency, lacking the standard equipment of most interest or pressure groups, and faced with great diversity of objectives among members and diversity of programs carried by the organization, Conference support was too diffuse to be used as a weapon in influencing policy.

Experienced in political action, James Cunningham understood these limitations clearly (as did Julian Levi). Moreover, Cunningham did not believe that democratic exchange, communication of views, and good will alone were sufficient sources of Conference influence, although he continued to apply these techniques in good measure.

Conference access to the Planning Unit was excellent. Jack Meltzer's responsiveness to the concept of citizen participation was an almost unique attitude among the personnel directing the actions of the University, the Commission, and the Planning Unit. Through his receptivity, the Conference staff, the Planning Committee, and block groups consistently found a willing listener in the chief planner. As we shall see, this resulted in substantial changes in the Preliminary Plan—changes that are more a result of the planner's own readiness to consider such suggestions, however, than an achievement of the Conference per se. Given a professional planner with views unlike those of the Conference, it might have failed to gain any leverage on the content of the plan at the local level.

The Conference achieved at least four kinds of influence upon the Conservation Community Council. Council members were appointed by the Mayor from nominees supplied by a variety of local associations. The slate of candidates, however, was screened by the Committee of Six, and at this point the Conference influenced composition of the Council. Thus, the eleven-man Council came to include three former Conference leaders, although they were appointed as individual, established residents, and not as representatives of the Conference. It was chiefly those Conference members on the Council, however, who kept alive the issue of public housing.

The work of the Planning Committee in preparing a special

report in favor of scattered public housing was conveyed to the Conservation Community Council informally through these members. These Conference members prepared a minority report favoring inclusion of public housing in the Final Plan, yielding the only nonunanimous vote expressed within the Council, and the Public Housing Report was transmitted to City Council.

As we have seen, the work of the Conference Planning Committee in establishing subarea public-information meetings was adopted as the pattern for public hearings by the Conservation Council. During 1957, furthermore, the Council cooperated with the Conference in arranging these preliminary hearings.

Compared with the access of Julian Levi to the Conservation Community Council, these Conference influences were limited. Mr. Levi attended Council meetings and acted in a quasi-*ex-officio* capacity. Although he exercised no vote, he expressed his views and wishes openly and directly there.

During the Planning phase, the Conference enjoyed its most influential external relations with the two local Aldermen, Leon Despres (5th Ward) and Claude Holman (4th Ward). As active Conference members, both aldermen publicly endorsed Conference actions and cooperated with the staff in its efforts to gain local code enforcements and physical improvements through municipal agencies.

Politically speaking, this close relationship may well have been more helpful to the aldermen than to the Conference. Neither alderman had significant personal influence over the content of the Plan. Under state law, the City Council had the power only to approve or to reject the Final Plan, not to modify it.

Alderman Despres worked vigorously during City Council Committee hearings to gain support for the idea of scattered public housing; and, indeed, he managed to secure verbal assurances from the Community Conservation Board and the planners to attempt to include at least 120 units "experimentally" in the final execution of renewal (see Chapter 9). But the relative exclusion of aldermen from the primary flow of influence—a matter which deeply perturbed both local aldermen—meant that, for them, support of the Conference was a demonstration of involvement in a matter of great public concern. It also meant that when challenged on policy positions, local aldermen could simply state: "The Conference represents my views by and large. I stand where they stand."

Conference access to the Office of the Mayor and to his Co-ordinator of Housing and Planning was excellent during 1956, 1957, and 1958. It was significantly superior to the access enjoyed by any other civic association, with the possible exception of the South East Chicago Commission, because Conference resources allowed greater investments of staff time in maintaining liaison. Mayor Daley is an official who takes particular pride in his accessibility to the public; that he can be reached for conferences is indeed a policy position he exercises most effectively, and it is a practice that extends to his executive agencies. Comparatively speaking, the South East Chicago Commission enjoyed identical access and the benefit of powerful backing from local institutions and interests. Access of the Commission to the Office of the Mayor was thus superior to that of the Conference, if one considers access a matter not only of communication but of influence.

The Role of the Conference in Renewal Planning—An Overview

The Conference, its members and staff, and affiliated block groups poured an extraordinary amount of energy and time into attempts to halt and reverse the trends of neighborhood deterioration. The role played by the Conference in its earliest period was to pave the way for renewal, and in the later period it provided a channel for "grass-roots" participation in the planning process. The exposition of the Conference's actions in this chapter has been interlarded with history and a good deal of organizational analysis. To highlight these roles is the purpose of this concluding summary discussion.

It is clear that the Conference did much to prepare the community for conservation renewal as a workable plan for saving Hyde Park–Kenwood. If one thinks of the local public as a pool of values with certain interests surfacing regularly and other concerns causing occasional ripples of response, the first ripples embodying the possibilities of conservation renewal were started by University of Chicago faculty members working through the Conference. Most of them were associated with the Committee on Planning and the Human Dynamics Laboratory, but some were from related social science faculties.

From 1949 through 1951 these men, and others like them outside the University, "stirred" the pool of public value as members of the Community Conference, especially through work on the Community Appraisal and the formation of block groups. The work of these men in the Conference also was part of the planning programs of the Illinois Institute of Technology and the Michael Reese Hospital. None of this denies the primacy of the Conference in disseminating the possibilities of renewal in the local community; it does mean, however, the dissemination was a function of the local manpower resources in the applied social sciences—a unique condition from which the Conference benefitted strongly.

By 1954 the initiative in redevelopment and renewal planning was seized by the South East Chicago Commission and the interests it represented. The Conference redefined its function and took on, as its primary responsibility, the work of educating the public about the meaning of the possibilities of conservation renewal. In 1956 this became the most absorbing task of the Conference as a service agency. Although its services here paralleled those of the Hyde Park *Herald,* the task of public education was inherently greater than could be managed by a newspaper alone, however competent. The task was vital simply because the success of renewal depended on the maintenance of relative residential stability. Although no one can definitely state that the white out-migration was stemmed through Conference educational efforts between 1955 and 1958, the fact of stabilization is at least consistent with this claim.

Concerning the dissemination of the idea of renewal, we can be certain of one thing. For two full years the Conference blanketed the community with opportunities for learning about every detail of the plans. In addition to block-group meetings, the subarea information sessions, the public hearings, and the block-group leader conferences with the Planning Unit and the Conference, the Conference, with funds provided by the Sears Roebuck Foundation, maintained for more than a year an Information Center within the staff offices, which undertook to answer accurately and authoritatively every question posed by residents. No other such special service existed in the community or downtown within the municipal agencies. The Center handled a wide variety of questions, of course, ranging from inquiries about acquisition and demolition schedules projected by the Plan to questions about opportunity for relocation and settlement within the community by outsiders. Copies of the excellent *Herald* issue reporting in detail on the Final Plan were available free for more than a year at the Conference office, as were related pamphlets and bulletins.

Another important educational task was the dissemination of a conception of the importance of renewal to large sectors of the metropolitan public. Here, again, the achievements of the Conference were greater than those of any other local organization. Actively affiliated with the Associtaion of Community Councils and the Area Welfare Planning Department of the Welfare Council of Metropolitan Chicago, the Conference provided speakers and press releases through those and other groups, such as the Metropolitan Housing and Planning Council. Conference staff officers worked diligently to maintain close contact with all daily newspapers in the city; press coverage was correspondingly outstanding.

We must not neglect the inherent news value of the renewal program itself, however, for we have already indicated it has been widely hailed as the first conservation program of its kind in the nation. In Greater Chicago it has been defined as a pilot program with precedent making importance to the renewal projects that may be undertaken in other areas within the metropolis. In this connection, it is relevant to note that Mrs. Abrahamson and James Cunningham were both experienced journalists, and Conference leadership included considerable talents in public relations and educational writing, mostly drawn from the University community and George Williams College.

The Hyde Park renewal story, as it came to be called, was important enough to be reported upon periodically in the Sunday editions of *The New York Times*. From 1957 on, the story "carried itself," as a news object of intrinsic fascination. It was a story of a project, a $30 million to $40 million renewal program. It was a story of a bootstrap operation being conducted by a world famous University facing a kind of deterioration that was beginning to plague metropolitan educational centers throughout the nation. It was different in kind from slum clearance projects and held the quality of a potential remedy for the problems of upper-middle-class urban living. And it was a story involving the high-energy theme of inter-racial living.

In the newspaper world only the Negro press held back from giving blanket approval to the Hyde Park–Kenwood Renewal plans. Although the leading Negro daily, the Chicago *Defender*, opposed the Final Plan as segregationist in intent and effect, the columns of the paper were open to statements from the Conference and from other supporters of the Plan. Though Conference efforts were not enough to secure all-out acceptance of the Plan, they were sufficient to get its point of view into print.

A major stumbling-block to obtaining Negro support was the fact that one implicit goal of urban renewal was to fix a balance between the races in the community. Whatever the motives of racial conservatives in supporting this stabilization of the Negro component as a minority, racial liberals quickly recognized that at this juncture in the history of Negro-white relations, an interracial community could only be attained un-der these conditions. This was a line of reasoning that could not be stated too openly for fear of misinterpretation of mo-tives. Yet it was fairly clear in the Plan proposals themselves that the effects of the Plan would be to limit the proportion of Negroes in the population. Upper- and middle-class Negroes, however, who had settled into some of the larger and expensive apartments and homes in Kenwood and North West Hyde Park, and who were fearful of finding themselves once again in the "ghetto," did approve of the stabilization goal.

Another factor that fostered the suspicion in the Negro community that renewal was directed specifically against them was the higher opinion Negroes as compared with whites held of Hyde Park–Kenwood as a place to live. As the attitude sur-vey data reveal (see Appendix), the community was viewed by Negroes as an almost ideal residential location, far from blighted or deteriorated. For Negroes from every class level the unrenewed community was so much better than the "ghetto" from which they had moved that the importance ascribed by

whites to renewal seemed only a flimsy excuse. Except at the
uppermost level of the Negro community, renewal plans were
seen as directed specifically against Negroes. Of course, individual block groups in some Negro neighborhoods came to view
renewal differently, often through the educational efforts of the
Conference.

Finally, Negro opposition to the plan crystallized into
hardness because of the actions of the University in pursuing
private redevelopment in South West Hyde Park. This sequence
of events (as told in Chapter 6) led many Chicago Negro
leaders to oppose certain features of the Final Plan, particularly relocation procedures. The failure of the Conference to
secure favorable acceptance of renewal in the Negro community was a failure in a situation in which success was nearly
impossible.[20]

We have shown how the Conference provided the organizational machinery and opportunities for citizen participation
in urban renewal planning. This apparatus of committees,
meetings, trained staff, and well-written publicity has been
amply described.

How well did this work? Exceptionally good opportunities
for participation were provided by the Conference. The case
studies of action in North West Hyde Park (in Chapter 7)
will indicate that when citizens wished, for whatever reason, to
take the opportunities presented, they were able to make significant gains as measured by their own interests. This conclusion, based on solid evidence, is a strong negation of the fancies
of those who believe that renewal planning is always a matter
of informal handclasps between hidden hands among "those who
are in power."

The opportunities presented, however, were not always

20. Depending on one's point of departure, the part played by Negro
leaders may be differently interpreted. James Cunningham has pointed out,
for example, that Alderman Claude Holman did support the passage of
the final plan, that many Hyde Park Negro residents testified in support
of the plan at all hearings, and—he adds—"The fact that no anti-plan
movement on the part of Negroes developed is significant. The great
emphasis at the public hearings before the City Council was that the plan
could help achieve an interracial community. I never remember the plan
being attacked at these hearings as anti-Negro." The authors agree that
this is an equally tenable interpretation, if one chooses to assume that the
absence of overt conflict signifies some degree of consensus.

grasped. If we apply the standard of *100 per cent participation*, often advanced by community organizers, populist theorists, and in some cases by the Conference itself, it is obvious from the record that the Conference cannot qualify as a total success. The actual proportion of citizens who were involved in the discussions and meetings concerned with the planning, probably falls short of 50 per cent participation. Furthermore, from our analysis of the area distribution of Conference membership, from interviews with block leaders, and from our questionnaire survey, we must conclude that full and open discussions occurred for the most part in those sectors of the community where the fewest changes were called for in the plan. Even in North West Hyde Park, where discussion was most effective, the bulk of participation occurred among citizens *adjacent* to pockets of blight (see Chapter 7).

But is the standard of full and complete participation the proper measuring stick to apply in the evaluation of the Conference's efforts to provide machinery for citizen participation? Certainly the Conference was at least as successful as other organizations in attempting to involve a large and heterogeneous body of citizens, and more successful than most. Furthermore, one might argue that the apathy found among residents in the sectors facing the greatest reorganization under the plan was their own responsibility. The Conference provided the machinery for expressing their interests: they were given the opportunity to present their views. If they did not grasp the opportunity, for whatever reason, their failure to do so was only their own fault.

On the other hand, it is also possible to raise the questions: Why should they participate? What could be accomplished realistically by such participation? Certainly participation through the machinery designed and set up by the Conference was not a guaranteed way of influencing the plan, although, as we shall see in Chapter 7, significant modifications were often made in this fashion. The apparatus of participation was not sufficiently empowered to press for the demands of local citizens. For the most part, residents participated who wished to express approval of the plans. Many of those whose dwellings were most affected perhaps saw no point of going through the motions of discussion when the outcome seemed already determined by the powers that were given to the Planning Unit of the University and the subordinate role of the Conference.[21]

Finally, we might ask what kinds of effects did citizens acting through the Conference have upon the contents of the Final Plan? On this score there exist no hard and fast data to bring to bear. Both the block directors and the planner endorsed the view that many changes in the plan were made as the result of block discussions of the Preliminary Plan and of the intelligence conveyed to the planners through the block directors. Since there are no records of these changes, however, it is impossible to evaluate these statements or to give them specific content.

However, records were kept of the Conference's representations at the hearings of the Conservation Community Council on the Final Plan. In the hearings held in March, 1958, thirty-two changes were requested by the Conference. Eight of these, or one-fourth, were accepted by the Council and the plan changed accordingly. Another four requests were listed by the Council as "recommendations" to the Community Conservation Board, and two of these were definitely enacted later by the Board. An additional thirty-six changes were requested by individual block groups, individual home owners, and other civic associations. About fourteen of these requests were accepted and introduced into the Final Plan by the Council.[22]

---

21. What is meant by a defined role for citizen participants is conveyed best by reference to the Detroit, Michigan, planning program: "After numerous block discussions and general public meetings, during which the citizens participated helpfully in decision-making . . . the delegates of the . . . blocks . . . voted four to one in favor of the proposed . . . plan recommended by the staff and as modified by the residents' suggestions. . . . (This) . . . has continued throughout the subsequent planning stages. It proved a most valuable experience of planning in a democracy." The important point here is that the citizen organizations had a formal vote which had the power of approval or rejection of the proposal. The same program includes citizen volunteers who work in the offices of the City Planning Commission. Maurice F. Parkins, *Neighborhood Conservation: A Pilot Study* (Detroit City Plan Commission, 1958), p. 94.

22. In his very fair-minded review of this chapter, James Cunningham commented as follows on the use of this measure: "You would seem to judge our program of citizen participation—its effect on the final plan— in terms of whether the political influence of the Conference at hearings could 'force' changes. But it seems to me that citizens acting through the Conference were shaping the contents of the final plan in *all* the meetings with the planner which you have described, in all the reports submitted to Jack Meltzer, in meetings of the Committee of Six, and in the entire process through the years. Influence is not something that takes place only at final hearings."

Although these proportions do not appear very impressive, it must be remembered that they refer to the actions of the Conservation Community Council on the Final Plan, which itself embodied many block group and Conference recommendations. The score and a half changes requested at this point represent those points still at issue between the Conference and the Planning Unit.

Perhaps the most sensitive measure of the success of the Conference is to consider how the Board of Directors answered the question raised in a June, 1958, meeting: Just how have "we" affected the plan? The Chairman's impromptu answer was: "The Conference was most important in getting the planning program started. Our specific impact since then has not been great. We all know that, and we know too that we have had some isolated successes." The nature of the failures and successes of the Conference in shaping and changing the contents of the Final Plan will be examined in minute detail in Chapters 6 and 7.

The important achievements of the Conference did not result from its direct influence on the Final Plan. Rather, they lay in other equally important directions.[23] First, the Conference initiated the movement that culminated in the renewal plan. Secondly, by keeping alive the issues of interracialism, housing for low- and middle-income groups, and proper relocation procedures for displaced residents, the Conference modified the planning process by introducing considerations of human needs and wishes. The plan might otherwise have been totally oriented toward institutional and commercial uses. Finally, and most important of all, the Conference effectively created a climate favorable to renewal both within the community and the city as a whole. The public-education role voluntarily assumed by the Conference undoubtedly helped assure successful public acceptance of the plan in general and approval by the city government.

---

23. In reviewing an earlier draft of this chapter in manuscript, former Conference Planning Committee Chairman William L. Frederick commented: "I would suggest that the areas of Conference success may be far more important in the long run than those areas in which it was not successful. The fact that a specific change in the plan was or was not made may well be of little significance twenty years from now. In contrast, the work of the Conference in building an interracial neighborhood and its continuing efforts to have middle-income and public housing included in the plan may have long-range significance."

CHAPTER 6

South West Hyde Park:
A Case of Failure to Achieve
Popular Consensus

*A*ccording to its advocates, citizen participation in planning and urban renewal contributes to the planning process in two ways. First, a better plan is drawn up because the real needs of the populace as expressed through participation can be incorporated into it. Secondly, the plan gains success in execution because citizen participation increases the amount of popular support. These are the functions which the Conference undertook as its role.

Judged in terms of whether these two goals of citizen participation were achieved, the case related in this chapter amounts to a failure of the Conference to perform its functions. In South West Hyde Park the Conference was unable to mediate between the populace and the planners, and popular consensus was never achieved.

We choose to present a failure in detail, because one learns at least as much from failures as from successes, and because this failure was part of the learning experience of the Conference. The lessons in South West Hyde Park were taken to heart and to

The ample documentation on which this chapter is based was prepared by Miss Patricia Denton after a skillful and painstaking search through Conference files and interviews with some of the major participants. A more detailed account of the case of South West Hyde Park will appear in Miss Denton's Masters Thesis, to be submitted to the Department of Sociology of the University of Chicago sometime in 1961.

some extent explain the organization's subsequent successes.

That we dwell so long on a failure should not be seen as a measure of the Conference's total score in leading citizen participation. South West Hyde Park is not fully representative of the Conference's experiences in mediating between the citizens and the Planning Unit. In any event, the next chapter will treat of a successful case in as much detail.

This case concerns the controversies surrounding the proposed redevelopment by a neighborhood redevelopment corporation of one sector of Hyde Park, termed the "South West," consisting of fifty-four and three-fifths acres running from 55th to 59th Streets, and from Cottage Grove Avenue to Woodlawn Avenue, excluding the University of Chicago campus. This area lies between the campus and Washington Park. Next to North West Hyde Park, South West Hyde Park between 1945 and 1956 experienced the heaviest infusion of nonwhite residents of any portion of the community. In terms of the sectors which we distinguished in Chapter 2, this area lies in the western portion of the University community.

The controversies surrounding this sector developed during 1956, a year when Redevelopment Project Number One (Hyde Park "A and B") was reaching its final stages and when the Planning Unit was heavily engaged in drawing up a preliminary plan for total conservation renewal of the community. Thus, the events reported in this case represent only a fraction of the planning effort in Hyde Park–Kenwood during this crucial year.

The South West Hyde Park Neighborhood Redevelopment Corporation

Early in 1956 the South West Hyde Park Neighborhood Redevelopment Corporation was formed with capital provided by the University of Chicago. Its trustees and officers were Norman Eaton, Corporation President; William B. Harrell, Vice President of the University of Chicago; Howard Goodman, University Trustee; Albert C. Svoboda, University Treasurer; Harold Moore, University Trustee; and Julian Levi. Two of these men live within the South West sector, on its easternmost boundary.

The South West Hyde Park Neighborhood Redevelopment Corporation was formed under the provisions of the Neighborhood Redevelopment Act,[1] as amended, of Illinois. The Act, as we described it earlier, was first passed in 1941 as a means for private redevelopment of slums and was amended in 1953, largely through the efforts of Julian Levi, to include conservation areas. The constitutionality of the Act was upheld by the Illinois Supreme Court in 1945 and in 1954.

The legislation provided as follows. Any three residents may form a private corporation for slum clearance or slum prevention in an area no smaller than two square blocks and no larger than 160 acres. The area must be more than 50 per cent residential; most of its buildings must be thirty-five years old or older; and the area must show signs of deterioration. The corporation must submit a development plan to the city Neighborhood Redevelopment Commission, and the plan must be shown to be nondiscriminatory. The Commission must hold public hearings on the development plan and then approve or reject it.

Crucial to the law is the requirement that *owners* of not less than 60 per cent of the land in the proposed corporation area must consent to be bound by the provisions of the development plan. Equally crucial is the granting of *eminent domain,* a right to be given by the Redevelopment Commission if the corporation finds it is unable to complete acquisition of properties by private purchases at fair prices.

The Redevelopment Plan

In June, 1956, the South West Hyde Park Redevelopment Corporation filed a proposed "Plan of Development" with the Chicago Neighborhood Redevelopment Commission. This was the first formal proposal (but not the first such corporation) to be submitted under the Illinois legislation permitting such corporations to be formed.

The plan itself had been drawn up by the Planning Unit of

---

1. It should be recalled that the nature of the emendation of this law was described in Chapter 3, where the early assessment of the Metropolitan Housing and Planning Council of the value of the legislative device was explaining as unfavorable. The Council had feared that a corporate redevelopment approach would have serious shortcomings because of strict dependence on local initiative, neglect of a comprehensive organizational framework, and problems inherent in "granting of eminent domain to private corporations."

the University. The core of the proposal concerned a fourteen-and-a-half-acre tract of four square blocks in the northwest corner of the corporation area. This tract—which we will refer to henceforth as the "acquisition site"—the corporation proposed to acquire and clear at the cost of an estimated $2.5 million. Once cleared, the Corporation would sell the site to the University of Chicago for immediate construction of five five-story buildings to be used for married student housing and for eventual erection of three additional structures for the same use. Only three existing buildings, already owned by the University, were to remain on the site. The acquisition site was to contain, when redeveloped, 394 dwelling units, as compared with its existing 660. More than four-fifths of the site was planned as "open land" for parking, landscaping and playgrounds. The University could be expected to invest $4.3 million altogether, in acquisition, demolition, and construction within the four-square-block site.

One distinction between the fifty-four-acre development area of the southwest sector and the acquisition site within it should be kept in mind. In 1956 the racial composition of South West Hyde Park was 54.3 per cent Negro, while the population in the acquisition site was 79.9 per cent Negro.

What of the forty acres surrounding the acquisition site but included in the development area? These would come under jurisdiction (not ownership) of the corporation, which would require modernization and rehabilitation of existing structures. The redevelopment plan, for example, would require that within one year of approval of the plan all necessary improvements be completed by owners to bring properties into compliance with existing building codes. Against those failing to comply, the corporation could sue in the courts for compliance and could even have property condemned. The corporation also proposed to write covenants into property deeds requiring future owners to maintain building standards, and proposed rezoning of the area to allow only multiple dwellings.

The Conference, Block Groups, and the Plan

The Hyde Park–Kenwood Community Conference staff first learned of University of Chicago proposals for a South West

Hyde Park Redevelopment Corporation in January, 1956. In a meeting of the Committee of Six, Chancellor Kimpton announced that proposals had been formulated but not yet submitted to the University Trustees. The Conference then had only two block groups in the area under consideration, one in the 5500 Drexel Block and one in the 5500 Maryland Block. Mr. Irving Horwitz, Staff Conference Block Director, sent letters to these block-group leaders at once, urging them to attend meetings of the Block Steering Committee.

In the same month real estate agents of the University of Chicago mailed termination of lease notices to about 300 residents in University-owned buildings along 5600 Drexel Avenue (as we reported in Chapter 4) and announced plans to use the released quarters for married student housing. The Community Conference office, the editors of the *Herald*, and the office of the South East Chicago Commission were promptly bombarded with bitter complaints from residents who had lived in these buildings many years, some of whom were unaware of University ownership.

Neither Chancellor Kimpton nor Julian Levi had been consulted by the real estate agents as to the manner in which leases would be terminated; both were thus caught in the contradiction of supporting residential stability in general and evictions in particular. Kimpton promptly sent individual letters to the tenants, apologizing for the abruptness of the first letter and offering a longer period prior to lease termination. The Conference staff spent many hours in "the mollification of the justifiable resentment of the tenants," in Mrs. Abrahamson's words to the Board, "some of whom have been in the buildings for over 25 years."

The lease terminations coincided with reports about University redevelopment intentions to produce a rash of rumors during the winter of 1956. The key rumor was that the University intended to clear the whole of South West Hyde Park for institutional use. University purchases of buildings in this sector (completed covertly to keep prices down) appeared to strengthen this wave of rumor and hostility toward the University.

In mid-February, Julian Levi and Jack Meltzer spoke before the Conference Planning Committee on the tentative redevelopment plans for the South West sector. Notes taken at the meeting reflected his rationale for the plan: "In terms of use, there really is no alternative since this is the logical area for University expansion.[2] In terms of technique, an alternative might be action through the Community Conservation Board (meaning, use of public renewal funds), although the corporation is an easier technique by which financing might become more readily available. If the corporation can do the job, this would also reduce the required public subsidy under the Community Conservation Board."

They emphasized that these plans would ultimately mean benefits for North West Hyde Park (the area immediately to the north of the corporation area) as well, claimed deterioration in the sector was extensive, and cited the University's needs for student housing, for academic buildings, and for a general campus expansion. Levi and Meltzer also indicated the Planning Unit was considering more extensive use of the neighborhood redevelopment corporation to achieve conservation and renewal.

Levi and Meltzer announced that while only a four-square-block area was under consideration for acquisition, eventually the entire South West area should be used by the University because there was need for additional facilities. Levi estimated that, with cooperation from other institutions, about one-third of the owners in the area would sign consent agreements.

In March Mr. William Frederick, Chairman of the Conference Planning Committee, described the corporation plans before the Block Steering Committee. Although all were urged to attend, only one block-group leader from the affected sector was present. Mr. Frederick stressed the potential benefits in the proposal, and only one committee member expressed open doubts about the redevelopment corporation approach. During the same month the Planning Committee decided to postpone making any recommendations to the Conference Board approving the proposals.

In March and April, nearly two months after first learning of the redevelopment proposals, the Conference began to transmit knowledge about the plans to the block groups in and around

---

2. Asked by our interviewer why the University did not consider expansion to the east, a respondent high in the University administration replied that the area to the east (the "Golden Square") contained "our people."

the affected sector. Reactions among residents varied from fatalism about the power of the University, through skepticism about realization of the plan, to approval.

There were no more organized contacts, other than discussion with individuals, between the block groups in the acquisition site and the Conference after April, 1956. Irving Horwitz recommended, on the basis of these meetings, that the Planning Committee delay further before recommending on the redevelopment proposals. He wrote: "There is a reservoir of great hatred and fear of the University, and for the Conference to recommend this at an early stage I think would make us vulnerable. . . . I am not suggesting that block groups make policy for the Conference, but that they be given a chance to voice their views." He noted in the same report that block-group activities in the acquisition-site neighborhood had "for some time" been at a low ebb in participating in community planning generally.

Public feelings in South West Hyde Park concerning University intentions were so heightened by mid-April that the role of the University in renewal was reviewed at a Conference Board Meeting. A Public Relations Committee representative reported that his committee felt strongly that the Conference should attack the University for any policies the Conference considered detrimental to the renewal program as a whole. A very influential Board member replied the Conference could not meet in private from week to week with University representatives to share views and negotiate differences and attack it in public at the same time. After much discussion, no decision was reached.

The Conference Planning Committee then set up a Subcommittee to study and report on plans for South West Hyde Park; Julian Levi and Jack Meltzer were invited to participate. In a meeting of the subcommittee held late in April Levi announced that the University Board of Trustees had voted funds to capitalize the South West Hyde Park Redevelopment Corporation and had decided to apply for federal funds to finance the proposed housing for married students.

Conference members expressed concern that this action was taken without wider public knowledge, that the proposed corporation boundaries did not include any portion of North West Hyde Park, and that the plant included nothing but University housing.

In May, 1956, the Planning Subcommittee began to discuss the details of the corporation plan. Subcommittee members asked whether the proposal would drive householders out of the community if they lacked funds for private rehabilitation. They asked about the specific procedures to be used in requesting owners to give consent, and whether home owners would get enough information to understand the full implications of the redevelopment project. Finally, the Subcommittee expressed general accord with the project proposal but stated that to take a stand at the present date would be premature, since a land-use plan and a copy of the consent agreement were not available.

Late in May Conference Staff Block Director Horwitz reported on block-group activity within the South West Hyde Park area since mid-1955. He concluded that of seven organized groups all but one was "weak in communication with the Conference." Only three had met on the corporation proposal, and reactions had been completely mixed. Within the acquisition site, he said, block groups had a total Conference membership of six persons. Only one had sent a delegate to more than one Block Steering Committee meeting. None attended the special briefing session for block leaders in the area on the proposal, and none responded to Conference communications advising them of the proposal. This report, written to the Director, was never given either to the Conference Board or the Planning Committee, judging from careful review of the records of these groups.

The Conference Planning Committee convened in June, and approved the corporation proposal—with certain provisos:

Sponsors of the proposed corporation should clarify the situation with respect to the following questions before seeking consents from property owners: (1) What policies will be followed in relocating residents . . . and what assistance will be given? (2) What efforts will be made to insure that property owners fully understand the meaning of the consent agreements . . .? . . . can property owners bring their structures into "full compliance" with the electrical code, for example? (3) What financial assistance will be available to property owners who desire to improve their properties . . .? (4) What will be done about properties which are in sound structural condition but which are unsatisfactory due to various factors of obsolescence?

The next week the Conference Board approved the general recommendation of the Planning Committee, but it deleted the above reservations and directed the Planning Committee "to study further some of the anticipated questions people will have and to seek answers in order to help smooth the way for the corporation as well as protect the rights of the people." The Board wanted the Planning Committee questions "rephrased, so they will appear as positive statements of the Conferences' views. . . ."

Thus, five months after learning of the redevelopment corporation proposal the Conference went on record as endorsing fully the needs and aims of the corporation, leaving to the future the problem of stating reservations. The Board took this action without reviewing block-group attitudes, without consultation with the staff Block Director, and without receipt of staff reports on local conditions.

At the end of June, the South West Hyde Park Neighborhood Redevelopment Corporation released its plans to the press. Its brochure, filed with the city Commission, emphasized the program would conserve the "development area," without public monies, for University purposes, and without racial or ethnic discrimination. The issue of the *Herald* devoted to the announcements included an interview with Julian Levi; asked why the proposals were not released in early Spring when they were being discussed with the Conference, Levi stated, "In view of the effect plans have on the market value of property, it would have been irresponsible to release plans before they had any sort of official status."

In July James Cunningham replaced Julia Abrahamson as Executive Director of the Conference. Cunningham solicited legal opinions regarding enforcement of the Redevelopment Act against noncompliers, and for the first time the Conference learned the corporation would not be able to condemn the property of those who signed consent agreements unless the property was substandard. The corporation would, however, be able to bring condemnation proceedings against owners who did not sign the consent agreement! This peculiar situation Cunningham shared with the Planning Committee early in July, 1956, when it convened to reconsider its reservations about the proposals. The Committee concluded that it still lacked guarantees from the corporation on means of informing owners of these and other implications of consent signatures. They voted to urge publication of a booklet to be distributed before signatures were sought.

The South West Hyde Park Neighborhood Association

That Conference contacts in and around the acquisition site were very weak has already been established. Moreover, Conference officials did not learn of the formation of a property-owners association until two months after its organization in April. This group, the South West Hyde Park Neighborhood Association, informed the Conference of its intent to disseminate information on redevelopment programs; to seek "a place in the formation of the plans"; and "to protect owners against wholesale demolition and movement out of the area." The group was initially sympathetic to and expressed a wish to work with but not through the Conference. The Association was formed under the leadership of St. Clair Drake [3] and was initially composed of forty-five members who lived on two of the blocks within the acquisition site.

At the time of the announcement of redevelopment plans for South West Hyde Park, St. Clair Drake (Ph.D. from the University of Chicago, Professor of Sociology at Roosevelt University, and a Negro) had just purchased a home on the 5600 block of Maryland Avenue. Until 1953 he had lived in a cooperatively owned interracial building just south of the acquisition site. Between 1953 and 1955 he had been on leave for two years. On his return in 1955 he had tried very hard to locate and purchase housing to the east of the University of Chicago and near the University Laboratory School which his children attended.

Drake was unable to buy or rent suitable housing for his family in spite of numerous vacancies in the area. Drake understandably became increasingly bitter as vacancy after vacancy was either sold or rented to others. Finally, Drake purchased a home just a few doors north of his previous apartment and half a block south of the acquisition area. The extent of his

---

3. Sociologist and author, with Horace Cayton, of *Black Metropolis* (Chicago: University of Chicago Press, 1945).

bitterness is measured in the following open letter he wrote to his friends and neighbors in July, 1956, after his election as President of the Association:

I just moved into 5618 Maryland a short while ago, and soon afterwards the . . . Redevelopment Corporation announced its plans for the area west of the University. This area "west of Ellis" has a fairly heavy Negro population—I wouldn't have been able to move in there if it hadn't been a neighborhood of this character. The problems of redeveloping the area are bound to raise questions in the minds of residents there as to whether it is going to be carried out with or without "integration"; whether the objective is to "roll back" the "Negro bulge" which extends across Cottage Grove and to restore the area to its former all-white character, or whether the objectives contemplae a *mixed* community of people cooperating . . . to maintain a clean, safe, orderly, quiet neighborhood . . . I am inclinded to cast a "protest vote" when I am asked if I will become one of the 60% needed to sanction the plan.

Drake concluded this letter with a page of "Unanswered Questions." He wrote:

The Negro property owners "west of Ellis" are, at the moment, disturbed, confused, and resentful. Much of this is due to the fact that neither the University, the Southeast Commission, or this recently formed corporation has been willing to explain to them just where they stand in this contemplated process of "urban renewal." There are no channels of communication. . . . There is a heavy-handedness about the operations of the University real estate office . . . which does not reflect well on a great University. . . .

The letter was written very shortly after Drake's election to the post of President of the Neighborhood Association. The unanswered questions became the basis for the Association's opposition to the corporation's Development Plan.

The Neighborhood Association and the Conference in Interaction

In midsummer of 1956, the South West Hyde Park Neighborhood Association presented to the Conference a memorandum outlining the policies of the Association on redevelopment procedures and on relationships with the Conference. It endorsed

the principle of planning for conservation; expressed its obliga-
tion to work for achievement of a "clean, safe, orderly, attractive community"; recognized the University's needs for increased
facilities and space; and asserted a "profound respect for the
Community Conference." The memo also stated: "We feel the
rights of resident owners in this area are every whit as important
as the rights of the institutions." The Association leadership
stated:

We think the Conference has made a serious error of judgment in
endorsing the Redevelopment Plan before re-examining the claim
that only demolition of the "four blocks" can meet the legitimate
needs of university housing . . . before iron-clad guarantees have
been given that amendments will not be made in the near future
to make "acquisition areas" out of the rest of Southwest Hyde Park;
before the realtors, the University and the Southeast Commission
have taken a clear stand for "open occupancy" east of Ellis Avenue
(in the Golden Square); and before the ethics and legality of the
methods being used for securing consent have been carefully
examined.

The memo concluded, "A fair price and 'painless relocation' are
no answers to people who feel they are 'Hyde Parkers'. . . ."

In response, Irving Horwitz prepared a memorandum for
James Cunningham, expressing his concern over the local situation and making recommendations for action:

I am still deeply troubled about this area. Somehow or other this
whole business of the redevelopment corporation will have to be
worked out. As far as I can see the complaints rest on two bases:
(1) The entire area to be cleared will be used for University
utilization—with nothing for the community. (2) Since the area
is predominantly Negro, the operation is seen as anti-Negro
clearance.

Horwitz proposed that he be allowed to contact the leadership in the area, to arrange a meeting with delegates to hear
complaints and objections, and to submit these to the Conference
Board and the Committee of Six. He commented:

I'm not kidding myself into thinking some aspect of the plan can
be changed—but I think the Conference should at least point up
as strenuously as possible to the powers that be the tremendous

emotional opposition that has been stirred up, opposition that can lead to horrible consequences. I think, moreover, it was a mistake for the Conference Board to make their endorsement of the corporation as early as they did.

He felt it was his duty to work for local support of the proposal, since the Board had already endorsed it, but he concluded:

If we can only get some aspect of the plan changed to include some housing other than married students' dormitories, I think the whole business would be easier to take. As it stands now, it is an impossible situation.

Cunningham then instructed Horwitz to make the rounds of the local leadership as the memorandum suggested. Horwitz reported on a series of individual interviews, in which he obtained as mixed a variety of attitudes as had been expressed earlier. One block-group leader's block, predominantly faculty personnel, favored the proposals as they stood. Other leaders favored everything from specific changes to radical revision of the entire proposal. Still others expressed strongly cynical distrust of the motives of both the corporation and the University.

Acting on Horwitz' recommendations, the Conference, on August 20, 1956, brought together leaders of the block groups and the Neighborhood Association. The important point to note about this date is that it fell five days after the *Herald* announced that owners of 32 per cent of the property in South West Hyde Park, including the University, had already signed consents to the corporation proposal—that is, half the necessary consents had already been obtained.

About thirty-five leaders attended the Conference meeting, presided over by a Conference Planning Committee member, a University of Chicago professor. The purpose of the meeting was announced as airing questions bothering local South West sector residents. Conference Director Cunningham took the floor at the opening of the meeting and explained in detail the Conference endorsement of the corporation proposal. Irving Horwitz followed by summarizing the questions that had been raised by leaders in his individual interviews.

The remainder of the meeting consisted of inquiries from area residents, most of them directed at and answered by Julian

Levi and Jack Meltzer. Among these, six questions received greatest attention from "both sides." Their content and the answers Levi supplied are of importance to our later analysis. (1) Would the acquisition site be extended by the corporation in the future? Levi assured everyone there was no intention of this, and said the corporation would ask that it be forbidden in the order of the Neighborhood Redevelopment Commission. (2) What would happen to nonconsenters? Levi replied that once the plan was agreed to by the Commission, nonconsenters would be given six months in which to sign consents. After this period of grace, nonconsenters would be subject to condemnation and acquisition in cases of noncompliance with standards of the corporation. (3) Questions on fair price were given general reassurance of fair procedures. (4) St. Clair Drake and others pointed out that the area could be rehabilitated through spot clearance and code enforcement. Levi and Meltzer answered that most of the buildings in the acquisition area had violations and would be uneconomical to rehabilitate, and that good planning required clearance of at least four square blocks. They added that to attract married students to the University, modern housing was necessary. (5) In reply to a Neighborhood Association leader's claim that the people in the site had never been consulted on the plan, Horwitz said that they had been invited to meetings for block leaders but that few people came. (6) St. Clair Drake said he would refuse to sign a consent if housing east of Ellis Avenue and south of 55th Street (the "Golden Square") remained closed to Negro occupancy. Levi replied, "Well, that is an academic question, since there are no vacancies or houses for sale in that area, and many people are waiting to snap up any that do occur." To Drake, who had failed on many separate occasions to find a way of buying properties within the "Golden Square" that were on the market, this was in no sense an academic question.

In a memorandum subsequent to this meeting Horwitz remarked to Cunningham:

I've been thinking over your remarks about the fact that people like Drake . . . [and] Hagiwara should feel they must organize their own group in order to be heard instead of working through the Conference. . . . you made particular reference to the fact that the Board never heard from any person in the area itself in opposition to the corporation and that the Board had made its recommendation without such hearings.

He proposed that in the future the Planning Committee should hold meetings similar to the one he had arranged, described above, in order to involve its members directly in local perspectives. He concluded, "I don't know, Jim, any way that we try it, it's going to be a rough deal."

Shortly after, Cunningham conferred with Redevelopment Commission Secretary Mackelmann, who explained that the Commission could *not* write in limitations to the acquisition area, as Levi had suggested, since this referred to future actions.

Early in September the Planning Committee recommended to the Conference Board that it testify at the forthcoming Neighborhood Redevelopment Commission Hearing in favor of the corporation proposal and that it express concern or reservation over relocation procedures and unresolved problems in financing acquisition and maintenance. The Board promptly and unanimously voted to support this recommendation. Except for a few brief meetings of a very routine nature, this concluded the first phase of Conference activities on the issue of corporate redevelopment of South West Hyde Park.

It should be stressed that from the time the Neighborhood Association was formed, for a period of nearly six months, the Conference staff engaged in only two important contacts with anyone in the ranks of the Association. Individual conferences with three leaders and one general meeting comprised the range of Conference negotiations in this instance. That the Association drew its key leadership and most of its members from two former Block Groups makes this low investment all the more significant. Cunningham and Horwitz note, however, that they tried but were unable to contact Association leaders during the controversy.

The Neighborhood Redevelopment Commission Hearings

After nine months of effort by the Planning Unit and South East Chicago Commission, during which the objectives of the

South West Hyde Park Neighborhood Corporation were prepared for formal consideration, the municipal Commission responsible for authorizing or rejecting the proposal took its
first steps toward a decision. During this same period, as we
have documented, the Conference, the Neighborhood Association,
and the local public engaged in a variety of peripheral and
indeterminate negotiations. Yet the Commission hearings were
conducted on the basis of the proposal as it had been announced
publicly in June, three months earlier. No changes had since
been introduced by corporation officials. It should be noted, too,
that this was the first such proposal to come before the five
unsalaried Commissioners. (All expenses for Commission hearings were paid by the Neighborhood Corporation.)

The first public hearing was held on September 28. In the
month that had passed since Julian Levi had announced that
he had half the necessary consents, he had collected enough additional ones to cover the owners of 61.06 per cent of the property,
or 1.06 per cent more than the proportion required by law. These
consents were filed at the hearings. He also assured the Commission that the corporation, in cooperation with the Mayor's
Housing Coordinator and the Chicago Housing Authority,
would provide good relocation service to residents. Other individuals, all of them associated with the corporation, testified on
behalf of the proposal, and these representatives were questioned
by area residents.

At a second public hearing, held two weeks later, Cunningham and Horwitz supported the proposal on behalf of the Conference. The Conference Board statement of support was read.
The reservations about relocation procedures and rehabilitation
financing suggested by the Planning Committee were expressed.
And reminders of Julian Levi's assurances that there would be
no extension of the acquisition site and that property owners
would recive sale prices amounting to at least as much as they
had paid for their properties, were introduced into the record.
In effect, then, four qualifications to the corporation proposal
were expressed by the Conference spokesmen.

More interesting, however, was this assertion by Cunningham:

The Conference believes that an important factor in determining

the future of an area is its response to community organization. While the Conference has been able to help 80 per cent of the blocks in Hyde Park–Kenwood to organize successfully for neighborhood conservation, these four blocks in question have a long record of apathy and resistance to community organization. A handful of people in these blocks have sincerely attempted to organize them but have met with cold indifference.

Following Cunningham's testimony, Commissioner John McCarthy said, "I am very much interested in your statement that the organization that you represent has attempted to interest the owners in the four block area to cooperate in conservation, and that many of them have failed. . . . Could you go into a little more detail for us what these efforts have been . . . ?" Cunningham then provided a block by block history of Conference efforts since about 1954 as it pertained to the acquisition site. He concluded as follows:

In the aggregate, the area has been very lax in taking up the matter of housing code violations. . . . The area showed little interest in discussing the plan early last year when the Conference was calling meetings and making information available. . . . Every month the Conference called together all of the block leaders in Hyde Park–Kenwood. From September of 1955 to the present, there was only one of these monthly block steering committee meetings at which any number of persons from the area in question appeared. And this was a meeting held in the late summer after the plan had been released . . . that is the picture of what we have seen in that area.

In the rather heated exchange with questioners that followed, Cunningham heard St. Clair Drake assert:

We can give evidence . . . that lack of interest in the Conference does not necessarily mean lack of interest in one's own property . . . [and] why would we expect people to come to a meeting to discuss their own extinction? . . . I think it is somewhat unreasonable for people to show enthusiasm at meetings to discuss how to eliminate themselves from an area.

Cross-examination of both Cunningham and Horwitz by southwest residents, who disputed and resented these assertions, was lengthy and bitter. About seventy-five area residents attended this hearing.

The next piece of testimony was presented by St. Clair Drake for the South West Hyde Park Neighborhood Association. Drake attacked Jack Meltzer's structural survey, which had been used to support the contention the area was deteriorating. Drake claimed that homes with minor and repairable damage were classified on the maps as deteriorated and that the several surveys of the sector differed as to the number of buildings classified as dilapidated. Drake also argued for demolition of dilapidated buildings in some portions of the acquisition site, and for spot clearance and conservation efforts in the remainder. He claimed the University should buy individual buildings on the open market in order to house students in this area.

Before the third public hearing was convened, Cunningham met with leaders of Drake's Neighborhood Association and, according to his notes, "restored some friendly relations." In these contacts, however, Cunningham was furnished with information revealing that two block groups in the acquisition area had in fact done more than Conference testimony indicated.

Another Conference staff employee, in charge of real estate affairs, completed telephone conversations with fifteen of the twenty-five property owners who had signed consent agreements and discovered that ten of the fifteen were white, upper-middle-class home owners, including five University employees. All ten whites lived outside the acquisition site proper, and all ten agreed that the acquisition site was deteriorated and overcrowded. The remaining five were Negroes: three of them said they had been planning to move anyway, and agreed that the neighborhood was deteriorating; two explained, "We figured if we played ball with the University we'd get a better deal."

Plainly, Conference testimony at the hearings was equivocal. It endorsed the corporation proposal, but it expressed reservations about four features of the proposal. At the same time, it discredited block group and Neighborhood Association opposition to the proposal. Cunningham was privately uncomfortable about this ambiguous posture and publicly embarrassed by the doubt cast on his evidence about weak public participation in the sector. He began to reconsider the entire issue.

Four days after the second public hearing, Cunningham presented a lengthy report to the Executive Committee of the Conference Board. In this report, he stated:

The Conference has given its approval to the plan of the Southwest Hyde Park Neighborhood Redevelopment Corporation, which plan has engendered tremendous bitterness and opposition in our community. We gave our approval by relying on certain data of the corporation. Serious doubts have been cast on that data by opponents . . . and the checking we have been able to do indicates those doubts may be justified.

Cunningham then emphasized, "The Conference may be in the position of supporting the University and the South East Commission on a project that is *not* in the public interest." Noting that the Conference as "the organization of the people . . . is estranged from a large part of the people" on this issue, Cunningham specified three "grave dangers" to the Conference implicit in its current stand. The Conference could become labeled as a "tool of the University of Chicago"; the race issue could be introduced into the situation and could "carry over to kill urban renewal" as a whole in the community; or, "Great bitterness to all urban renewal" could be stimulated by the issue of redevelopment through neighborhood corporations.

He asked the Executive Committee to consider whether the Conference needed to do some independent research before it made decisions about endorsing the proposal. He also asked:

Don't we have to take more initiative independent of the University and the Commission? In presenting renewal plans to block groups, are we more than merely messengers? Are we really the peoples' organization? Or do we represent only the well-educated, somewhat liberal, mostly white, middle class and upper middle class? How can we broaden our base?

Cunningham concluded that the Conference had to choose between standing strongly behind its original position or announcing to the press that doubts had been raised as to the validity of the data supporting the corporation proposal. The Conference real estate affairs staff director announced that on personal inspection, he had found eight buildings marked as dilapidated in the proposal to be in "excellent condition."

The Executive Committee reached a decision to continue to support the proposal, but to have the Planning Committee Chairman and staff employees review the Planning Unit data with Jack Meltzer. At a later meeting, the Conference staff offi-

cial reported the classification of "dilapidated" in the corporation data was used loosely to apply to violations found in initial
surveys. These violations had been promptly and inexpensively
corrected by property owners, but Meltzer reported he intended
to stick by his conclusion that the acquisition sites were headed
for blight, even if some buildings had been recently improved.

A week later, the third public hearing was convened by the
Neighborhood Redevelopment Commission. Drake was rigor-
ously cross-examined by an attorney for the corporation on his
earlier testimony that the corporation's survey data were
invalid. Drake criticized "the type of definition of dilapidation
which shifts backwards and forward and under which it is
possible for a building to be classified as dilapidated merely
because a window has been boarded up for a week."

In a move apparently made to discredit testimony about the
condition of property within the acquisition site, Drake called
several property owners to the stand. Each testified to an impressive number of repairs and improvements which he had
made on his properties. Some testified that the code violations
listed for their properties had been corrected.

However, under cross-examination, the attorney for the
redevelopment corporation was able to establish that property
after property was "converted through usage." In one three-
decker apartment building, meant to house three families, six
or seven separate households lived in doubled-up conditions.
The evidence on conversion by usage made a considerable impact on the Commissioners, judging from the questions which
they put to the witnesses.

This testimony given by the property owners expressed in
a poignant way the conflict of housing values between Negroes
recently moved from the "ghetto" and upper-middle-class whites
who establish housing standards. The witnesses were indignant
that their properties, into which they had poured so much
energy and scarce capital, were designated as dilapidated. They
also clearly felt that two couples related through blood or mar-
riage and their children could occupy a four-room apartment
without necessarily being overcrowded. The fact that more than
twice as many individuals as had been the intent of the builder
occupied some of the property holdings did not signify to the
witnesses that anything had been lost in the way of housing

standards. Obviously, compared to the incredible overcrowding in the old "Black Belt," the housing in the acquisition site was luxurious.

Philip Hauser, Chairman of the Department of Sociology at the University of Chicago, testified for the corporation and presented data that he claimed added up to "The pattern of an area in transition," a trend toward deterioration and blight. Hauser reported that:

On the basis of the survey of the area made by the National Opinion Research Center and the Chicago Community Inventory of which I am director, it contained 652 dwelling units in March to May of 1956 . . . there has been an increase without any new construction . . . of 103 dwelling units or an increase of 19 per cent over 1940. . . . This . . . is conversion detectable by the Census enumerator and not conversion by use. . . . Second . . . the acquisition area had 18.5 per cent of the dwelling units sharing the bath. I present that as an item relevant to the nature of the occupancy of the area. . . . With respect to evidence of crowding . . . what is normally accepted as an index among experts in the field, crowding is occupancy of more than 1.5 persons per room. This is the classification used in the official United States Census practices. . . . In the acquisition area, there are about 9 per cent of dwelling units so occupied in terms of overcrowded conditions, whereas, in the remainder of the development area this Corporation is interested in, it was only one third as great.

Dr. Hauser continued to assemble evidence of overoccupancy in the site. He noted that use of a 1.25 persons per room standard yielded a 24 per cent proportion in the site, compared to 6 per cent in South West Hyde Park outside the site. At least 65 per cent of the residents of the acquisition site moved from the sector between 1950 and 1956, indicating extremely high transiency. More than one-third of the 1956 inhabitants had lived there for less than one year. He summarized as follows:

If you take each of these statistics to which I have referred, they add up to mean that you have the symptoms of an area in transition, symptoms of the kind which, under the purposes of this Act, as I think the intention of the Counsel here is to show, indicate that these are symptoms and point to a trend of deterioration and blight.

The third hearing as a whole reflected the underlying differences between redevelopment corporation perspectives and perspectives of leaders within the resident neighborhood association. The corporation and the area property owners it represented brought *upper-middle-class* standards of occupancy thresholds and transiency rates to bear in their approaches to renewal. These were generally in accord with standards followed by professional housing and census specialists. Local residents —most of them recently moved from the incredibly extreme overcrowding of Chicago's "Black Belt," and most of them (51 per cent) employed as domestic servants, factory operators, and manual laborers—viewed the acquisition site as a relatively ideal residential locale. The gulf between perspectives here was insurmountable.

At a fourth hearing Cunningham represented the Conference. He reiterated endorsement of the corporation but retracted his earlier testimony discrediting the local block groups.

At the same hearing, Attorney Michael Hagiwara summarized the position of the Neighborhood Association, as follows: (1) The corporation had not proven the area is blighted or in need of clearance, as required by state law. (2) The proposal does not accomplish the public use required by law: "The need here is only that the University of Chicago must have housing. . . ." (3) The planning had not been done with the cooperation of neighbors for the benefit of the neighborhood, as envisioned by the Redevelopment Act. (4) The Corporation had failed to show that execution of the plan would not result in undue hardship to area residents. To underscore the racial importance of this claim, Hagiwara asked a Negro block leader, a widow with four children, to testify: "Must we always be on the move," she asked, "Must we always be afraid to invest in anything except expensive cars? Must we be told in an undertone that we are not needed?" (5) Finally, the proposal did not satisfy the law which specifies that "no property is to be acquired because of race, creed or color." "It is our belief," Hagiwara reported, "that the basic purpose of this plan . . . is to allow the University of Chicago to set up a buffer against the presence of Negro residents in large numbers."

At the same fourth hearing 5th Ward Alderman Leon Despres testified, saying neither party had consulted with him.

He claimed the key question for decision was, "Do the needs of a great university . . . justify this use of public power?" He also noted the University's activities in the promotion of racially restrictive covenants before 1948. But he concluded the Commission should approve the plan, expressing substantially the reservations expressed by the Conference about relocation, fair purchase prices and nondiscrimination.

One week before the fifth and final public hearing the *Herald* carried a letter from James Cunningham for the Conference, which included the following remarks bearing on Conference views on the corporation proposal:

It has to do with saving a neighborhood. . . . The most potent factor of stability in making this area attractive is the University of Chicago. . . . No doubt, it would have been much better if the University had consulted the people of the community when the need for student housing was first realized and before any plans were developed. But the fact that this did not happen does not mean the present plan is not a sound one. . . .

The same issue of the *Herald* carried a feature story based on interviews with acquisition-site residents, who explained that they had invested hard work and money in improving their property and felt resentment at having their homes termed "dilapidated" or "deteriorated," denied charges of apathy, and expressed their feelings about the hardships moving would entail for them.

Cunningham's *Herald* letter elicited a strong letter of opposition from a former Conference Board member and resident of the South West sector. He did not publish the letter, but sent it privately to the Conference office. He complained:

The Conference does not bargain for its support. . . . In Southwest Hyde Park it puts itself in the position of having to explain because it treads on shaky ground . . . Who are you saving the neighborhood for? If you are saving the neighborhood for the University, many of us would like to know, because we can start another organization to do the work you are supposed to do. . . .

Just a few days prior to the final decision of the Redevelopment Commission, the city's largest Negro newspaper, the Chicago *Defender*, rose to judge the issues in corporate redevelopment. Cunningham used Conference prestige to arrange a meeting between Chancellor Kimpton and *Defender* Publisher and Editor Louis Martin, in the hope of "promoting understanding." Kimpton explained to the *Defender* that the University's admission policies were nondiscriminatory, that he personally did not believe that the presence of Negroes created slums, and that the University's concern was only to prevent blight. The *Defender* published this statement and added a commentary by St. Clair Drake: "Kimpton's statement evades the whole issue. . . . The issue is whether a law designed to conserve a neighborhood should be used to reduce the proportion of Negroes in the area." This reply established the tone toward Hyde Park renewal issues taken by the *Defender* throughout 1957 and 1958, culminating in stories impugning the motives of the University and in editorial opposition to the Final Renewal Plan.

The final public hearing was held in mid-November of 1956. At this meeting, the Commissioners directed questions at Julian Levi concerning the proposal. On the issue of extension of the acquisition site, Levi said the University had no plans for doing so "within the next five or ten years."

On rehabilitation financing Levi produced assurances of bank support and said federal loans might also become available. He said relocation would be handled through a municipal agency, promised independent appraisals to insure fair purchase prices, and further assured the Commission that the corporation "will seek permission to acquire property by . . . eminent domain only after all attempts at negotiation have failed."

Drake and Hagiwara testified again for the Neighborhood Association. Drake proposed that either the corporation should be broadened to include residents of the area and a new plan drafted, or that the residents should be allowed to form their own corporation. He emphasized that the first alternative was preferred. Hagiwara added the claim that married student housing was "just another kind of private use." Levi disagreed and produced remarks made by congressmen stating that student housing is "in the national interest."

The Neighborhood Redevelopment Commission approved the proposed plan of the South West Hyde Park Redevelopment Corporation on November 26, 1956, by a vote of two to one. The opposing vote was registered by the one Negro member of the Commission—a resident of Hyde Park who was not convinced the corporation had proved the acquisition site was deteriorating fast enough to require demolition.

The Aftermath

The approving vote of the Redevelopment Commission, however, was not to be the final go-ahead signal for redevelopment. The South West Hyde Park Neighborhood Association petitioned the Neighborhood Redevelopment Commission to reconsider. Failing in this move, the Association conducted a mass meeting in the neighborhood and then launched a court fight. After one unsuccessful appeal after another, the law suit challenging the constitutionality of the corporation ended in October, 1958, when the United States Supreme Court refused to accept jurisdiction of the case. In effect, the Supreme Court upheld the right of the neighborhood redevelopment corporation to use condemnation procedures in blighted areas.

Julian Levi announced to the press: "Some clearance has been completed and construction will start soon on the new apartments. The corporation will apply at once to the Redevelopment Commission to proceed with the rest of the work." The litigation started by the Association delayed the plans of the University nearly two years.

Neighborhood resentment of the Conference was slow to die down. The Conference Staff Block Director who replaced Irving Horwitz discovered during 1957 that the Conference was regarded with some hostility by many former block-group members in and around the acquisition site. Of three block organizations that had been somewhat active in this area, only one —predominantly faculty—continued to meet during 1957. Not until the middle of 1958 was the Conference able to resurrect block activities in this locale.

Finally, after the death of the Association Attorney, Michael Hagiwara, during the proceedings of the case, St. Clair Drake left Hyde Park and America for Africa, "to fight the germs of malaria in preference to the germs of prejudice." In a letter to the *Herald* Drake concluded:

Conference activities cannot be a substitute for frank, cards-on-the table, behavior by the Southeast Chicago Commission itself. It is unfortunate that fate has cast University and Southeast Commission officials in the roles of King Canute and the Little-Boy-With-His-Finger-in-the-Dike, or that Conference officials (white and colored) have been put in a position where they have to defend their racial liberalism while trying to build an interracial community. And every Hyde Park Negro leader is almost driven schizophrenic trying to decide whether to act as a "Race Man" or in terms of his social class position.

Perhaps expressing their chagrin at being without direct authority in the decision-making process, Aldermen Leon Despres and Claude Holman (of the 5th and 4th Wards, respectively) submitted a resolution to the City Council calling for an amendment to the Redevelopment Act which would give the City Council rather than the Neighborhood Redevelopment Commission the power to approve or reject any future corporate proposals in the city.

Future neighborhood redevelopment through private corporations seems a very remote possibility at the present time. The incidents in South West Hyde Park have made public officials and community leaders wary of the device.

An Interpretation

To some citizens in South West Hyde Park urban renewal appeared as a significant threat to their interests. The resulting popular movement was able to force a reconsideration of the neighborhood redevelopment corporation as a tool of community renewal, although it was not able to modify its use in the community.

In any pioneering attempt to employ a new social device, questions inevitably arise out of the uncertainties that stem from the lack of precedent. Indeed, some of the questions that residents and the Conference raised were the same as those *Conservation* (the earlier report of the Metropolitan Housing and Planning Council) had posed: adequate safeguards around the use of eminent domain, organizational machinery to coordinate the activities of the neighborhood redevelopment corporation with other planning activities, and the like.

Some fears of the residents concerning South West Hyde Park redevelopment centered around the private use of eminent domain. The substance of much of the controversy as it unfolded throughout the hearings revolved around this point. Would signers of consent agreements have full knowledge of what this involved? Would fair prices be given? How would compliers and noncompliers be handled by the corporation? These questions reflected the uncertainty over the transfer of public power to private institutional hands. Furthermore, adequate provisions for relocating displaced residents had not been developed; indeed, it was only after public pressure that Julian Levi announced that relocation would be handled by contract with a municipal agency.

From a political viewpoint, the most serious deficiency was the absence of mechanisms for allowing residents to express their views. Unlike the case of Urban Renewal, no local body comparable to the Conservation Community Council existed to review the redevelopment proposals and to give approval or disapproval.

The Chicago Neighborhood Redevelopment Commission amounted to an *ad-hoc* decision-making authority: no other specific redevelopment plan had ever been submitted to it (since 1941); it had no set of precedents and had only temporary status within the framework of the city government. Although the Commission's Executive Secretary, D. E. Mackelmann, was experienced in planning and housing, no one had had experience with this particular device.

This interpretation in no way reflects discredit on the quality of the Neighborhood Redevelopment Commission's deliberations. The publicly available transcripts of the Commission hearings, from which we have quoted so liberally, suggest grave concern for sound and equitable judgment based on meticulous attention to all the facts in the case. More than 600 pages of testimony were recevied. Procedural regulations were agreed upon in advance, and full courtesy appears to have been shown every registered participant.

Perhaps most significantly, no officials had responsibility for evaluating the proposal in relation to conservation planning for the community or the city as a whole. As Commissioner Robert Landrum commented at the first hearing:

There are many other areas that are conservation areas or slum and blight areas, that may do the same thing (e.g., submit plans to the Commission). This plan happens to be one that was submitted to us, and this plan has gone through all the various processes to reach this stage for hearing . . . you may attack questions and object to this plan, but you cannot state generalities concerning other sections of the city.

No one was authorized to decide whether the corporation's goals could be achieved just as well within the Final Renewal Plan, which was being prepared concurrently. No one was empowered to *delay* the application of the corporation to pose this question.

Thus, the tool of private corporate redevelopment is a highly problematical instrument. One experienced downtown legal informant commented during an interview:

The Neighborhood Redevelopment Corporation is what we call a one crack execution. The city will have one successful corporation project and will then let the tool rest . . . the stock held by residents peters out . . . even the University of Chicago has found itself unable to raise sufficient stock purchasing support for similar corporate programs elsewhere in the community.

As summarized in Chapter 4, the characteristic mode of action of the University and the South East Chicago Commission was to develop plans quickly, announce proposals in general terms, and then obtain quick approval through political leverage downtown. This mode of action was also characteristic of the neighborhood redevelopment proposal in South West Hyde Park. However, of all the renewal proposals that were made in connection with the conservation of the community, this one called for the most cautious handling. For one thing, the special interests of the University as an organization were closer to the surface in this proposal. In "Hyde Park A and B," the redevelopment plans were not to the direct benefit of the University but involved the razing of obvious slums and their replacement with public facilities and residential structures. The plans for South West Hyde Park, however, involved the removal of structures not clearly deteriorated, with University facilities replacing them. This surfacing of special interests intensified the public-relations stresses that had been stimulated in the case of other projects. Heightening this effect further is the difference between proposals made by a private corporation and those embodied in plans sanctioned by federal scrutiny.

Residents were inevitably suspicious of University motives. Attempts on the part of University officials to prove their good intentions only served to increase suspicion. Irving Horwitz' suggestion that at least one land use other than student housing should be introduced into the plan makes this point: consensus could only have been achieved at the price of demonstrated good intentions—"good" as defined by the opponents to private redevelopment. One of the questions posed at a Planning Committee meeting was, "Will children in the surrounding neighborhood be able to use the student families' playground equipment?" The reply: "Yes, until some unpleasant incidents occur." This captures the sense in which a private corporation's proposal to eliminate an existing neighborhood of 100 buildings and to construct an institutional community was bound to raise the issue of whether private groups should gain rights to eminent domain.

The population living in the Development Area of the neighborhood corporation reflected in its composition a kind of microcosm of the larger Hyde Park–Kenwood community. The acquisition site proper is located in a border zone. A four-square-block site situated directly in one of the main paths of in-migrations, it contains aging three-story walk-ups, for the most part, interspersed with small private dwellings and bordered on two sides by commercial uses and transportation routes. In the surrounding development area are located both a stable nonwhite residential community, and to the east is the University faculty community.

Thus, the corporation proposal placed the question of an interracial community squarely on the voting block by putting property owners in the University community development area in a position to vote for acquisition, demolition and relocation of the impinging nonwhite property owners. Irrespective of questions of motive [4] (which are not assessable in events of this

4. St. Clair Drake, seeking as a participant to assess motives, was himself unable to do more than raise this issue. He asked: "What is the *real* thing the University and the others have against us? Is it that our buildings aren't kept up, is it our selection of tenants, is it our behavior, or is it because we are black—period?"

sort in any case), the invitation to sign consents had the undisputed effect of producing a vote for the demolition of the predominantly nonwhite acquisition site. And this did indeed occur. The great majority of consent agreements were signed by owners residing in the development area but outside the acquisition site.

It is also interesting to observe that the Neighborhood Association was formed and led by residents located between the acquisition site and the remainder of the development area— from those blocks which had one foot in the University community (as Drake himself) and one foot out, and from those with racially mixed populations. More than any other segment, this intermediate population understandably felt, as Drake said of the renewal program of the University as a whole, "The next bite might be me."

The Neighborhood Redevelopment Corporation, therefore, did not speak on behalf of a "neighborhood" in any social sense. Communication between these heterogeneous sections within the South West had always been nonexistent.

That acquisition-site owners improved their properties so promptly after the Planning Unit's first surveys of violations is perhaps expressive of the intended stability of these residents. But their border-zone neighborhood was certainly not so perceived by the surrounding upper-middle-class whites.[5]

In part, the public reaction flowed from the differences in housing and living standards of Negroes and whites, as these were described from attitude survey findings (see Appendix). A Negro who had worked his way slowly out of the conditions described in St. Clair Drake's famous study *Black Metropolis*, and who had managed to place his family in only slightly overcrowded quarters in the Hyde Park acquisition site near 55th Street, was bound to perceive his new neighborhood with relatively high satisfaction. If, moreover, this Hyde Parker had arrived about 1952 and had been settled in the South West sector for even one year prior to the corporation proposal, by

---

5. The term "upper middle class" is intended in this chapter to refer more to subculturally prescribed life styles and values than to income levels. Many University personnel cannot afford high rentals or expensive homes; in fact, in western sectors of Hyde Park they tend to live in University subsidized housing.

his standards he was certainly not a transient dweller. In social-class terms, this resident was upwardly mobile if one used the criteria of his own segregated group. The heavy investment in home improvements made by property owners in this group during 1956 simply strengthened self-definitions of self-reliance, family and residential stability and desirability.

The idea that the same buildings, for the most part simply aging or potentially "obsolescent," would not be suitable to house married students was unacceptable to this recently "ghetto"-ized population. To faculty residents and similar upper-middle-class whites in other portions of the South West area, the attractive plans for housing for married students—sketches for which included little children romping along broad white sidewalks sheltered by handsome elms—projected an image of the quasi-suburban life in the city that they themselves might hope to enjoy under eventual redevelopment of the entire area. (Their reactions to hasty University eviction earlier in 1956, of course, were not unlike the reactions of acquisition site Negroes later in the year.)

The failure of the Hyde Park–Kenwood Community Conference in South West Hyde Park stems from two basic organizational inadequacies. First, Conference connections in the acquisition area through block groups and membership were weak. Secondly, the Conference had not yet fully devised means of communicating to and receiving comments from the unorganized portions of the Hyde Park–Kenwood citizenry. The transmission-belt organizational devices described in Chapter 5 were perfected after the South West Hyde Park redevelopment controversy.

In the absence of strong "grass-roots" opinions adequately transmitted to the policy-making organs of the Conference, this organization all too quickly endorsed the redevelopment proposal. Since no loud voices of objection were heard by the Conference supported the proposal in the hope of encouraging Planning Unit interest in North West Hyde Park area (a hope that Julian Levi stimulated on more than one occasion). Conference approval was also predicated on the conviction that provision should be made for expansion of the central institution in the community. Thus the Conference played the issue of private redevelopment "by ear" without sufficient recognition that the residents directly affected had not been adequately "negotiated" to communicate their opinions to the organization.

This occurred despite the fact that communications between the Planning Unit, the Conference, and the South East Chicago Commission were quite good. Levi and Meltzer shared in the deliberations of the Conference Planning Subcommittee. The University duly notified the Conference of its tentative plans within the Committee of Six, several months before these plans were made public. At the request of Conference leaders, Levi and Meltzer tardily released the proposals, maps, and, ultimately, copies of the consent agreement. The early period of secrecy surrounding the proposals was characteristic of University and Commission activities. When challenged firmly enough by the Conference, the latter often responded cooperatively.

Internally, the Conference was not organized to cope with the issues raised by the neighborhood redevelopment proposal. The Block Director's reports did not always reach the Planning Committee or the Board of Directors. The Conference had not clearly worked out the locus of responsibility for policy on the proposal. The Planning Committee delegated partial responsibility to its subcommittees. The Conference Board occasionally assumed control and occasionally operated only through its Executive Committee. In the midst of the negotiations, the Executive Directorship passed from Mrs. Abrahamson to James Cunningham, and the latter delegated field responsibility to Block Director Horwitz, until very late in the year. The result of these inadequacies was an equivocal policy position and an embarrassing error—in discrediting the block groups—before the Redevelopment Commission.

The Conference made its only attempts at negotiation with the corporation under pressure of countering opposition to the plan. These attempts occurred only after the Conference had officially announced approval of the proposal. And they consisted, not of attempts to change the proposal itself, but of requests for humane procedures in implementation.

In effect, the Conference was coopted by the University corporation as far as the exercise of influence was concerned. We noted this was also the case in the Conference's role in the

Redevelopment Projects One and Two ("A and B") during 1954 and 1955. Exceptions to this performance of supplementary and auxiliary rather than primary influences will be reviewed in Chapter 7.

At its special meeting in August, 1956, the Conference Executive Committee, responding to Cunningham's appeal to reconsider the role of the Conference, decided to "keep open" the possibilities of (1) retaining some housing in the acquisition site for use by present residents, (2) saving some good buildings slated for demolition, and (3) insisting on assurance from the corporation that displaced residents would have free entry to housing in other portions of the University community. It should be noted that these were all policy demands of the Neighborhood Association. The record indicates, however, that these reservations were entertained primarily as proposals designed to lessen the protests of local citizens and not as items valued as such by the Conference. Also, they were not included in Conference testimony.

In short, this late moment of revaluation by the Conference was induced by the emergence of the new citizen group. Coopted by the University from above and, in effect, dispossessed at the "grass-roots" level by the Neighborhood Association, the Conference Staff underwent an "eleventh hour" phase of reconsideration. Following this late soul searching, Cunningham changed his expressed reasons for endorsing the proposal. His letter to the *Herald* a week before the final hearing made it plain and unequivocal: "The most potent factor of stability in making this area attractive is the University of Chicago."

The Conference was also cut off from, and strongly pressured by, the Neighborhood Association. It failed to exercise strong influence here as well. At the root of this powerlessness was the Conference's inability to negotiate effectively. The Conference failed to bargain with the University representatives.

What the Conference "learned" from its experiences in South West Hyde Park will become clearer in subsequent chapters. Some of the items, however, are evident in the closing portions of this case itself. Citizen opposition stimulated the Conference to undertake independent investigations of the acquisition site and to re-evaluate its own position in the final hour. The experience sharpened Conference awareness of the University's mode of action and made it critical of these procedures. It disillusioned the Conference about the potentialities of the redevelopment corporation as a tool for conservation. It stimulated Conference efforts to erect much more adequate machinery for organized communications with the public, including formation of a formal program of block group and subarea conferences. According to both Horwitz and Cunningham, it was this experience that prompted the Conference to establish, for the future, a general practice of avoiding policy stands on specific plan proposals, as we shall see.[6]

As one final observation—it is difficult to evaluate the relevance of the political process in this case study, where negotiations and public hearings may be little more than a small feature set against a backdrop of intergroup differences. This case occurs within constraints fostered by the cultural gulf between the rather transient residents in and around the acquisition site and the remainder of Hyde Park–Kenwood. The complexity of divergent perspectives is reflected in the following exchange between Commissioner Landrum and Association Attorney Hagiwara:

HAGIWARA: I would like to have established what *conversion by use* is, what the specific definition of conversion by use is. The fact that two unrelated people are living in one apartment does not necessarily mean that it is a conversion by use . . . two related families living together in one apartment does not necessarily mean that it is a conversion by use.

6. In a review of an earlier draft of this chapter, Julia Abrahamson provided the following helpful résumé: ". . . The Conference . . . challenged the Commission and University . . . whenever it appeared necessary but . . . usually . . . privately in order not to divide the community further. They were challenged on public housing, by the Conference insistence over and over again that plans must be shared before public appearances on them . . . this happened before the initial survey for blight in the redevelopment area, in dealing with redevelopment plans, in refusal to appear before the City Council to endorse plans that had had no public discussion, in connection with the research park proposal, and in other instances. . . . Conference leaders repeatedly asked for documents in connection with the South West Hyde Park Redevelopment Corporation and were told just as often that they were not yet ready. This also interferred with full-fledged discussion. That the Conference did not thereupon insist that *no action whatever* should be taken on the corporation until thorough investigation could be made was a failure on its part *in this instance*."

LANDRUM: Are you making the definition? . . . What Mr. Mc-Carthy is saying is that a conversion by use definition would be difficult, and we are not disposed to make it now. What we want are facts and we will determine whether a particular apartment or building is guilty . . . [of] misuse . . . over-occupancy, and so forth . . . do you think that is unfair?

CHAPTER 7

Successful Citizen
Participation: The Case of
North West Hyde Park

While in the South West sector the Community Conference failed to mediate effectively between the planners and the residents, in North West Hyde Park the Conference scored a notable success. Through Conference efforts, residents were able to communicate their needs and desires to the planners, modifying the latters' actions, and the Final Renewal Plan met with widespread acceptance among residents. This was achieved despite the fact that North West Hyde Park was among the most deteriorated sectors of the community and scheduled for widespread changes. A careful analysis of the features of this case, particularly the actions of the Conference, can help us to specify the conditions under which citizen participation can be stimulated and in which it can be effective.

The North West Hyde Park Sector

The North West Hyde Park sector (the western portion of the Village Core) consists of a rectangle bound on the north and south respectively by 51st Street and 55th Street, and on the east and west by Woodlawn and Cottage Grove Avenues,

Miss Patricia Denton collected and analyzed the major part of the data on which this chapter is based. The section on Victor Towns was prepared by Nelson W. Polsby.

an area of one-quarter of a square mile. In 1956 about 17,000 persons made their homes there, with a density of about 68,000 per square mile, almost double the over-all Hyde Park density of 36,000.

Overcrowding was not the only form of deterioration here. It contained about twice as many dilapidated structures as the rest of Hyde Park–Kenwood. The area was heavily overbuilt. Its public schools had inadequate facilities and were rapidly deteriorating in quality. Crime rates were among the highest for the community, especially along the area's border.

From the start of urban renewal planning, the Community Conference and the Planning Unit alike defined North West Hyde Park as the most difficult sector to conserve. Both organizations gave it special attention. Described in Chapter 2, North West Hyde Park consists of a conglomerate of three-story walk-ups, stone and brick two-flat dwellings, aged and oversized single-unit houses, and three-story sun-parlor apartment buildings. Many structures were erected before 1921 and hence are outmoded as well as dilapidated. Expensive apartment buildings built since the twenties are randomly interspersed with these deteriorating structures.

This neighborhood experienced a more rapid infusion of Negro residents than any other part of the Hyde Park–Kenwood community. As Chapter 2 shows, the in-migration began in 1948, spearheaded by upper-middle-class Negro families, who settled in the expensive, well-maintained apartment buildings or purchased and renovated some of the least dilapidated two-flat structures.

In the center of the neighborhood are clustered large, well-maintained brick and frame single-family homes, similar in quality to those in Kenwood. These have always been occupied by whites, many employed at the University of Chicago and George Williams College.

Between the little enclave of white family dwellings and the western edge of North West Hyde Park there are about three square blocks of institutional property, occupied by George Williams College, the Chicago Osteopathic Hospital and Chicago College of Osteopathy, and the Kozminski Elementary School.

Under the Final Renewal Plan, North West Hyde Park

will be considerably transformed. Scores of buildings will be acquired and demolished, hundreds of families will be relocated, and land uses will be radically changed.

For our purposes, it is not necessary to give the details of the many changes to be made. Rather, we shall concentrate on three major acquisition sites within the area. These are chosen as the focus of this chapter because each was significantly shaped by citizen action.

The first acquisition site consists of almost two square blocks of buildings between Cottage Grove and Drexel Avenues, directly north of 55th Street. The Plan schedules the site for erection of a therapeutic center for disturbed children by the Jewish Children's Bureau. The second site consists of about ten acres of commercial and residential property surrounding George Williams College, the Kozminski School and the Chicago Osteopathic Hospital. It is proposed to clear this area, creating a "Campus Park" to allow for institutional expansion. The third site is the location of the former Rodfei Zedek Temple, near the center of the neighborhood, on which a park is to be created. Each of these extensive conservation projects will be considered as a subcase of planning and citizen participation. To simplify matters, the three will be referred to henceforth as the "Maryland Site," the "Kozminski School Site," and the "Rodfei Zedek Site."

We need to do more than trace how citizens engaged in shaping the plans for neighborhood renewal. This chapter examines the special interests several institutions had vested in North West Hyde Park and relates these "institutional stakes" to some of the unique human resources available there. In addition to reviewing subcases of land use planning, this chapter also considers neighborhood involvement in improvement efforts by taking a close look at the activities of one highly successful block-group leader and by comparing neighborhood organization in North West Hyde Park with organization in the South West. The aim here is to uncover the factors that best explain the success of participation in this neighborhood.

Motivations for Renewal in North West Hyde Park

As the sector in the total community undergoing the most rapid transformation, North West Hyde Park was one of the centers of attention on the part of planners and the Community Conference. Neither the University to the south nor the Conference with heavy membership in the east could afford to ignore the area. In addition, strongly motivated interests within the area itself looked to urban renewal as a means of conserving their stakes in locating in North West Hyde Park.

As early as 1955, Julian Levi had defined North West Hyde Park as an area to which the long-run plans of the University of Chicago looked for room for expansion. When Julian Levi first revealed the South West Hyde Park Neighborhood Redevelopment Corporation proposal to the Conference, he said:

If the University moves to 55th Street, it must commit itself psychologically to the north because it cannot have the kind of development it wants with structures like the Schwind Building across the street. It seems reasonable to believe that the University's physical expansion will make it essential to move as far north as 54th Place or possibly 54th Street. From the standpoint of North West Hyde Park, this would be highly desirable.[1]

Within North West Hyde Park there were other institutional interests. Both the College of Osteopathy and George Williams College were located at its core. Both had accumulated sizable physical plants, which were then hemmed in.

Another important group with vital stakes in achieving conservation of the North West Neighborhood was a small group of white and Negro upper-middle-class residents, some home owners and others occupying many of the newer and most spacious apartments. The white group consisted mainly of faculty and staff of local institutions.[2] These professionals owned the large houses in the center of the neighborhood. They were

1. Conference Planning Committee Records for February 14, 1956.
2. The Planning Unit *Survey and Planning Application* (March 8, 1955) states that there is a concentration of deteriorated buildings in west North West Hyde Park, "immediately adjacent to the single family home blocks along Greenwood and University Avenues which are occupied principally by University and hospital faculty and professional personnel."

stable citizens, most of them having lived there for at least ten years and many as long as thirty.

The upper-middle-class Negro group was centered for the most part in Drexel Square, an expensive apartment complex along Cottage Grove Avenue on the western edge. They too were stable residents. Most of them had moved into the area between 1948 and 1953, immediately after the lifting of restrictive covenants, and were among the earliest arrivals of the nonwhite in-migrants. They were, by and large, educated professionals and businessmen—journalists, teachers, social workers, realtors, and the like.

This biracial upper-middle-class group shared the common objective of protecting their fine homes from the threat of blight spreading inward from the western edge of the neighborhood. They also formed the backbone of the Kozminski Parent Teachers Association, a group manifesting strong desires to improve school conditions.

Contrasting South West and North West Hyde Park, there are several crucial differences in the kinds of interests motivated to seek renewal in these two areas. In the first place, although the University of Chicago expressed an interest in long-run expansion into the North West, at the time its plans were not definite and did not require specific sites. Secondly, the institutional interests represented by George Williams and the Chicago College of Osteopathy were not powerful enough to dominate their environments. To the residents they appeared as almost on a par with themselves and subject to the same kinds of pressures from the University of Chicago and its Planning Unit.

Finally, the upper-middle-class whites and Negroes had more in common. This was not a white group maintaining an informally restricted residential enclave, as was the case for those whites who voted for private redevelopment in the South West. Furthermore, as we shall see, through the Conference many sought to reach out across racial barriers and communicate with their fellow residents.

The North West Hyde Park Neighborhood Redevelopment Corporation

The ability to mobilize conservation resources rests in part on the availability of experienced leadership and on ties between citizen groups. The unique human resources of North West Hyde Park can best be understood through a brief look at the North West Hyde Park Neighborhood Redevelopment Corporation, its founders, and its connections with the Community Conference and the Planning Unit.

In 1953 the Illinois Neighborhood Redevelopment Act was revised to cover deteriorating neighborhoods (see Chapter 4). Shortly thereafter Julian Levi and the SECC formed the Maryland–Drexel Neighborhood Redevelopment Corporation in North West Hyde Park, which took no action beyond testing in the courts the legality of the new legislation.

Six months after the new legislation had been enacted, a group of North West residents began to discuss the advantages of forming a redevelopment corporation, an idea initiated by members of the Conference Block Steering Committee. In February, 1954, Maynard Kreuger—Professor of Economics at the University of Chicago, charter member of the Conference, and a North West resident for more than twenty years—presented a proposal for creation of the North West Hyde Park Neighborhood Redevelopment Corporation to a committee of neighborhood leaders assembled for this purpose.

Chairing this first meeting was Willard Stout, University of Chicago Professor of Chemistry, Conference leader, and a local resident for many years (whose block group activities we shall mention later in this chapter). This and the many subsequent meetings before the corporation was a going concern were heavily attended by top-echelon Conference leaders.

The new corporation was formed late in 1954 and a year later had amassed caiptal funds of about $4,000 through shares purchased by neighborhood residents. Unlike the South West Hyde Park Neighborhood Redevelopment Corporation this organization was a neighborhood venture. It was an outcome of Community Conference support and leadership. Seven of the twenty-one founders of the new corporation were active as Conference officers. Among the leaders of the corporation were not only Kreuger and Stout, and Conference Board members, but Elmer W. Donahue, Chairman of the Conference Board (1954–1958) and a resident of the North West neighborhood for more than thirty years, and James D. Braxton, Conference Planning Committee member and professional city planner.

However, the corporation never obtained sufficient capital to develop specific redevelopment plans. Moreover, private redevelopment became obsolete with the development of urban renewal plans in 1956. But the North West Hyde Park Neighborhood Redevelopment Corporation, because of its ties with the Conference and its working relationship with Julian Levi (who was delighted to see his legislation implemented and fostered the group's emergence), became a strategic resource for neighborhood leaders in influencing the planning process.

The corporation's leaders were able to perform as lobbyists, as it were, for their neighborhood before the Planning Unit, the South East Chicago Commission, and the Community Conference.

All in all, the corporation helped stimulate renewal planning for the community. Its shareholders (about 150) and leadership were home owners who worked effectively to orient renewal planning toward conservation of housing. The corporation was also instrumental in influencing Conference policy recommendations on the specific plans for the neighborhood.[3]

In other words, the North West had resources in individuals who could and did supply leadership. The particular importance of this lay in providing interlocking relationships between the neighborhood and community-wide civic associations. Block groups, the neighborhood redevelopment corporation, the Kozminski Parent Teachers Association, and the Hyde Park Neighborhood Club were thus interlocked with the Conference and the South East Chicago Commission. Elsewhere in this study we have noted that membership overlap and interlocking organizations are general characteristics of the community—of the Community Conference in particular (see Chapter 5). Here we want to stress that this was especially true for North West Hyde Park—and, significantly, on an interracial basis.

3. For example, the corporation was active in revising the Kozminski Site proposals; in saving the Cottonwood Co-op Building; and in getting specific properties selected for clearance by the Planning Unit.

The Kozminski School Site

As early as 1951, four years before official planning began, the Hyde Park–Kenwood Community Conference and the Kozminski School Parent Teachers Association had identified the physical plant of this old elementary school as inadequate. The Community Appraisal (1951), sponsored by the Conference, pointed to the need for recreational space in North West Hyde Park and suggested that the Kozminski School grounds be expanded. Roughly ten months before the Planning Unit issued its Preliminary Project Report (August, 1956), the Kozminski P.T.A. formally proposed demolition of buildings north of Kozminski School and the closing of one street to provide play space. Three adjacent block groups immediately endorsed this proposal. The Planning Unit meanwhile had developed its own proposal: in its Preliminary Report, the Unit proposed three times as much clearance of housing surrounding the school and the closing of two additional streets to create a "Campus Park" connecting the Chicago College of Osteopathy, George Williams, and Kozminski. Planner Jack Meltzer proposed that the "Campus Park" should be large enough to accommodate another public school in the future.

Two adjacent block groups and the P.T.A. objected to the size of the "Campus Park." Three months after the Preliminary Project Report appeared, these groups forwarded to Jack Meltzer an alternative proposal. They asked that the area directly east of the school be cleared in preference to Meltzer's plan to clear a larger area directly west and north of Kozminski. They also suggested that a new school eventually could be constructed side by side with the old Kozminski.

At a meeting with Meltzer to discuss their alternative, block-group and P.T.A. leaders claimed their approach would put the "Campus Park" directly adjacent to Kozminski, would save one entire block of good housing from demolition, and would utilize an existing vacant lot as part of the clearance site. Jack Meltzer replied that there was a great need for increased open space in the neighborhood, that the federal agency reviewing his Preliminary Project Report had already criticized it for lack of sufficient clearance in North West Hyde Park, and that his park proposal would free a now overcrowded block and yield more open space than the block group's alternative proposal. But he admitted that his proposal emphasized clearance for institutional use more heavily than slum clearance. He also said he had himself considered the residents' alternative approach before devising the preliminary plan. He then agreed to resurvey the site and to review the issues before developing his final plan.

This meeting, like most others, had been arranged by the Community Conference Planning Committee. The Conference followed a cautious path in handling policy exchanges about the Kozminski Site. Although the Conference had declared its intent to remain neutral on the specifics of planning until the appearance of the final plan, Conference records show the staff and Planning Committee members continually emphasized the Planning Unit's assertion of the need for increased open space and sought to increase citizen support for over-all community conservation. For the most part, however, the Conference served in the Kozminski Site negotiations "as a channel through which individuals and block groups could negotiate," to quote Planning Committee minutes.

A year later, the Planning Unit released its Final Urban Renewal Plan. There, the proposal advanced by the Kozminski P.T.A. and two neighborhood block groups had replaced that made earlier by Jack Meltzer. The citizens' alternative had been accepted with only a slight enlargement of the clearance area.

This revision netted a great deal for the Planning Unit and the future welfare of the over-all plan. The change amounted to reducing slightly the original scope of proposed clearance and to shifting its location from one side of Kozminski School to the other. Concessions by the Planning Unit on a matter of great local saliency but perhaps small technical significance prevented public controversy and heightened local feelings of effective involvement. In addition, this gratifying change in the plan apparently gained local acceptance for the part of the plan that called for clearance of more than one entire block of standard housing and closing of a street in order to provide for future expansion of the College of Osteopathy, a feature of the Campus Park Plan that received very little attention during or after negotiations over Kozminski.

Whether tactic or coincidence, the Planning Unit did not include in its Preliminary Project Report a provision for expansion of George Williams College. When the final plan appeared, a large site was included for this purpose. At this point, one block group expressed suspicions that the "Campus Park" proposal as a whole constituted an intent to erect a "racial barrier" between the western edge of the neighborhood and its virtually all-white center, but no organized opposition to any part of the Campus Park plan for open space around the three schools ever developed.[4]

Rodfei Zedek Site

The Rodfei Zedek congregation vacated its large Temple in North West Hyde Park in 1954. For two years the question of how to reuse this site was widely discussed in the neighborhood. Before the Preliminary Project Report of the Planning Unit appeared, the Kozminski P.T.A. proposed that it be used for a branch library and a small park.

The Planning Unit, however, first proposed use of the site for a new elementary school, a small park, and extra parking space. Meltzer proposed to clear the Temple and a surrounding block strip of houses. As in the case of the Kozminski Site, the planner sought clearance of a larger area than did the citizens' group.

Soon after the Preliminary Report appeared, the Kozminski P.T.A. announced its objections to Meltzer's proposal for the Rodfei Zedek Site and reasserted its suggestion that the Temple be used for a branch library. This alternative proposal was made jointly with the 5400 Ellis–Ingleside Block Group, which included residents whose homes would be demolished under the Meltzer proposal. Home owners within the Zedek Site also objected independently. The nearby 5400 Greenwood Block Group, however, led by Dr. Willard Stout and composed in

4. This is worth noting because it was during this period that doubt was being cast on the legitimacy of using public funds and powers to provide space for institutional expansion (see Chapter 6). However, the Osteopathic Hospital administrators emphasized, "We have no designs on neighboring property and homes," in their testimony. As a service hospital with a biracial clientele, this institution faced a more sympathetic public than did the University of Chicago with its plan for housing married students.

part of owners of the cluster of expensive Kenwood-type homes mentioned earlier, met to discuss Meltzer's Zedek proposal and publicly announced support for it.

The central objection of the P.T.A. and Ellis–Ingleside Group was that Meltzer's proposal would extend clearance beyond the half-block immediately surrounding the Temple and would involve demolition of some good structures inhabited by long-term residents. These groups also claimed that a second elementary school would prove unnecessary when Kozminski was expanded, thus linking the Zedek reuse issue to the Kozminski Site negotiations.

The Conference Board and Planning Committee took no formal stand on the Zedek Site question, but the Planning Committee tended to support Jack Meltzer by emphasizing publicly that a second elementary school would prove essential to maintain high local standards and that the proximity of the two schools was a minor issue. Again, the contribution of the Conference was chiefly to bring organized citizens and official planners into productive contact.

In the final plan the Planning Unit compromised with the two objecting citizen groups. The plan to construct a school on the Temple site was eliminated. But the planners did not reduce the extent of clearance around the Temple as citizens had requested. As a means of reducing controversy, the Planning Unit also eliminated its earlier specifications for use of the Zedek Site and simply listed it as a prospective general "park site." Thus the changes made by the planner were very minor but were important enough to eliminate controversy on the issue. With publication of the final plan, objections to the extent of the Zedek clearance ceased. Apparently broad agreement among citizens was achieved on the requirement for more open space in the neighborhood. One small revision by the Planning Unit—removal of designation of use for the site—increased public acceptance of the most painful of all features of conservation renewal: demolition of good housing.

The Maryland Site

North West Hyde Park contained some of the worst deterioration in the entire community in the site centering on the corner of Maryland Avenue and 55th Street. Along 55th Street from Cottage Grove to Drexel and extending one block to the North the Maryland Site formed the southwest corner of the area. From the very beginning of attempts at renewal this site received attention. The 1951 Community Appraisal report identified the site as severely blighted.

One building in particular achieved considerable notoriety in the press. A huge structure known as the Schwind Building stood at the corner of Maryland Avenue and 55th Street, its brick and stone facade cracked and crumbling, its areaways littered with broken glass and refuse, and its interior crammed with migrant tenants. This building and its surroundings very early became an important neighborhood-wide symbol of the need for basic conservation.

Julian Levi had used this site in 1953 as the base for organizing the Maryland–Drexel Neighborhood Redevelopment Corporation, and in 1955 the North West Hyde Park Neighborhood Redevelopment Corporation, the Kozminski P.T.A., several block groups, and the Conference Planning Committee had all agreed that this site required thorough clearance and reuse. The Preliminary Project Report shared this long-standing opinion and proposed total demolition along the two thoroughfares and clearance inward at several points. Meltzer proposed replacement of the blighted properties with high-rise apartment buildings, parking lots, and a convenient shopping center.

This consensus on clearance, however, obtained only among residents *outside* the two square blocks of blighted dwellings. Upon publication of the Preliminary Project Report, the owners of five row houses within the proposed acquisition area objected to their being cleared for reuse as a parking lot. The Community Conference forwarded their objections to the Planning Unit and also resurveyed these buildings. The Planning Committee reported that four of the five row houses could be retained as sound structures if they were rehabilitated.

Aside from this brief flurry of suggestions, the Planning Unit's preliminary proposals were received as acceptable within the community. Of course, it should be noted that most of the Maryland Site consisted of commercial structures, that the homes most severely affected were not organized in block groups, and that the Planning Unit called only for spot clearance and rehabilitation in those blocks surrounding the Maryland Site where block groups had been organized.

Although there was wide community agreement that the Maryland Site be cleared, there was still room for disagreement about the uses to which the cleared site should be put. Early in 1957 the Conference Planning Committee learned the Planning Unit was considering a proposal for a "Research Park" on the Maryland Site. Industrial research laboratories, social agencies, and academic research organizations, it was suggested, would secure locations here because the area was close to the resources represented by the faculty and facilities located on the University of Chicago campus. The suggestion also included a radical change in the scope of clearance, adding three more block-strips of residences to the Maryland Site. Thus, the new suggestion included enlarged demolition and a switch from use for housing to use for institutions.

This was introduced by the South East Chicago Commission and the Planning Unit as a tentative suggestion. Within one month the Conference had arranged a meeting of North West neighborhood block-group leaders to consider the suggestion. Three block leaders opposed the suggestion without further review, and other neighborhood residents, following this meeting, introduced individual objections.[5]

Opposition to the "Research Park" suggestion grew rapidly. It culminated in an appeal from several block groups and many individual residents to the Community Conference to take a public stand against the park before the Planning Unit published its final plan. They urged the Conference to act swiftly to avoid a later public dispute during the hearings. The Conference Board of Directors met the day after this appeal was received and, after strong debate, voted to pass this motion:

It is the sense of the Conference Board that on the basis of the information available to it at this time, in regard to a tentative proposal for a research park, the Board is opposed to it.

---

5. They observed that institutional use would not bring new white families into the Kozminski School area to balance that school's increasingly nonwhite population, that this would further institutionalize an already overinstitutionalized zone, and that many good dwelling units would be sacrificed without replacement elsewhere.

The deciding factor appears to have been a report from the Committee on Maintaining an Interracial Community that "the construction of attractive new housing in the area in question . . . introduces the best chance it could see to revitalize interracial occupancy in North West Hyde Park."

Early in 1957 the Conference had set up a Special Housing Committee to consider the question of how public housing could be fitted into the renewal program. This Committee was most active during the period in which the "Research Park" was being discussed. It issued its report shortly after the Conference had taken its stand against the "Research Park." The Committee report touched upon the Maryland Site:

The Committee did not discuss the more recent suggestion that the Cottage Grove–Maryland Site be developed as a Research Park. It considered only the question of housing re-use from the standpoint of the kind of housing which might contribute to good community standards and to accomplishing interracial occupancy in the North West Hyde Park.

The committee then recommended "the fullest possible enlargement of the site . . . development of a mixture of row housing and elevator apartments . . . and construction of high-rise buildings on the original site (the two square blocks). . . ." It asserted that this reuse would achieve high standards and interracial occupancy.

The Conference Board deleted the recommendation for fullest possible enlargement of the site and sent the report to the official Planning Unit. Ironically, however, the Planning Unit had already sent word to the Conference Planning Committee that the "Research Park" suggestion had been given up "for now."

The formal actions of the Conference Board and its committees, then, did not directly cause withdrawal of the "Research Park" proposal. The Planning Unit itself had decided to withdraw the idea as quickly as it had advanced it.[6] The ma-

6. One University administrator in his interview asserted that the "Research Park" proposal was dropped because of lack of interest on the part of businesses and institutions. We believe, to the contrary, that readiness of groups to invest in a research park could not have been assessed in a matter of a week or two. We prefer the account given by one highly informed Conference leader: "Meltzer knew as soon as it happened that the

chinery of the Community Conference, however, had been set in motion on the question of how the Maryland Site should be reused, and this machinery continued to examine the issue from late 1957 throughout 1958.

When Planning Unit released its final Urban Renewal Plan in February, 1958, Conference groups noted the "Research Park" proposal had been dropped and the Maryland Site reduced to its original size. Two changes had been introduced: on the Maryland Site the Planning Unit had designated part of the site to be used for a psychological treatment and research center to house thirty children and some staff, to be built by the Jewish Children's Bureau; to the north of the Maryland Site new clearance was planned to allow for expansion of George Williams College.

From the day after release of the final plan until the last Conservation Community Council public hearings in March, 1958, North West neighborhood block groups met regularly with members of the Conference Planning Committee. All but three of the many block groups involved supported the Urban Renewal Plan as it was endorsed by the Conference at this time. The three remaining groups requested inclusion of scattered public housing and some middle-income housing in North West Hyde Park, and two of these urged low-cost housing in preference to a treatment center for the Maryland Site. A Block Steering Committee report to the Conference Board also recommended housing for the Maryland Site. The Board rejected the Steering Committee recommendation but supported in its testimony at the hearings a recommendation from the Planning Committee urging general inclusion of scattered public housing and middle-income housing in Hyde Park.

After the Conservation Community Council hearings, the same two block groups continued to object to use of the Maryland Site for institutional purposes. The most active of these groups, the 5300-5400 Drexel Avenue Block Group, was led by Victor Towns, whose influential leadership is reviewed below. Both block-group leaders personally brought their objections

Conference Board had opposed his Research Park proposal. Only after this decision, and a big blast from the *Defender,* did he send word that the proposal had been given up 'for now.' The University ran into a citizens' stone wall on this one, and they pulled out fast."

before the Conference Planning Committee in April, 1958, and the Committee appointed a new subcommittee to investigate possible alternative uses of the Maryland Site.

In his appeal to the Planning Committee for review of this site, Victor Towns argued that in the Final Plan North West Hyde Park was slated for "drastic changes." He noted that of 17,000 persons residing in this neighborhood 3,500 were to be relocated, about twenty-five acres of buildings were to be torn down, and ten acres of land were to be given to four institutions for expansion. Towns said, "The need of all worthwhile institutions to expand is recognized, but there is a strong feeling that no more are needed or wanted here." He pointed out that the five acres within the Maryland Site could house more than 500 persons and that good housing there, coupled with general rehabilitation of surrounding structures, would induce white families into North West Hyde Park's western sector. Towns had received a letter from Alderman Leon Despres, which read:

Since the Jewish Children's arrangement was made behind closed doors, I have no information on it at all. . . . I can conceive no more severe indictment of the policy of dealing with such questions from behind closed doors.

The Planning Subcommittee to investigate reuse of the Maryland Site began work in earnest in May, 1958. Subcommittee members interviewed local real estate dealers and similar "experts" to obtain their estimates of the possibility of successful housing ventures on this site. They also discussed the issue in detail with planners, including Jack Meltzer. Before the subcommittee reached its decision, it conducted a small hearing at which Jack Meltzer spoke and was questioned by Victor Towns and other block group members. The subcommittee voted three to one to report to the Planning Committee that:

. . . institutional use would be the most effective use for the site in question . . . even if the Jewish Children's Bureau were not to be interested in using the land. . . . In addition, the Conference Legal Panel should be asked to look into the legal possibility of giving some guarantees to the residents of the area that there would be no further expansion from this new institution.[7]

---

7. The subcommittee, in support of this conclusion, reported the Maryland Site was a doubtful one for successful housing; even with clearance

The next day James Cunningham sent a copy of the sub-committee report to Victor Towns. Towns replied in a letter, following a block group meeting:

> There was some resentment because of the manner in which the Planning Unit and the Conference Planning Committee handled the 55th Street and Cottage Grove (Maryland Site) proposal in its earlier stages. Doubt was expressed that the same approach would be used in some other area of Hyde Park or Kenwood. A preliminary discussion and study of the situation—as was done later—might have lessened or have caused little or no opposition to the proposal . . . [but] a majority vote of the block group supported a proposal to withdraw opposition to the use of the land by the Jewish Children's Bureau provided agreement can be reached on the following conditions.

Towns then asked for a legal guarantee that there will be no expansion of the Bureau's site for twenty-five years, and for an agreement that if major changes were made which would affect local residents in the future, these residents would be consulted immediately through their block groups. This letter was read to the Conference Board, with Towns present.[8]

The Conference then arranged a meeting of Alderman Despres, three block-group delegates (including Towns), and the Executive Director of the Jewish Welfare Federation. The Director, Samuel Goldsmith, was very sympathetic, agreed with the proposed guarantees, and promised to obtain legal counsel to arrange contracts promptly. One month later, mutually satisfactory covenants were agreed upon, limiting expansion of the Children's Bureau and promising notification of residents of all major plans.

Although there are some similarities between the Maryland Site transaction and problems of negotiation in South West Hyde Park (for example, the abrupt revelation of the plan to allocate the property to the Children's Bureau, the subsequent suspicions among local neighbors of a University "plot" to displace Negroes by institutionalizing the area, and criticism

---

for institutional use, density in the neighborhood would remain extremely high (68,000 per square mile for the one-fourth-square-mile neighborhood). The plan intends to reduce this density to 60,000 per square mile.

8. Towns characterized the new plan as a definite defeat of the interests of his block group when he spoke before the Conference Board.

of the Community Conference for its hasty support of the proposal), Victor Towns' block group did not react as groups in the South West neighborhood did. In opposing the Children's Bureau proposal, Towns consistently pointed out his group's support for urban renewal and repeatedly thanked the "planners for the consideration given our proposal in connection with the preliminary plans." His block-group members expressed their determination to rehabilitate their own properties and emphasized their high regard for the Children's Bureau. Towns personally felt that he had met with "just about everyone," that the report of the Conference special subcommittee was "a thorough one," and, generally, that he had won significant concessions on behalf of his neighborhood.

What is of crucial importance in this case is that, although the citizens did not get what they wanted, they were also not alienated from the Final Plan. The sympathy with which residents felt the Conference, the planners, and other authorities listened to their demands and desires, giving them careful consideration, led to satisfaction with the outcome. The perception of the Plan among residents within the Maryland Site was conditioned by the opportunities to have their views heard and seriously considered. The long history of close ties between the Conference, the Planning Unit, and the Maryland Site block groups had created a climate of cooperation. When strong conflicts of interest finally appeared, these favorably perceived relationships transformed conflict, tension, and suspicion into negotiation and relative satisfaction among the participants. Note the contrast with South West Hyde Park.

Victor Towns—A Successful Block-Group Leader

The case of citizen participation in the Maryland Site renewal plans has been reviewed as an instance of mutually satisfying interaction among the Community Conference, the Planning Unit, and neighborhood block groups. It is also an excellent example of effective "grass-roots" leadership. Even a cursory reading of the Maryland Site case would show that much of the "grass-roots" initiative stemmed from the 5300-5400 Drexel Block Group, led by Victor Towns. The quality of Towns' leadership and the resulting vigor of his group are crucial elements in any account of citizen involvement in North West Hyde Park.

Victor Towns is a Negro, a middle-aged dining-car waiter who works for the Baltimore and Ohio Railroad. He lives in a one-story frame house on Drexel Avenue, one of the most congested residential strips in the community. Victor Towns is married and has four children, only the youngest of whom still lives at home. He has lived in the same house for nine years and is without question one of the most settled residents of the neighborhood. Drexel Avenue between 53rd and 54th Streets is populated almost entirely by recently arrived Negro families; it is in this sector that Negroes first began extensive inmigration into Hyde Park between 1950 and 1952.

The block group for this area was organized under Towns in 1956. Twice before block groups had been formed in this strip, but both times they failed when officers moved away and others lost interest. The need for an improvement-oriented group in this block strip was obvious: deterioration was already well advanced, city services were comparatively skimpy, garbage collections were irregular, streets were left uncleaned, there were many abandoned cars on the streets, and parkway trees were dying and diseased from neglect. The delinquency and petty crime rate was excessive.

These and other facts would lead one to assume that very little citizen action could be expected in this neighborhood. The block was in the area of greatest population turnover and most severe physical deterioration. Local leadership was episodic and inexperienced. The low-status residents were unskilled at maintaining an organization or using an organization effectively.

Yet, the Drexel Block Group was among the most successful of all citizen groups in Hyde Park in setting goals which were meaningful and important to residents and in attaining their goals. Although many of these goals had little to do with the grander features of the Urban Renewal Plan, they were significant in improving the life of residents in the block. For example, a grocer displaced from "Hyde Park A and B" moved his store to the corner of 55th Street and Drexel Avenue and began to run his business as he had always done. He piled bushel baskets full of vegetables along the sidewalk and installed above his door a loudspeaker that blared radio music to the neighborhood. The Drexel Block Group immediately formed a committee and had a talk with the merchant, who readily agreed to change his business habits to accord with the new living standards the neighborhood was striving to achieve.

Under the leadership of Victor Towns, the Block Group began to inspect buildings and to register complaints about substandard conditions with the municipal Department of Buildings. This effort brought eventual results. The Block Group managed as well to arrange direct agreements with owners of several large multiple-unit apartment buildings, without recourse to city agencies or other legal action.

The Conference, of course, often acted as a go-between, legitimizing and backing up the agreements between the Block Group and the landlords. One such agreement provided that the landlord would screen incoming tenants more carefully, would take special pains to enforce rules and regulations, would evict objectionable tenants, and would institute a clean-up and rehabilitation program. Thus, in an appeal almost entirely to good will, albeit with faint overtones of legal pressure, the Block Group was in a number of cases able to induce absentee owners to spend considerable money improving their property.

At the same time, the Block Group successfully ran a fix-up, clean-up drive in which owners of small homes participated. Walking up and down Drexel Boulevard in summer, 1958, one observed a steady stream of workmen and materials going in and out of the small houses there. From his front porch Towns could point to almost every building in sight and describe with considerable pride the improvements that had been made within the last two years.

With respect to the plan, the members of the Drexel Block Group had several goals. First, they sought the removal of the three overcrowded "kitchenette" apartments in their block. To replace these, they wanted off-street parking and a park area. Second, they wanted no expansion of land used for institutional purposes but rapidly accommodated themselves to the proposition that those institutions presently located in the area should have limited rights to expand, as was provided in the plan. The Block Group was adamant, however, in opposing the inclusion in the plan of the Jewish Children's Bureau Treatment Center.

In negotiating the Maryland Site issue, Towns mobilized the support of the Urban League and the NAACP of Chicago, made representations to Alderman Despres, and carried the fight to the SECC and the Board of Directors of the Conference.

Considering the substantial effectiveness of this group, it seems appropriate to ask what the secret of its success was. We turn now to that question, discussing in passing the process by which this group made its decisions and mobilized itself for action.

In many respects, the power of the Block Group stemmed directly from the activity of Towns himself. There were a Secretary-Treasurer and an executive committee, but most of the work was done by Towns. He personally conducted inspections of properties about which complaints had been received, he personally saw to it that the proper city and community agencies were notified when an abandoned car or inadequate street lighting was reported, and he personally negotiated the support of extra-block influences, drafting the letters and memoranda. In short, Towns led the fight for what the block wanted from the plan.

One should not get the impression, however, that Towns is in any sense a dictator. He is in close contact with the Block Group Executive Committee and his immediate neighbors; and members of the Executive Committee, in turn, are in close contact with their neighbors. In this way, so far as Mr. Towns can judge, the sentiment of the entire block is easily tapped and in some cases alerted on issues. While these issues were hot, the Block Group held regular and rather well-attended meetings. When the plan became frozen, the Block Group reverted to a system of meeting when necessary, with quarterly business meetings.

There are several unique features in Towns' situation. He is not, as we have noted, a high-status member of the community. In fact, although his name has been twice proposed as a member of the Board of Directors of the Conference, he was not elected either time, while considerably higher-status (but certainly no abler) Negroes regularly held office.

Towns is preoccupied with and earnestly dedicated to his neighborhood. He has no particular political ambitions, and no organizational interests outside of his neighborhood. He has never been active in metropolitan Negro civic groups and professes no interest in them. He is a "localist" in every sense of the term. Thus he has one great advantage over so many other actors in the urban renewal drama: he is wholly preoccupied with his role in this drama and so is not torn, as are so many others, between their roles in this context and their businesses, their other community responsibilities, their careers, and so forth.

Secondly, Towns knows what he wants. Just as his preoccupation with these problems is great, his claims are modest and are restricted to proposals designed to benefit directly the neighborhood he loves. He is willing to agitate and negotiate endlessly to accommodate the wishes of other interests as well, insofar as they impinge on his block's claims in the community; but few leaders can match his vigilance and diligence, and few care enough about promoting outcomes different from those Towns has in mind.

Third, Towns leads a group that is firmly behind him. There are some apathetic members in his Block Group, but all those who are mobilized on the issues with which Towns deals favor his position. In fact, Towns clearly stands ready to formulate his position in the first place along lines congenial to the great majority of his block members. And, of course, the issues are clear-cut. Just as the issues are clear and nonsalient to decision-makers outside the block, they are clear and highly salient to members of the block group, and they have no trouble reaching unanimity on them.

The techniques Towns used are for the most part familiar enough: he contacted his alderman, testified at hearings, conferred privately and publicly with planners and with Conference and Commission officials, and formed *ad hoc* committees of citizens to make representations before boards to meet with landlords and with the perpetrators of neighborhood nuisances. One further advantage is perhaps unique to Towns, and—though one may doubt its importance—it yields an insight into what an ingenious and dedicated citizen, of whatever status, can accomplish.

We noted earlier that Towns is a dining-car waiter. While he is out of town a good part of each week, he has many hours at home as well—at all hours of the day—and this enables him to contact people at their offices. But, moving as he does between Chicago and the large cities of the East, Towns occasionally serves dinner to one or another of the top decision-makers on urban renewal in the community. On the occasions when this has happened Towns has availed himself of the opportunity to speak informally and at length with these top decision-makers, and they have in turn welcomed his interest. The boredom of long-distance, overnight train travel conspires to aid Towns in promoting his position informally. Certainly not all lower-status people who wish to be active in community affairs can be expected to breach the preserves of the rich so effectively.

Minor Planning Examples

The three major elements of the Urban Renewal Plan for North West Hyde Park have been reviewed. The consistency with which the residents, the Conference, and the Planning Unit worked in meaningful harmony in this neighborhood carried as well into the minor elements of planning for this area.

One of these minor planning points was concerned with reserving some land for commercial use. Through each stage of discussion about the renewal plan, various North West block groups urged inclusion of locations for neighborhood convenience shopping centers. This concept was not favored by Jack Meltzer and other planners who were concerned with reducing the excessive number of commercial strips in the inner community. The Preliminary Project Report proposed to eliminate many neighborhood stores, auto repair services, and the like.

Several block groups proposed establishment of at least one convenience center, and the Conference Planning Committee agreed with this appeal. In the Final Plan two sites were designated for neighborhood retail facilities. The Final Plan also specified that retail commercial uses would be permitted on the first floor of the proposed high-density residential buildings. Without doubt, addition of scattered commercial facilities represents an instance of successful citizen influence upon the planner.

Another minor point concerned off-street parking. Just before release of the Final Plan, the Conference Planning Committee reported to the Conference Board that more off-street parking was needed in North West Hyde Park and elsewhere, and that further demolition was needed to provide the necessary land. A Planning Subcommittee then took this question to Jack Meltzer, who explained it was very difficult to select buildings for clearance for this proposal in a way that would achieve public acceptance. He suggested leaving all designations for spot clearance out of the Final Plan, since "it is very difficult to justify such clearance." Thus, in the Urban Renewal Plan few small "spot-site" parking-space designations were mapped, but the federal government was asked for funds earmarked for parking space and playlots on additional sites to be designated later. This arrangement was supported by the Conference in its public testimony.[9] The block group led by Victor Towns, incidentally, also proposed that one lot in its block scheduled for acquisition be used for parking space, and this suggestion was incorporated into the Final Plan by the Conservation Community Council.

The provision of adequate recreational facilities in the North West neighborhood was early defined as a major task. Most discussion on this topic concerned the Kozminski School and the Rodfei Zedek Sites, already discussed. But, in addition,

---

9. With ironic contradictions, however. Before the Conservation Council with hearings in December, 1958, a Conference spokesman said: ". . . most residents opposed demolition to provide off-street parking space. This has resulted in insufficient space for parking in the plan. The Conference recommends that the Community Conservation Board sponsor further studies to find ways to obtain, maintain, and operate parking for residential areas, including . . . new legislation." Also, "that a very sizable sum of money be set aside . . . to provide for needed spot clearance." Yet, in September, 1958, before the City Council, the Conference urged: "Make it crystal clear in the text of this plan that any property not now scheduled for clearance which is kept or brought into full compliance with codes, will be exempt from future acquisition and demolition." Thus, the solution to more parking space through spot clearance was greatly limited. As Meltzer had told the Planning Committee of the Conference a year earlier, spot clearance would have to be made on the basis of owners who refuse to rehabilitate. Part of the rationale for the Planning Committee and for Meltzer was the expectation that there would be many owners who could not or would not rehabilitate, and whose pre-empted property could then be used for spot clearance. There was also the belief that those owners who did rehabilitate should be protected.

four special playlot sites were included in the Final Plan. These were an outcome of suggestions made by block groups and the Conference. The Conference Board endorsed the Planning Unit's designations for the playlots, and four months before the City Council hearings the Board supported a proposal from the Conference Parks and Recreation Committee to work with city agencies to develop plans for the layout of these new lots. By the time of the final hearings this Committee had, in an extremely short time, completed detailed blueprints for these playlots of the future.[10]

The demolition of specific buildings was also a point for special negotiations among residents, Conference, and planners. An outstanding example of a successful appeal to save a building otherwise destined for demolition was that of the Cottonwood Cooperative Building, located on a site initially slated for parking space. The 5400 Woodlawn Block Group objected to the proposed demolition of the cooperative. The Conference Planning Committee and James Cunningham both acted as liaison between the Block Group and the Planning Unit. Cunningham wrote Meltzer that the cooperative residents had recently rehabilitated the Cottonwood, which "is making a fine contribution . . . to the community." Meltzer accepted this appeal, but to do so, it apparently became necessary to reorganize an entire section of the Final Plan.[11]

The Cottonwood Cooperative is an instance where the Conference prevented clearance, but there were also many instances in which block groups, through the Conference, urged clearance of specific buildings. Thus, in cases of planning for convenience shopping inside the neighborhood, planning for play space, and planning for specific clearance sites, citizen participation as it

---

10. This, incidentally, is an especially good example of the ability of Conference volunteers to identify and resolve a community challenge. The Committee managed to obtain the special services of a planner within the City Park government. He developed the original plans "on public time," and these were integrated with play equipment designs developed by a University of Chicago metallurgist—a Conference volunteer—and other professionals fully informed about matters ranging from botany to child development. The final plans for these little lots have a distinctive, award-winning character, and they were devised at "no expense" to the Conference.

11. At least the entire plan for the 5400 block of Woodlawn was changed in the Final Plan to the extent of six basic revisions.

was sustained and organized through the Conference played a meaningful part in shaping the Urban Renewal Plan.

Successful Citizen Participation—
Structure and Process

Citizen participation in North West Hyde Park stands as impressive evidence of the ability of the Hyde Park–Kenwood Community Conference to achieve the goals it set for itself in this area. The Conference widely and effectively distributed planning information to the residents and provided access to the planners within the Planning Unit. The outcome of communication was satisfactory to all sides: the planners were able to work out a plan which satisfied their professional standards, and the citizens were able to modify the planners' actions to produce a plan which met some of their most crucial needs.

This instance of effective functioning occurred in a neighborhood that was severely affected by blight and deterioration. Between one-fifth and one-fourth of the inhabitants would be displaced as their dwellings were demolished in the years to come. Others might be "priced out" of the area as rents and prices increased with the upgrading of the neighborhood. The degree of success attained by the Conference in North West Hyde Park must be considered all the more impressive because of the conditions under which this success was won.

Measured by influence upon the contents of the Urban Renewal Plan, organized citizens successfully influenced the choice of planning targets, contributed suggestions for handling those targets that the planner incorporated into his preliminary proposals, modified other preliminary proposals in the direction of their interests, and effectively supported city officials in their decision to approve the Final Plan. Although North West Hyde Parkers did not get public or middle-income housing on the Maryland Site, they did achieve two other major features of the plan for the neighborhood on which planners and citizens were in substantial agreement from the start.

The general approval given to the plan by the citizens of North West Hyde Park was not obtained by catering in every instance to citizen desires. On the contrary, in some instances the planners, for technical reasons, pressed for solutions which the citizens did not relish. However, the citizens accepted the planners' proposal despite the fact that for some of them drastic changes would result. The citizens of North West Hyde Park accepted personally unpleasant future consequences without conflict. They pursued their special interests through regularized channels provided by the Community Conference, using the tactics of negotiation rather than those of combat.

What were the reasons for this success? Specifically, what were the crucial differences between this area and South West Hyde Park which fostered success here and failure there? Although each neighborhood is to some degree a unique case, there are contrasts along several lines, some of which are crucial. These contrasts are summarized below:

1. *Local Initiative:* In North West Hyde Park the citizens had very early engaged on their own in attempts to renew and conserve their neighborhood. The North West Hyde Park Neighborhood Redevelopment Corporation and the Kozminski P.T.A. both had started to work on neighborhood problems before urban renewal planning got under way. In a sense, neighborhood leaders had already become familiar with the notions of planning long before they had to confront the solutions put forth by the professionals. In contrast, little or no experience of this sort had been accrued by the leaders in South West Hyde Park before they were confronted with the proposals of the professional planners.

2. *Leadership Cadre:* The leadership of North West Hyde Park was tied in very closely through overlap with the leadership of the Community Conference. The leadership therefore had good access to the organizations and institutions of the community. The base of the leadership among the white home owners of the eastern edge and the upper-middle-class Negroes along the northern edge provided a biracial leadership group. For this reason, urban renewal proposals for the North West sector did not take on the appearance of Negro clearance for this reason.

3. *Citizen organization:* In contrast to the area to the South, the North West Hyde Park block groups had been well organized before urban renewal got underway. Furthermore, the groups had been successful in making small improvements

to their own blocks, successfully started clean-up and rehabilitation drives, won a local option election, and the like.

Organized blocks became inactive in the South West in 1956, as they began to fail to influence corporation plans for redeveloping the neighborhood. Prior to 1956 the 5500 Maryland Block Group—located inside the redevelopment clearance site—had attempted two action programs. It had tried to prevent the opening of a pool hall on 55th Street a half-block away, and it had tried to swing a local option election in an effort to eliminate liquor stores in the immediate neighborhood. The 5600 Maryland Block Group also was active in the local-option campaign. Both action programs failed. From April, 1955, through 1956 Horwitz' activity reports on block groups in the South West are filled with such evaluative remarks as, "poor communication with Conference," "weak meeting," "no response shown," and during the same period reports on the North West include twice as many evaluations of a positive order: "good leadership," "active communication." These reports are, of course, of uncertain reliability.

Table 7.1—Proportion of Organized and Active Block Groups

	1955	1956	(Total Block Strips in Area)
North West	76%	82%	(100)
South West	72	44	(32)

Table 7.1 shows that in 1955, the year prior to official planning for either neighborhood, both sectors were extensively organized and active. By 1956, when the redevelopment corporation plans for South West Hyde Park were made public, active block organization declined abruptly from 72 per cent to 44 per cent. During the same year activity was extended from 76 per cent to 82 per cent in the North West neighborhood.

4. *Planning Goals:* The physical plant of North West Hyde Park was such as to direct planners toward "public use planning." Expanding the Kozminski School Site, new use for the Rodfei Zedek Site, and planning for play space, for instance, were unquestionably plans for public facilities, in contrast to plans for married student housing in South West Hyde Park. Expansion of the Osteopathic Hospital was only quasi-public,

but more public by far than use for married student housing. Site expansion for George Williams College was not introduced into the plan until the last moment, thus avoiding the public-versus-private-use question, and this space was drawn mostly from a commercial rather than a residential block. The only major controversy in the entire process surrounded the Maryland Site, where citizens fought for public use and planners for sale to the Children's Bureau. Relating this point to item 1 above, Planning Unit definitions of conservation problems and citizen definitions were highly convergent from start to finish, leaving little room for public conflict.

5. *Institutional Stakes:* Several institutions were heavily interested in conserving this neighborhood, but the interest and power of none of them was dominant. This distribution fostered cooperative negotiations among the institutions and between them and neighborhood residents. Institutions were on the scene and involved, but, most important, the balance of local power was not concentrated.

6. *Conference Machinery:* The Conference leadership learned much from South West Hyde Park during 1956. Most of the bargaining in the North West occurred during 1957, and the Conference had by that time improved its own machinery. Its Planning Committee was strengthened, and procedures for communicating up to the Planning Unit and down to the block groups were perfected. Furthermore, the constituency of the Conference in North West Hyde Park was clear. Overlap between block-group membership and Conference membership here was very high, and, with such block leaders as Victor Towns, the citizens' desires were directly expressed to and through Conference machinery. This time the neighborhood redevelopment corporation was a by-product of the Conference and the block groups rather than the University and the South East Chicago Commission. Most important of all, what was to happen in conserving North West Hyde Park was highly salient to key leaders inside the Conference.

CHAPTER 8

Some Voices of Dissent

*W*hen winter ended in 1958, it appeared that the Final Plan was headed for quick approval by the City Council. Hearings before the Council were scheduled for May. The considerable effort expended by community organizations, institutions, and individuals appeared to have borne fruit. Consensus obtained within the local community, and there were no major sources of opposition in the greater metropolitan community.

But just at this point, when success seemed so clear, two sources of dissent began to be heard. First, disagreement appeared within the community in the form of a Tenants and Home Owners Association, which began in April, 1958, to bid for membership and support on the basis of opposition to the Plan. The formation of the Association, however, was not as serious a threat to the eventual success of the Plan as was the other dissenter. In the middle of April, 1958, the *New World*, the weekly newspaper of the Roman Catholic Archdiocese of Chicago began a series of articles on the Plan which strongly criticized its provisions. This sign of opposition from one of Chicago's most powerful institutions brought governmental machinery to a halt. It was not until October, 1958, that public hearings were begun on the City Council Ordinance on the Final Plan. Almost to the very last, there was serious doubt on the part of some of the participants that the Plan could be approved against such powerful opposition.

We treat the stories of these two dissenting organizations in some detail in this chapter because they illustrate a number of important points concerning citizen participation in urban renewal planning. The case of the Tenants and Home Owners

Association illuminates many of the dilemmas of planning that were given emphasis in Chapter 3. Any plan calling for significant transformation of some portion of a residential neighborhood is bound to threaten the interests of certain residents. If at the same time these residents are articulate in their desire to remain in the neighborhood, then one can expect some serious opposition to develop.

A second point made by these examples concerns metropolitan limitations on the renewal of individual neighborhoods. Urban renewal in any subcommunity has city-wide impact, and the metropolitan scene at some point becomes the crucial setting for decision making. The ability of the Catholic Church to bring about a last-minute reconsideration of the entire plan places obvious limits on the effectiveness of citizen participation within the affected area alone.

Finally, these cases illustrate the effect of opposition upon the major participants themselves. Perhaps the most important effect was the creation of any even stronger unanimity within the community. At no point were the University, the South East Chicago Commission, the Hyde Park–Kenwood Community Conference, and other institutions more closely allied than when significant opposition began to arise.

The Hyde Park–Kenwood Tenants and Home Owners Association

In Chapter 5 we reported how in the early years of its existence, the Hyde Park–Kenwood Community Conference was primarily the representative organization for the liberal, intellectual elements in the Hyde Park–Kenwood Community. This was manifested in its strong interest in integration and in the methods of "grass-roots" participation it employed. We have documented how, as time went on, the Conference was transformed from an interest group into a fiduciary institution, acting less on behalf of a specific group within the community and more on behalf of "the community as a whole." While this transformation undoubtedly made it possible for the Conference to grow in membership and influence, at the same time certain of the population, who were initially attracted to it because of its philosophy of organization and its liberal goals, became increasingly disenchanted.

Before the details of the plan were released, much of the dissatisfaction with the Conference on the part of small groups within the membership was well contained within the organization. However, as planning got under way, the impact of the Plan began to make itself felt. The very specific interests of particular home owners began to be affected: the properties of some of them were to be acquired and demolished in order to provide land for the projected renewal of the community, while others had their properties described as blighted, deteriorated, or beyond rehabilitation.

When these two sources of discontent coincided, as was the case in a small neighborhood close to the area to be acquired under "Hyde Park A and B" (see Chapter 4), some property owners there became a particular source of discontent. This neighborhood, centering around Dorchester and 54th Street, contained a number of active Community Conference members of strong liberal persuasions. In addition, on several occasions the planners had made gestures in the direction of acquiring additional property in that area. The first sign of disaffection that was to lead eventually to the formation of a Tenants and Home Owners Association arose in connection with "Hyde Park A and B." A group of liberals, joined by other home owners in the area, broke away from the Conference to testify at the public hearings in opposition to the Plan. The individuals involved were active members of the Conference, and several had served on important committees. At this time, however, they did not form a separate organization, but continued to work within the Conference.

At the 1954 public hearings on "Hyde Park A and B," as individuals they offered testimony against the proposal. Their testimony touched upon three major themes: (1) too much housing suitable for rehabilitation was being demolished in view of the severe housing shortage in Chicago; (2) the plans for the redevelopment of the cleared area would price them out of neighborhood; and (3) the clearance threatened a Buddhist Church. From the testimony it could be seen that their major emphasis was upon the *housing* implications of urban renewal. This group was not particularly sympathetic to the notion of the renewal of community facilities. From their point of view, to tear down rehabilitable houses and replace them with a shopping center seemed a travesty of social justice.

As discussed in Chapters 4 and 5, when the planning unit of the South East Chicago Commission in 1954 proposed a park on the west border of "Hyde Park A and B," the same group agitated strongly within the Conference for that organization to oppose this project. The arguments put forth in defense of their position were the same as those marshaled in opposition to "Hyde Park A and B." On this occasion the Conference and this group were not very far apart.

Up to this point the small group of dissenters within the Conference took no organizational form. The leaders of the group were in close contact with each other as neighbors and as workers within a block group. They did not attempt to form a separate formal organization.

When the Final Plan was released early in 1958, this group —apparently feeling that their position was too much in disagreement with the Conference to make themselves heard and listened to within the organization—formed the Hyde Park–Kenwood Tenants and Home Owners Association. On March 26 the Association was formed, with Mrs. Hilda Mason and Eugene Turner elected as cochairmen. The Association soon opened offices in a prominent Hyde Park business building.

Within a month after its formation the Association claimed between 100 and 200 members, a testimony to the organizing experience of its leaders. The Association opened its campaign against the Plan by placing an advertisement in the *Herald*. Leaders contacted public officials—General Holland of the Community Conservation Board, Alderman Despres, and Congressman Barrett O'Hara. On the "grass-roots" level, the Association held "parlor meetings" and prepared testimony to give at the forthcoming City Council hearings on the Final Plan.

As manifested both in their publicity and in the testimony that they were later to give at the City Council hearings, the basic criticism of the renewal plan offered by the Association centered around three main issues. First, the plan as they saw it was intended to produce a high-income community by displacing lower- and middle-income families. Second, the effect of the plan would be to increase the severe housing shortage in the City of Chicago by destroying rehabilitable housing. Finally, the plan was viewed as "Negro clearance."

In the first two months of its existence some public attention was given to the Tenants and Home Owners Association by newspapers and by other community organizations, particularly the Hyde Park–Kenwood Community Conference. After this brief notice, the Association quickly faded away as a recipient of publicity. In large part, this eclipse occurred because a much more formidable opponent, the Catholic Church, appeared upon the scene, with similar criticisms to offer and with an ability to command a considerably larger metropolitan audience. In addition, the campaign of the Association was geared to reach a climax at the time of the public hearings initially scheduled for May. With the postponement of the Council hearings, the momentum generated by the Association was dissipated.

The story of the Tenants and Home Owners Association points up that end of the spectrum of opinion on the meaning and goals of urban renewal which could not be covered by either the South East Chicago Commission or the Hyde Park–Kenwood Community Conference. The Association attempted to represent those who felt that the urban renewal plan as finally drawn up did not meet the housing needs of the lower-income segment of the community. It sought to attract to itself householders and tenants whose housing would be drastically affected by the plan.

The ideological roots of the Association can be seen in the close connection between its leaders and certain left-wing militant unions in the Chicago area—the Packinghouse Workers Union in particular. Its social base in the householders whose homes were being demolished is shown in the fact that its strength came so heavily from around the borders of "Hyde Park A and B."

Once effectively organized, interest groups often have amazing durability. This citizen-action group, first formed in schism from the Conference in 1954 and active in 1958, came to life again in April, 1959. It distributed a pamphlet to all demolition-slated addresses, describing the relocation rights of inhabitants and offering to assist relocatees in securing their rights. Continuity of concern with housing and human needs is manifest, and this protest movement, however undermanned, has become a useful watchdog.

The Cardinal's Committee on Conservation and Urban Renewal

It is a tribute to the organizational skills represented in the community organizations of Hyde Park–Kenwood that the only powerful opposition to the plans for renewal arose from outside rather than inside the community. The Conference particularly managed to cover so wide a range of neighborhood interests and groups that whatever dissatisfaction there was with the final version of the planning was largely limited to reservations rather than public opposition. In the final months of decision, however, a very important source of dissent appeared from without the local neighborhood and for a time threatened municipal approval of the Final Plan.

The opposition to the plan represented by the Cardinal's Committee was a formidable one. In Chicago Roman Catholics are the largest single denomination, and, as elsewhere, they are strongly organized. An authoritative statement on some local issue voiced by a Church body and widely circulated among Catholics cannot fail to receive some response from city officials, many of whom are Catholics and all of whom are sensitive to the "grass-roots" and organizational pressures that such a statement might generate.

The weight of the Catholic Church in Chicago can be assessed in the response that developed to criticisms of the Plan which were widely circulated by the Cardinal's Committee on Conservation and Urban Renewal. Final City Council approval of the plan was delayed for five months while the meaning and determination of the Committee was measured and tested. Only when the city officials were reasonably certain that the local Church clergy and laity were not fully united on this opposition did the Mayor's office proceed with the presentation of the Final Plan to the Council.

The late Cardinal Stritch organized the Cardinal's Committee on Conservation and Urban Renewal in 1954. The Cardinal's interest in this topic was stimulated by both organizational and social problems. Many of the parishes located in older urban neighborhoods had begun to feel the impact strongly of the rapid population shifts of the postwar period. Cardinal Stritch was also concerned with the housing problems of low-income groups. When state and federal renewal and conservation legislation was passed in 1954, the Cardinal was quick to set up a committee to consider the implications of this legislation for the organizational and social concerns of his diocese. At least some of the stimulus for the foundation of the Committee came from persons outside the clergy who sought to obtain Church backing for local renewal and conservation projects. (Ironically, Julian Levi was one of those who sought in 1954 to obtain the Cardinal's backing for the neighborhood redevelopment corporation legislation then before the state legislature.)

The functions given to the Committee were to explore the meaning of renewal legislation as a basis for conserving parish environs and to advise the Cardinal on policy stands on local renewal and redevelopment proposals. The Committee was composed of Catholic clergy, with Monsignor Reed as Chairman. Members were chosen because of their interest and knowledge in the fields of housing and race relations.

During the first few years of its existence, the Cardinal's Committee was not a particularly active organization, in part because the forms to be taken by neighborhood renewal and conservation in Chicago had not yet evolved and partly because the Committee had not evolved its own mission and organization. Its most significant public action was to testify strongly in favor of the new housing codes at hearings held in 1956.

In 1957 Monsignor Egan [1] was asked by Cardinal Stritch to

---

1. Monsignor Egan had held a fellowship in community organization with the Industrial Areas Foundation in 1956. The Industrial Areas Foundation, a Chicago Organization headed by Saul Alinsky has been concerned with ways and means of stimulating the "grass-roots" organization of underprivileged groups, growing in great part out of the very successful organization of the largely Catholic Back-of-the-Yards neighborhood during the thirties. The style of organizational tactics developed by Alinsky is very different from that developed in the more usual community organization manuals. Alinsky has adapted the organizing tactics of labor unions to the organization of communities seeking for issues that would stimulate residents to band together. The communities organized by the Foundation often take postures of combat that are far from the search for consensus that more frequently characterizes at least the language of community organization as practiced in the Hyde Park—Kenwood Community Conference and is described in the more traditional manuals of community organizers.

become executive director of the Committee. Monsignor Egan was best known at that time for the vigorous direction he gave to the Cana Conference on Family Life, an organization devoted to the support of Catholic concepts of family values.

When the Final Plan for Hyde Park–Kenwood was released in 1958, Monsignor Egan turned his attention to analysis of the plan. He met with Julian Levi and Planner Jack Meltzer. He visited Hyde Park–Kenwood and listened to tape recordings of the hearings before the Conservation Community Council. Shortly before Cardinal Stritch left for Rome early in 1958, Monsignor Egan reported to the Cardinal on his evaluation of the plan; his report recommended over-all approval of the plan with reservations on housing for low- and middle-income groups and relocation procedures and presented criticism of the lack of a tie-in between the local plan and some larger plan for the city of Chicago. The Cardinal authorized Monsignor Egan to announce publicly these criticisms of the Plan.

The meeting between Monsignor Egan and Cardinal Stritch became of critical significance. The outcome of the meeting was the basis of the Monsignor's campaign against certain features of the plan, for it gave official approval to public criticism in the name of the Cardinal. The death of the Cardinal during his visit to Rome and the subsequent period without permanent headship for the Chicago Archdiocese gave Monsignor Egan more than usual latitude in action. At the same time, it undermined the authoritative nature of his pronouncements. It should be noted that it is the strongly hierarchical structure of the Catholic Church that makes the problem of sanction for a spokesman so important.

In April 1958, shortly before the Conservation Community Council approved the Final Plan, the Cardinal's Committee began public discussion of the plan's merits. The start of the campaign was a series of articles in the *New World*, official newspaper of the Chicago diocese. The first articles immediately received wide attention in the metropolitan press and in

---

There are some who saw in the tactics pursued by Monsignor Egan lessons learned in his apprenticeship at the Industrial Areas Foundation. While there may be some similarity in style, the content is certainly quite different. Monsignor Egan was not organizing a community but carrying out a power struggle at a level far removed from the "grass roots."

the Hyde Park *Herald*. Even more important was the heavy concern in the local community with the Committee's actions. Community leaders and University officials pondered the meaning of the criticisms and tried to assess their impact on city officials.

The first reaction of the local organizations was to draw closer together to work out a strategy for countering the Committee. A dramatic illustration of this period was the luncheon meeting called by Julian Levi for local Protestant and Jewish clergy. Levi suggested that some action be taken by the clergy to counteract the Catholic attack. Partly growing out of this meeting and partly on his own initiative, Kenwood Rabbi Jacob Weinstein wrote an open letter, which the *Sun-Times* published, sharply criticizing the *New World*'s attack on the plan.

As more articles appeared in the *New World* and as the metropolitan press took up the discussion with feature articles on the plan and its critics and supporters, progress toward official approval of the Final Plan came to a halt. First, the City Council hearings of the plan, tentatively scheduled for May, were postponed. The Community Conservation Board proposed a cutback in funds for the project, necessitating a referral of the Plan back to the Conservation Community Council. The cutback in funds was widely interpreted as a concession to the Cardinal's Committee. (A full account of these reactions to the Committee is contained in Chapter 9.)

There is no doubt that the Cardinal's Committee and Monsignor Egan were central actors on the stage of urban renewal politics during the summer of 1958. The setting of the drama was mainly downtown in municipal agencies and offices where there was concern with the ambiguous meaning of the Committee's criticisms, an ambiguity which stemmed not so much from their manifest content, for all these criticisms had been offered before, as from their latent meaning. How much did statements of the Committee represent the views of the Church officialdom and what steps would be taken by the Church to prevent passage of the Final Plan in the form approved by the Conservation Community Council? It was only when the city fathers felt sure that the officials of the Church were not in total agreement with the Committee, and that the Committee had failed to find great response among lay Catholics or other significant groups, that the Final Plan was brought before the City Council.

In the City Council hearings Monsignor Egan made his final plea for reconsideration of the Plan, urging the Council's Committee on Housing to devise changes. Although some members of the Council Committee listened with manifest sympathy to his suggestions, the Committee reported favorably on the Plan.

In connection with the Cardinal's Committee campaign, there are two questions which must be raised. First, why did the attack develop? Here we must consider not only the content of the criticisms but also the motivation behind them. Essential also to the answer to this question are the tactics which the Committee employed, for tactical matters often condition content. Secondly, we must ask why there was such a strong reaction to these criticisms. Certainly many of these specific points had been made before, both by organizations within the neighborhood and elsewhere. Yet the Cardinal's Committee gave these old objections new strength.

To answer these questions, we must consider the criticisms voiced by the Cardinal's Committee and its spokesmen. The Committee pointed to the following defects in the Plan. They saw the Plan as primarily benefiting the University of Chicago, just as previous redevelopment surrounding Michael Reese Hospital and the Illinois Institute of Technology primarily benefited these institutions. The interests of the University of Chicago were regarded as legitimate but to some degree in conflict with the interests of residents of the area, whose major concern was housing.

The Cardinal's Committee assessed the plan in terms of its housing provisions. They believed that too much housing that could be rehabilitated was scheduled for demolition, needlessly lowering the amount of housing available in the city. The housing being demolished was primarily occupied by low-income groups and Negroes, whose housing stock, already in short supply, would be further reduced.

The Committee also suggested that provisions in the plan for the relocation of displaced residents were not sufficient. Property owners whose property was not taken initially were not adequately safeguarded against later acquisition under regulations which permitted acquisition on such grounds as the "obsolete layout" of a structure.

The Committee also struck a metropolitan theme, claiming concern with the cumulative impact on the rest of the city of the reduction of density in older neighborhoods. Dislocation resulting from previous redevelopment projects and the coming dislocation in Hyde Park–Kenwood would send thousands of low-income and Negro families out on the housing market, to their detriment and to that of already established older neighborhoods. In addition, funds used in Hyde Park–Kenwood would delay renewal of other neighborhoods in the city with greater need for consideration. Finally the *ad-hoc* renewal of neighborhood after neighborhood might hopelessly compromise any attempt at constructing a master plan for the entire city.

One by one these criticisms had been made before. Certainly, the Hyde Park–Kenwood Community Conference in its testimony before the Conservation Community Council had been concerned with housing and had urged more public housing and provisions for middle-income housing. The Conference was also concerned with relocation and the adequate safeguarding of rights of property owners whose property was not yet to be acquired. The Conference's attention to racial integration was long-standing. And it had made a consistent fight against racial discrimination in housing within the community.

Perhaps the only "new" themes in the Cardinal's Committee indictment against the Plan were concern for the impact upon the metropolitan area of urban renewal in Hyde Park–Kenwood, and certain matters of emphasis. The differences in emphasis can be sensed from the following quotation from Monsignor Reed, Chairman of the Committee, written to the Conservation Community Council just before the cutback decision on July 23:

In the opinion of the Cardinal's Committee, the plan failed to provide: 1) An adequate amount of housing for low income families; 2) guarantees that a substantial amount of new residential construction will have rentals and sale prices that a modest-income family can afford; 3) safeguards that will prevent housing from being demolished until the land cleared is actually needed for re-use; 4) adequate relocation procedures. . . .

The Committee scored the lack of comprehensive planning for the city and raised the question of how widespread neighborhood conservation along the lines of Hyde Park–Kenwood was going to affect other neighborhoods in the city. The protagonists of the Plan had offered it as Chicago's pilot project in renewal to serve as a model for other neighborhoods.

In the spring of 1958 there was much speculation about the meaning of the Cardinal's Committee criticisms. There was concern to assess to the extent to which the Church officialdom fully backed the Committee. The sudden death of Cardinal Stritch in Rome severely complicated matters by obscuring authority lines within the diocese until his successor could be appointed. Much effort on the part of community leaders and city officials went into ascertaining the extent to which Monsignor Egan had the support of some significant segment of the Catholic clergy. In the end, the proponents of the Plan were convinced that Monsignor Egan was without such backing, while Monsignor Egan continued to refer to his mandate from the Cardinal as a clear indication that the Archdiocese should follow his lead.

What lay behind the Committee's indictment of the Plan? It is obvious that the Catholic Church had real and substantial interests in the fate of aging and deteriorating city neighborhoods. Many of Chicago's parishes, representing a great investment in physical plant and accumulated organizational effort, were located in neighborhoods that were then or could be shortly affected by renewal efforts. It was also obvious that the families to be displaced from Hyde Park–Kenwood or other renewed areas would increase the pressure on the low-rent housing market. Indeed, it was partly a recognition of these strong material interests which prompted the Cardinal to set up his committee.

A second source of motivation for the Committee was located in a strong liberal wing among the Catholic clergy of Chicago, represented vigorously in this particular case by Monsignor Egan, the executive director. It was this liberal element among Chicago's Catholic clergy that had resulted in strong lay social-action movements, by close connection with militant labor unions, notably the Packinghouse Workers. The liberal wing of the church was sensitive to the plight of Chicago's Negroes and other underprivileged groups.

As Monsignor Egan pointed out to our interviewer, he saw the Hyde Park–Kenwood Plan as an opportunity to awaken interest among Catholic clergy and laymen in urban problems by raising questions concerning the Plan. He raised these questions with the understanding that it was neither desirable nor possible to stop the Plan's progress toward eventual approval. It was his hope, as he expressed it, to focus some attention on *human* aspects of urban renewal.

His initial plans for the Committee's campaign misfired to an unanticipated degree. Although he expected to reach mainly a Catholic audience, it quickly became apparent that he was reaching a much wider one. Furthermore, his attack was misunderstood. Many saw it as directed toward a total defeat of the Hyde Park–Kenwood Plan, an interpretation which was aided by the strong form that the criticisms in the *New World* articles took.

Once it became clear that the *New World* series had achieved a wider impact than intended, the Cardinal's Committee was quick to take advantage of the situation to draw more and more attention to their reservations on the forms taken by Chicago's pilot project in urban renewal. It was at this point that the Committee hired a public-relations expert and began to seek ways of directly reaching a larger audience through the metropolitan press. At the same time the criticisms of the plan became stronger.

It was probably the case that the period of ambiguity of authority within the Chicago diocese served to give Monsignor Egan more than routine latitude in carrying out a campaign. Monsignor Egan, aided by his public-relations adviser, pursued the tactics of militant labor organizations. As we have shown, these tactics were to overstate one's objectives in public, to stir up as much controversy as possible, and then to negotiate a compromise that was close to one's initial objectives. The sharper the controversy, the more was to be gained in the final settlement by negotiation. Hence the all-out attack on the Plan in public at the same time that Monsignor Egan expressed support for the Plan.

One of the consequences of the Cardinal's Committee cam-

paign was unification of the community organizations within
Hyde Park–Kenwood and activation in support of the Plan of
individuals who might not have been so concerned. The Conference and the South East Chicago Commission drew closer together. On the metropolitan scene Protestant and Jewish
groups were quick to counter another "power move" on the
part of the Catholic Church by public support for the Plan.
The metropolitan newspapers also entered the scene, finding
that the controversy was news; most of their coverage favored
the Plan.

Surprisingly, little public support for the Committee's position appeared either within the Catholic group or from without. Despite the fact that the Committee explicitly spoke on
behalf of other neighborhoods and of such potentially powerful
groups as low-income Catholics and Negroes, no strongly res-
onant chord was struck among either prominent labor or Negro
interests. Even among Catholic lay groups the Cardinal's Committee did not meet with a solidly sympathetic audience. For
example, an editorial in *Work*, monthly publication of the liberal Catholic Conference on Working Life, written by Ed
Marciniak, an official of the local Newspaper Guild, announced
support of the Plan. Several prominent Catholic laymen identi-
fying themselves as such made statements which were designed
to indicate in public that Chicago Catholics were not all of a
mind with the Cardinal's Committee. Indeed, James Cunningham, executive director of the Hyde Park–Kenwood Community
Conference and prominent liberal Catholic layman, offered direct refutation of Catholic unanimity at the hearings of the
City Council Committee on Housing. Undoubtedly the lack of
consensus among lay Catholics on this question further
strengthened the decision of city officials to push for final approval of the Plan.

Nor were clergy within the Church of a single mind on the
stand of the Cardinal's Committee. Some were concerned with
the effect on relations between Catholics and non-Catholics,
believing that a "power play" on the part of Monsignor Egan
could only deteriorate relations which had been very good under Cardinal Stritch. Others with liberal persuasions were convinced that Hyde Park–Kenwood was sufficiently aware of the
housing plight of Negroes and low-income groups and that to

attack the plan was to attack a step toward progress, particularly in interracial living. According to Monsignor Egan, many pressures were brought to bear upon him from within the church to soften his criticisms.

Reaction to the campaign of Monsignor Egan was both more and less than might have been expected. It was greater in the sense that the articles in the *New World* could easily have been ignored by proponents of the Plan as directed mainly at an internal audience. The initial interpretation of the campaign invested it with more strength than it either intended or later demonstrated.

The reaction to the campaign was also less than might have been anticipated, in the sense that the Committee was unable to rally about itself support from the strong interests which the Committee tried to activate.

Part of the reaction to the Committee's campaign can be explained on the basis of the widespread interpretation with which it was met. Few persons took the criticisms offered on their own merit. Rather, there was much concern with the "real" motives behind the attack.

There were several reasons why the Committee was not taken at face value. For one thing, the Catholic Church of Chicago, despite its prominent liberal wing, did not have an established reputation as the defender of rights of underprivileged Negroes. Indeed, in many respects, the practice of the Church in regard to Negroes in Catholic communities left much to be desired from the liberal point of view. The anti-Negro record of the heavily Catholic Back-of-the-Yards neighborhood particularly contributed to suspicious or skeptical attitudes toward the Committee's view. As a recent sympathetic review of the achievements of the Back-of-the-Yards Council has stated the matter:

So there is a case to be made that the Back of the Yards is not so much anti-Negro as it is pro-nationality church. Whatever the inner truth, the practical effect is the same: Negroes are unwelcome as residents . . . many a savings and loan officer, many a businessman, many a householder in Back of the Yards will tell you privately that the neighborhood is "determined to keep Negroes out." [2]

2. Martin Millspaugh and Gurney Breckenfield, *The Human Side of Urban Renewal* (Baltimore: Fight-Blight, Inc. 1958 p. 211). While it is

The heavy praise given by Catholic clergy to Back-of-the-Yards as a model of neighborhood organization to be emulated by other Catholic parishes contributed toward suspicion of the Committee. Because of Monsignor Egan's association with the Industrial Areas Foundation, in turn closely connected with the Back-of-the-Yards movement, this area was chosen as a concrete manifestation of "real" Church practice in the realm of race and housing.

A second reason for the widespread discounting of the Committee's views was its late arrival on the scene. Many of the issues raised by the Committee had been thrashed over inside Hyde Park–Kenwood for a long time. The Cardinal's Committee opened its attack after it appeared to those on the local scene that these were settled issues that had been fully negotiated. In addition, the Committee had not established its legitimate right to enter the controversy by participating in the long and difficult struggle to achieve consensus. The same criticisms offered within the community by persons who had participated all along might have met with more sympathy: from an outside organization, criticism appeared only as trouble making.

A major reason why the Cardinal's Committee appeared so late on the scene is that the administrative machinery surrounding urban renewal did not provide means for the participation of metropolitan groups until the very last stages. Thus, while the Conservation Community Council was the setting for intra-community appraisals of the Final Plan, the metropolitan groups had to wait until the Final Plan was reviewed by the City Council before being afforded an opportunity to make public pronouncements. By that stage too much had been invested in the specific proposals by planners and the local community for much serious consideration to be given to metropolitan criticisms. Furthermore, the City Council was not empowered to do more than give blanket endorsement or rejection of the

---

true that Negroes are not welcome in the Back-of-the-Yards Council, it is not a unique neighborhood in this respect. The Back-of-the-Yards Council has had quite an impressive record of fighting for equality on other fronts, however. Nondiscrimination in employment was strongly supported by the Council, as were equal treatment in stores and other public facilities.

Plan, and the latter appeared to all as too drastic a step to be seriously considered.

For these reasons, proponents of the Plan concerned themselves with finding out the "real story" behind Monsignor Egan's opposition. Despite Monsignor Egan's own well-known liberal opinions, Plan proponents found the most congenial (to them) interpretation to be the material interests of the Church in the maintenance of all-white parishes in the areas potentially threatened by the influx of Negroes.

This interpretation was particularly attractive to the liberal elements within the community. It enabled them to disregard the cogent aspects of the Committee's critique. By adopting this interpretation, the Conference was brought into closer cooperation with the South East Chicago Commission.

The same interpretation in terms of material interests was also held by Negro leaders, preventing them from giving much support to the Cardinal's Committee. Indeed, the Negro press and interest groups, while making many of the same criticisms of the Plan as the Committee, were in general careful not to associate their opposition with that of Monsignor Egan. Urban League and N.A.A.C.P. testimony before City Council in particular closely paralleled Monsignor Egan's.[3]

The lack of mass response to the Cardinal's Committee left Monsignor Egan with only the authority of the Catholic Church and its internal discipline as his major weapon against the Plan. If he spoke with the full backing of the Archdiocese and parish priests were urged to put pressure on aldermen and other local officials within their parishes, his committee could still represent a major threat to the plan. At the very least, many aldermen would be faced with local pressures against the Plan. Some, if faced with a choice, would undoubtedly honor local pressures aganist the city administration. Thus in the end, the major effective weapon remaining to the Cardinal's Committee was a "power play"—a tactic that was too dangerous and one to which the Committee never resorted.

The tactics of the counterattack on the Cardinal's Committee were directed at ascertaining the power position of Monsignor Egan within the local church officialdom and sought

---

3. The Chicago *Defender* did give high praise to Monsignor Egan on at least one occasion.

to bolster those elements within the church hierarchy who would not go along with the Committee in an all-out "power play" either to stop approval of the Plan or force serious modification.

Although the Cardinal's death and the consequent clouding of lines of authority made a determination of the power position of Monsignor Egan difficult, enough "evidence" had been accumulated by late July to convince city officials that this was not an attempt by the Church as a whole to scuttle the Plan. Some small gesture toward meeting the objections of the Committee would suffice to "save face" for an official organ of the Church. The safe passage of the Final Plan, essentially untouched, was thus secured.

While the Cardinal's Committee did not succeed in officially modifying the Plan and the forms of urban renewal as represented by the Hyde Park–Kenwood Plan, it did succeed in another sense. Attention was drawn to problems of relocation and to the rights of property owners. In future renewal efforts, some modification of procedures can be expected. Ironically, Monsignor Egan achieved the goals he started out with, but the enlargement of his objectives as the struggle proceeded and the acceptance of these wider goals by the protagonists left him and the other actors with the final impression that he had failed.

There are several important lessons in the case of the Cardinal's Committee on Conservation and Urban Renewal. From the viewpoint of local organizations pressing for amelioration of local conditions, the case of the Committee highlights the fact that urban renewal takes place in a metropolitan context. It is not enough merely to obtain the sympathetic approval of city officials; it is also important to negotiate with other important sources of metropolitan power. In the large urban centers of the northeastern part of our country, for example, the Catholic Church, with its disciplined clergy and wide influence among the faithful, represents a power of the first magnitude.

The efforts of the local leaders in Hyde Park–Kenwood went toward achieving consensus within the community, the support of the business community, and the consent and approval of city officials. Negotiations with the powerful Church hierarchy was correspondingly neglected. This is not to say that the local interests of the Church were neglected: The Plan contained provision for some expansion of the physical plant of St. Thomas Parish, and the local pastor was a member (if somewhat inactive) of both the Conference and the South East Chicago Commission. The approval of a local pastor, however, is not necessarily relevant to the officialdom of the Church.

This is, of course, a retrospective assessment and, as such, contains all the false wisdom of hindsight. There are at least several good reasons why local leaders might have reasonably neglected to negotiate the high level support of the Church. For one thing, the local neighborhood was not one in which the Church had manifested much interest in the past and was not one of the major parishes in the Archdiocese. Secondly, efforts had been made to satisfy the interests of the local parish pastor. In addition, once the Cardinal's Committee had started its attack, the death of the Cardinal made it unclear with whom negotiations should be conducted.

A second important lesson to be drawn from the case of the Cardinal's Committee concerns one of the strengths of an organization such as the Hyde Park–Kenwood Community Conference. The wide and interracial coverage of Conference membership gave its approval to the plan particular weight when measured against the criticisms of the Cardinal's Committee. The participation of the Conference in urban renewal planning was assurance to the City Council that the interests of Negroes and lower-income groups had some sympathetic representation.

Finally, there is a lesson to be drawn *for* such organizations as the Cardinal's Committee. If some sort of impact on the course of urban renewal is desired, it is not a good political move to appear on the scene after the other major interests have already settled upon some solution to their differences. The effect of such last-minute opposition is to draw together the former antagonists into a solid front and to arouse suspicions about the motives of the latecomer. The Cardinal's Committee probably could have had a greater influence on the Plan (although not achieving as much notoriety) if it had expressed a position on renewal while the major features of the Plan were being formulated. At this more congenial time local organizations and city officials might have made a more serious effort to meet some of the reasonable criticisms of the Committee. The tactics of the Committee were more militant and aggressive than those of the well-disciplined negotiator.

The case of the Cardinal's Committee also shows up a flaw in the administrative machinery surrounding urban renewal. Essentially, the machinery is overdeveloped in the local community, providing many mechanisms for sounding public opinion on that level. But the development of metropolitan consensus is left until very late in the game, when a critical comment on the developed plans appears to be a total rejection because there is too much at stake to compromise.

In Chapter 3 we discussed the additive process by which support for renewal plans accumulates in a community. We suggested that the wider the support becomes, the less attention is focused on the particulars of plan content—technical, financial, consequential, or otherwise. The lack of heightened responsiveness to the Cardinal's Committee exemplifies this paradox, we think. With but isolated exceptions, supporters of the Final Plan had ceased to attend critically to the particulars of the proposal by the summer of 1958. The points raised by Monsignor Egan were specific, grounded in review of the plan maps, and essentially technical and procedural; they seemed by this time irrelevant to the diffuse concerns of supporters for over-all approval. When the criticisms were voiced, attention switched from the particulars cited to the imputation of underlying motives and to the ready assumption that anyone who was not "all for" approval was against conservation. The meaning in this situation for programs of citizen participation in other communities will be explored in Chapter 10.

CHAPTER 9

Municipal Government and Renewal Planning

Although in the main citizen participation in urban renewal was centered on the local scene, some of the most significant steps in attaining urban renewal involved municipal officials and agencies. At every juncture on the way to approval of the Final Plan, city officials and agencies played some decisive part: correspondingly, relations with the municipal government were neglected by neither the South East Chicago Commission nor the Hyde Park–Kenwood Community Conference.

Urban renewal in Hyde Park–Kenwood would have been impossible to achieve against the disapproval of municipal authorities. City officials had to give approval to local activities at many points. City agencies had to facilitate the work in drawing up the plans, and they would carry an even greater burden in their implementation. Under the conditions of a lukewarm acceptance of local urban renewal by municipal officials, something could be achieved, but only after lengthy delays and perhaps not on a large scale. City officials and agencies were more than acquiescent in the urban renewal of Hyde Park–Kenwood, however; there was great enthusiasm "downtown" for the project.

Chicago's city government is reputed to have a flavor all its own, which some regard with considerable gusto and which others dislike. The view of the municipal structure which has emerged from our research converges closely upon that expressed by Meyerson and Banfield in their astute analysis of the politics of public housing in Chicago:

> As they actually work . . . Chicago's governmental institutions achieve a high degree of centralization *and* a high degree of decentralization: they put a great deal of power over some matters in the hands of the city administration while leaving a great deal of power over other matters in the hands of the neighborhood and ward leaders. . . . Most of the matters that were decided locally were of local interest. . . . Some matters were on the border between being of local and of city-wide interest or were of both. . . . In these matters there would be friction. . . .[1]

Meyerson and Banfield also concluded that the political machine, for the most part, performs vital functions in safeguarding against both bureaucratic tyranny and extreme localism. Our review of the role of Chicago's city government in the case of renewal planning for Hyde Park–Kenwood generally bears out their analysis. From evidence gained in asking knowledgeable and influential citizens about their activities "in city hall" and from observation of the Chicago City Council as it deliberated over passage of the first Conservation Renewal Application, we must conclude that the decision to approve urban renewal in Hyde Park was reached in the best tradition of democratic politics.

This chapter provides the evidence for this conclusion. It summarizes the complex organization of Chicago city government, where this is relevant to renewal planning, and singles out the units where critical decisions were made in the case of Hyde Park–Kenwood. Then it traces the path of influences upon these units and examines the "crisis of the 'cut-back' "— the point at which the Mayor intervened personally to attempt to insure approval of the Plan.

Because the dominant concern of this study is with local citizen participation, this analysis has been compressed into a minor theme. This must not lead to the interpretation that the role of municipal government was in any way passive or minor. The City Council and, most important, the Office of the Mayor played decisive parts in approval of the Plan.

---

1. Martin Meyerson and Edward C. Banfield, *Politics, Planning, and the Public Interest* (Glencoe: The Free Press, 1955), pp. 288-289.

The Relevant Structure of Chicago
Municipal Government

Although in the early fifties, as we indicated in Chapter 4, the structure of Chicago municipal government had few provisions for carrying out renewal and conservation, by 1955 agencies for taking on the task had evolved. In part, the structure evolved because of the efforts of such civic associations as the Metropolitan Housing and Planning Council. In part, it evolved in response to the expressed needs of localities such as Hyde Park–Kenwood. The agencies arose, too, because of the requirements of state and federal legislation on urban renewal and conservation.

In many ways the structure is complex and unwieldly. Indeed, civic groups such as the Metropolitan Housing and Planning Council and the League of Women Voters have proposed repeatedly that the agencies responsible for planning and renewal be reorganized. These groups, emphasizing the dangers of the decentralized arrangement, are convinced that consolidation would conserve political and administrative energies and would stimulate swifter decision-making. We shall indicate that the existing structure possesses a special wisdom of its own—namely, responsiveness to divergent interests and publics —but the logic of the civic groups in pressing for centralization appears on first impression to be borne out by the complexity of the structure.

The components of the structure of the Chicago city government that are relevant to renewal planning constitute a complex of relationships. The Mayor, as the city's chief executive officer, with the advice and consent of the City Council, appoints the heads of city departments and other agencies. He presides over the City Council, where he has no vote except in case of a tie. He has veto power over ordinances passed by the Council, though the Council may repass ordinances over his objections by a two-thirds majority.

From a formal perspective, the fifty aldermen of the City Council govern Chicago. They make appropriations, award franchises to and regulate the rates of public utilities, pass on all appointments made by the Mayor, and may create new city departments at will. In principle, each alderman is the independent agent of his ward. Informally, however, the alderman's independence is greatly limited by several controls. Leadership of the City Council tends to consist of a group of the most powerful Democratic aldermen who, working with the Mayor, control the Council when matters of special interest to them or to the Mayor are at stake.[2]

Another related set of controls operates through the Democratic Party. Most aldermen must stay in favor with their ward committeemen (ward party leader) or else be committeemen themselves. Within the wards, the committeemen tend to make many of the important decisions for the party.[3]

Significantly for Hyde Park–Kenwood, Aldermen Leon Despres and Claude Holman were comparatively free of party controls during 1957 and 1958. Despres was elected as an independent candidate with the support of the Independent Voters of Illinois, and Holman had effectively challenged Congressman William Dawson, the political "boss" of the "Black Belt" and a great power within the Democratic Party, for local control over the 4th Ward during this period.[4]

State and federal legislation place another important limitation on City Council authority in the case of urban renewal. Under the law, the City Council has only the power to approve or to reject an ordinance calling for the renewal of a conservation area. This limitation proved important in this case, as we shall show. The effects of these controls, however, are to place considerable formal authority and even greater informal power in the hands of the mayor—*if he chooses to exercise it.*

The City Council does a great deal of its work through committees, setting up standing committees, each of which has a particular jurisdiction. The legislation covering the Hyde

---

2. *Ibid.,* pp. 66-67.

3. For a full description, see *ibid.,* pp. 65-69.

4. Leon Despres was elected in 1955. The Administration of the University of Chicago gave strong and open support to his opponent for office, Mrs. Dorothy Morgenstern, who was both the wife of the University's Director of Public Relations and the candidate endorsed by the Democratic Party, and by Mayor Kennelly's party faction in particular. Mayor Daley's party faction supported a second candidate, and thus, with strong I.V.I. support and a margin of liberal Republican backing, Despres had the advantage of running against a split vote. Some political observers considered this a reflection of the Kennelly-Daley-University of Chicago mutual support pact discussed in Chapter 3.

Park–Kenwood Final Plan, for example, was first sent to the Housing and Planning Committee for preliminary consideration. Council action on the plan was formally limited to consideration of the ordinance by the committee and a single vote by the council as a whole. Actually, as we shall see, this action alone was sufficiently influential to change some features of the Plan.

For the most part, the Office of the Mayor tends to exercise determining control, formal and informal, over matters of planned renewal. The Mayor oversees the Department of Buildings, the Department of Streets and Sanitation, and the Department of Water and Sewers, each of which is responsible for execution of portions of the renewal plan.[5] Among the many other sources of control, the Mayor has very immediate influence over the Office of the Housing and Redevelopment Coordinator (James Downs), the unit through which all others cleared actions relevant to renewal until late in 1957, when this office was dissolved and Downs became the Mayor's consultant on housing. The Coordinator had had no authority other than that delegated to him as a deputy to the Mayor. If, therefore, the Mayor chose to give strong backing to a given project, his deputy had considerable administrative and political strength.

The strong position of the Office of Housing and Redevelopment Coordinator sprang from several sources. First, it was established in 1947—quite early, compared with other city units dealing with planning and renewal. Second, the Coordinator, James Downs, and Deputy Coordinator (1947–1957), D. E. Mackelmann, were well known in professional planning circles as persons with wide experience. Many of the municipal officials located in other units did not have strong professional reputations but were appointed because of their demonstrated concern for public affairs and achievement in *local* neighborhoods of the city. The Coordinators, furthermore, were concerned primarily with policy decisions and were free from the long-term burdens of housekeeping administration of, for ex-

---

5. The Department of buildings, for example, is responsible for examining and approving plans for all buildings being constructed, altered, repaired, or removed. It issues permits for such activities and makes inspections of buildings.

ample, the sort carried by the Land Clearance Commission.
Until 1956 the chief planning agency was the Chicago Plan
Commission, an advisory department assisted by a City Advisory Board. The Commission had thirty-five members, fifteen
of whom were appointed by the Mayor, the remainder being
officials of the various local governments. Proposals of the
Plan Commission were submitted to the Advisory Board for
discussion and comment. After 1956 a Department of City
Planning was created, and Ira J. Bach, formerly Executive Director of the Land Clearance Commission, was appointed Commissioner of this new department early in 1957.

Prior to the establishment of the Department of City
Planning, the city government, as we have mentioned earlier,
had no unit with adequate funds or staff within which professional planning for renewal could be carried on.

In 1953 the Community Conservation Board was authorized
by the City Council under powers granted by the Urban Community Conservation Act of Illinois, but it did not begin operations until 1955. At that time it functioned without a division
of professional planning. Its five members are appointed by the
Mayor, with the approval of the City Council and the Illinois
State Housing Board.

Although the Commissioners appointed to the Community
Conservation Board have not been persons with backgrounds of
extensive experience in either city planning or municipal administration, they have tended to be persons with strong concerns with civic improvement and with records of involvement in
community problems. Indeed, a staff of professionally trained
persons could easily supply the technical know-how which could
complement the integrity and involvement of the Commissioners.

When the Board was first set up, however, a well-trained
technical staff was yet to be recruited, and a full complement of
staff members was finally assembled only in 1958. This lack of
a professional staff materially reduced the Board's ability to
influence the details of urban renewal in Hyde Park–Kenwood
during the planning stage. But of even greater importance than
the lack of organization was the task immediately facing the
Board when it was set up.

In its first stages the most important task of the Board
was to locate and designate neighborhood conservation areas.

Initially, designation requires the expenditure of resources in exploring subcommunities to find those that fit the specifications of "conservation areas," stimulating local interest in applying for formal designation, and guiding local groups through the maze of application regulations involved in achieving designation. During the first years of its existence the Board was oriented away from "downtown" and toward voluntary organizations on the neighborhood level.

What action the Board stimulates on the neighborhood level must then be translated into plans by its new planning unit. The conservation plans must then be approved locally by a Conservation Community Council appointed by the Mayor from among local residents, half of which must be property owners. Such Councils have the power to make changes in the plans. The Board transmits such plans to the City Council. The execution of the Plan, assuming approval by federal agencies involved, then falls to the staff of the Community Conservation Board.

The effect of these arrangements is to subject the Community Conservation Board to important neighborhood and "downtown" checks. In order to accomplish anything, the Board must get the Mayor's backing and the approval of a Conservation Community Council and the City Council, not to mention passing the scrutiny of the federal agencies involved.

In the case of Hyde Park–Kenwood the functions of the Board were narrowed further by subcontracting the planning function to the University of Chicago. Furthermore (as we showed in Chapters 4 and 5), the University and South East Chicago Commission enjoyed more than ordinary access to the Mayor, whereas in the usual case the Board would serve as the communication link to the chief executive of the city government.

Among the long-established municipal agencies relevant to conservation are the Chicago Land Clearance Commission and the Chicago Housing Authority. Some of their activities were discussed in Chapter 5. The Land Clearance Commission—its five members appointed by the Mayor with the approval of the State Housing Board—has authority over acquisition, demolition, and relocation operations in the redevelopment of slum areas. It may also contract to handle relocation for a conservation area; of course, in a complex plan of the sort involved in Hyde Park–Kenwood the Commission played an influential role at numerous times. At the same time the South East Chicago Commission and its Planning Unit were preparing the Preliminary Plan for renewal, for example, they also were negotiating almost daily with the Land Clearance Commission on the redevelopment projects.

The Chicago Housing Authority was created in 1937 as an independent public corporation with special powers from the state for action in slum clearance and low-rent public housing. Governed by a five-man Board of Commissioners appointed by the Mayor and approved by the State Housing Board, the Chicago Housing Authority had to be consulted with at great length on the question of its projected role in conservation of Hyde Park. Its willingness to erect public housing of various types in this neighborhood had to be estimated and guaranteed, and the Final Plan had to be closely coordinated with the special programs of the Authority.

The Neighborhood Redevelopment Commission (described in Chapter 6), the Chicago Park District (a partially autonomous local government), and the Chicago Zoning Board of Appeals complete this skeleton outline of the municipal governmental units most directly involved in influencing the Hyde Park–Kenwood Urban Renewal Plan and the projects associated with it.

We have tried to make two points, essentially, in presenting this descriptive outline. First, authority within the Chicago city government over the fate of a renewal plan is divided among a number of officials and agencies; at this date (1959) this division is still undergoing change. Secondly, this authority structure certainly may be labeled as decentralized, insofar as power is diffuse, controls are contradictory and shifting, and even ultimate authority is divided between the Democratic Party, the City Council, and the Office of the Mayor.

The political wisdom embodied in this complex, decentralized authority structure, however, is not sufficiently appreciated by those who propose reorganization. The complexity imposes a heavy overhead of time and resources in "getting things done" through city hall, but the same complexity opens to the citizen a variety of municipal avenues through which assistance may be obtained. Citizen groups with sufficient vigor, such as the South East Chicago Commission and the Hyde Park–Kenwood Community Conference, are free to tackle their problems through a wide variety of political agencies that, when marshaled under a unifying local plan, amount to formidable resources for action.

The decentralized condition also introduces some confusion and uncertainty into the decision-making process, but at the same time it provides for enhanced flexibility to both local actors and city hall. The *rigor mortis* common to so many bureaucracies, for example, is in this structure distributed among the single units. When rigidity is confronted in one unit, response to imaginative proposals may be available in another. Most important, before a decision is reached, decentralized organization guarantees that all interests will be heard that seek a hearing. Proof of this last feature is offered in the remainder of this chapter.

The Office of the Mayor

Under the conditions of this type of city government, the Office of the Mayor is well situated to make a choice of its own between support or neglect of a renewal proposal. Mayor Richard Daley has this aphorism printed on a large card placed in a corner of his office: "When I'm right, no one remembers. When I'm wrong, no one forgets." However true this may be of a metropolitan mayor's office, it is also true that the Mayor is somewhat free to choose to be neither right nor wrong. The Mayor may galvanize his vast organizational resources on behalf of a proposal, or he may let the proponents of the plan themselves carry it to his commissions, departments, and boards. Not even this choice needs to be final; it may instead be a matter of degree.

Mayor Kennelly had strongly endorsed policies favoring expansion of housing and planned reconstruction of the city, but, unlike Mayor Daley, he reputedly espoused the role of a "weak mayor—" meaning that he fostered full decentralization of authority during his regime.[6] Though under Kennelly (as we

---

6. Cf. Meyerson and Banfield, *op. cit.,* pp. 61-88 (ch. 3).

reported in Chapter 4) the University of Chicago, the South East Chicago Commission, and the Community Conference obtained a kind of broad go-ahead signal from the Office of the Mayor, the difficulties experienced in obtaining passage of the Redevelopment Proposal within the City Council demonstrated that Kennelly's support was comparatively passive.[7] Mayor Daley's decision on the Hyde Park proposal for renewal apparently was to direct his administration to work with the community without immediately or directly committing himself to all-out support. City hall was "made available"; its offices were opened to the reception of local and "downtown" proponents.

Mayor Daley did more than open his facilities to local interests in Hyde Park and Kenwood, however. He accepted the broad commitment made by Kennelly and went several steps further. First, Daley brought to life the Community Conservation Board. This agency had been created by act of the City Council under Mayor Kennelly's regime in 1954, but, typically, Kennelly did not make appointments of staff until October, 1955, when General Richard Smykal was appointed full-time Commissioner.

According to experienced observers, had the Hyde Park–Kenwood project been delayed until the Conservation Board put together a staff, it would still be in the preliminary stage. That there were some political reasons for such a delay can be seen from some of the criticisms raised about contracting the planning function. These criticisms reached a climax when in 1957 Alderman Claude Holman of the 4th Ward (which includes Kenwood) challenged the wisdom of the city's contract with the Planning Unit of the University of Chicago. Before the City Council Holman charged that the city was turning over excessive authority to a private institution. The City Council passed a resolution that if the Conservation Board intends to engage an outside planner, the Alderman of the ward concerned and the City Council should be advised.

Mayor Daley apparently did not involve himself much

7. Mayor Edward J. Kelly, Kennelly's predecessor, had been a very strong mayor, with undisputed control of the city's Democratic Party and of Cook County. Kennelly's style of leadership was apparently a reaction to the fourteen years of boss rule which preceded him.

beyond this preliminary support for the Hyde Park project during his first two years in office.[8] With publication of the Preliminary Plan, and the wide national and metropolitan publicity that attended it, the city administration became more convinced of the general significance of the project. Strong local involvement was also assured—an assurance which stands as one of the great achievements of the citizen participation through the Community Conference.

Accordingly, "downtown" interest in the project grew. Daley took two additional steps toward facilitating the renewal plan. In appointing the Conservation Community Council, the first to be organized in Illinois, he still left some power on the local scene in taking this step, for (as we have seen in Chapter 5) the appointments to the Council were made by the Mayor from a list agreed upon by the Committee of Six. Secondly, he organized an informal Mayor's coordinating committee to over- see renewal programing for the city as a whole. Symbolizing his concern with the success of renewal projects, he assumed leadership of this committee.

The Mayor's informal committee consisted of the Com- missioner of the Department of Buildings, Phil A. Doyle of the Land Clearance Commission, two representatives from the newly formed Department of City Planning, James Downs and D. E. Mackelmann from the Coordinator's Office, the Executive Director of the Chicago Housing Authority, and one of the Mayor's assistants. From 1957 on, this group met about twice monthly for about one and a half hours a session. Significantly, the committee undertook its own field work, going out to local neighborhoods—including Hyde Park—to study conservation problems at first hand. In Mayor Daley's own words, "This committee and my administration as a whole has given high priority to problems and opportunities for renewal."

8. Two other supports should be cited. Daley activated the Neighborhood Redevelopment Commission under the direction of one of the city's most experienced planning administrators, D. E. Mackelmann, to review and approve the proposals of the South West Hyde Park Neighborhood Rede- velopment Corporation in 1956. Daley also actively endorsed Redevelop- ment Project Number One in the City Council, action which Kennelly did not take as forcefully. Thus, Daley assisted in the birth of Chicago's first redevelopment corporation project and he implemented redevelopment of "Hyde Park A and B." Neither support committed the Mayor to direct leadership in passage of the Final Renewal Plan, however.

In a municipal government organized like Chicago's, the Office of the Mayor assumes the role of "signal giver." The Mayor can establish priorities to which underfinanced and undermanned administrative units then turn for a clear definition of immediate goals. Until 1957 the Office of the Mayor for the most part encouraged but did not itself directly oversee renewal efforts in Hyde Park–Kenwood. After 1957 the Office of the Mayor continued to encourage local efforts and established a high priority for the project within city hall, though it did not identify itself directly with the fate of the project.

The Political Stakes

Perhaps Mayor Daley and his advisors underestimated the political value of strong identification with renewal objectives during their early months in office. Chicago was experienced in land-clearance operations in blighted areas, but the politics of public housing had proved dangerously rich with conflict for Mayor Kennelly. Since conservation renewal was totally untried before 1955, Mayor Daley may have been understandably cautious about direct engagement in this arena when he first took office.

Hyde Park is not Chicago's most problematic neighborhood, as Chapter 2 reveals. There are many blighted areas in much greater need of redevelopment, and many conservation areas in equal or more serious need of renewal. This was fairly well understood within the city government, which meant that the mayor's support of renewal in Hyde Park–Kenwood could easily be misinterpreted. It might have appeared to some that one community less in need than others was to use up a large part of Chicago's share of federal funds for renewal. The Mayor might easily be accused of neglecting the fair share of other locales. However, this criticism was unlikely to arise, since no other local community had arrived at a point where it was ready to have application made for it by the city for federal funds. In terms of his record as a mayor capable of renewing Chicago, some strong advantage would lie with execution of the Hyde Park–Kenwood Plan, for this was the only conservation project that stood a chance of being realized as more than a proposal during his four-year term of office.

In another way, renewal in Hyde Park amounted to a peculiar opportunity for close rapprochement between groups ordinarily rather cool and distant from one another in Chicago —the professional party officialdom represented by the Mayor and a powerful private university represented by trustees drawn from business corporations and the professions. As we have shown, the basis for cooperation had been laid by Mayor Kennelly. Unique and advantageous as this must have appeared to party officials at the time, it was certainly worth sustaining and insuring by Mayor Daley.

These considerations added up to a problem in strategy for the mayor—how to negotiate decisions that would satisfy both local and metropolitan interests at once. This problem is perhaps easily understood from the testimony given by Mrs. Anneta Deackmann, who spoke before the Council Committee on Housing and Planning as a representative of the North Kenwood Oakland Community Conference, a group centered on the border of the planning area:

We are getting a great many relocated persons in our area from various city projects already underway. Building ordinances are being enforced in our community, which is too dense already. . . . More housing should be retained in the Hyde Park–Kenwood Plan. . . . Existing housing needs to be conserved in Chicago. An open occupancy policy throughout the city is needed. Other old neighborhoods need conserving also.

Woven through this abbreviated testimony are references to the special needs of Mrs. Deackmann's community. On top of these are placed references to over-all metropolitan requirements, such as the need for more housing and for open occupancy.

We shall return to consideration of some of the issues in greater detail. Our point here is that Mayor Daley repeatedly made it clear that he intended to "hold the reins" over the eventual decision on the Final Plan. His strategy, however, was to facilitate the decision-making process and yet to remain ready at all times to gallop or dismount. It was therefore widely publicized throughout 1958, in the press and through government officials, that Mayor Daley favored conservation of Hyde Park–Kenwood. Whether he would intervene in the City Council

in the event the ordinance appeared about to be rejected remained an open question until the last week of the negotiation.

The "Cut-Back"

In mid-July, 1958, two months before City Council's final
deliberation over the ordinance approving application for federal renewal funds, the Community Conservation Board sud-
denly and unexpectedly shifted its position and announced its
intention to "cut back" the request in the Final Plan for $29.8
million from the federal government to about $26 million. The
manner in which this took place within the city government
reveals much about the workings of this complicated structure.

Groups anxious to influence the content of the Final Plan
had to allocate their limited resources wisely. Both supporters
and opponents, local and metropolitan—like participants in
any decision—knew that timing was essential to securing a voice
in the ultimate decision. One of the most effective moments
for action was the point immediately after the Final Plan was
approved at the local level by the Conservation Community
Council and transmitted to the Conservation Board. While
numerous groups could boast of a history of active involvement dating back to formation of the Planning Unit, many
others could give full attention to the issue only toward the
final phases of decision-making.

Some of these—such as the Hyde Park Chapter of the
National Association for the Advancement of Colored People,
the Tenants and Home Owners Association, and individual property owners anxious to save their properties from demolition—
were strictly local actors. They were also limited by their slim
memberships and resources.

Other actors—such as the Cardinal's Committee on Conservation and the Urban League—were interested in securing a
voice in the decision over the plan but, as metropolitan organizations, could give only limited priority to the negotiations. Conse-
quently, opposition to the plan became vocal when in April,
1958, the Final Plan was approved by the Conservation Council.
Similarly, supporters of the plan heightened their campaign
for passage at this time—not only in reaction to new voices
of resistance but because the plan was leaving the local com-

munity, about to face the vicissitudes of the City Council.

The Cardinal's Committee (discussed in Chapter 8), through Monsignors Egan and Kelly, opened its program of criticism of the plan during April. By mid-May, 1958, opposition groups generally had mobilized their members and their resources. Monsignor Egan announced "three principles that I consider absolutely essential to a successful urban renewal program." "First," he said, "urban renewal must be part of our democratic process." Making this point, Monsignor Egan challenged the representativeness of the Conservation Community Council and indirectly accused it of acting as a "rubber stamp for smaller, tactfully silent groups which actually control the planning." His other two principles concerned an appeal for provision of low- and middle-income housing and guarantees for equitable relocation procedures.

The Chicago *Defender*, the largest Negro newspaper in the nation, had withheld its opinions on the question of the plan, aside from occasional feature stories, news reports, and jibes by columnists. Less than a week after Monsignor Egan's speech before the Association of Community Councils on May 22, the *Defender* published its decisive editorial under the title "Urban Renewal for Whom?" The two arguments against the plan in its current form were:

First, low and middle income housing both private and public, is in short supply in the city of Chicago, and secondly, the prevailing pattern of segregation denies Negroes free access to the housing market.

Clearance as proposed in Hyde Park–Kenwood, the *Defender* concluded, would displace Negroes who will be able to be rehoused only in the "already overcrowded ghettoes." The editorial asserted that new housing will be so costly as to literally price Negroes out of the local market. The editorial implication was unmistakable, playing on two of the themes to which municipal office holders would be most sensitive. Would not this plan benefit most of those people least in need of federal assistance? The *Defender* asserted that it would unless revised. Second, was not the plan unfairly neglectful of lower class and Negro housing needs in the city as a whole?

At the same time in late May, 1958, the Tenants and Home Owners Association in a series of paid advertisements in the *Herald* spelled out its two themes of dissent:

The Plan has never and *does not now* provide for . . . middle income housing. It says only three sites "may become available" . . . in part or in whole. . . . The Community Conservation Board . . . has made no formal request for CHA (public housing) and CDA (middle income) units. . . . THE REAL PURPOSE OF THE RENEWAL PLAN IS TO CREATE AN UPPER INCOME COMMUNITY!

Other voices of opposition could be heard elsewhere—from the Garfield Park–Austin Community Council, the Chicago Urban League, the N.A.A.C.P., and the policy unit of the C.I.O. Packinghouse Workers Union.

At first the brunt of the opposition was borne locally. The Conservation Community Council heard from all the dissenting voices. When it had finished its hearings and presented an approved version of the Final Plan, the target of opposition forces moved "downtown." It was at this point that the opposition appeared in greatest strength. From the viewpoint of the municipal administration, this was the point of decision. Should the plan receive firm support from the Mayor's office, should it be allowed to go through without strong support, or should it be opposed by the Mayor? The answer to this question depended on the political costs incurred by each alternative.

The advantages of supporting the renewal plan were very well known and had formed the basis for the considerable support the municipal administration had given to renewal efforts. But the strength and determination of the opposition were not known; to ascertain these factors was the next move of the administration. The important political device in the hands of the administration was timing, the scheduling of decisions.

To encourage plan supporters, the Mayor's Office repeatedly announced from April to July that the Final Plan would be brought before the City Council "within a few weeks." To "satisfy" opponents of the plan, the Mayor began to negotiate a reduction in the amount of funds to be employed in the Final Plan. In April, 1958, Mayor Daley indicated the plan would probably be presented to the City Council in May. Late in May he announced that he planned to schedule a special summer session in June or July to obtain a Council vote. By July the administration had achieved enough delay to secure local as well as city-wide likelihood of consensus on the content of the Plan, and within one month the ordinance came before the Council.

The "cut-back" in funds, then, apparently was devised as a way of satisfying opponents of the plan, particularly the Cardinal's Committee, whose strength had been estimated as significant enough to require careful negotiating. It was clear in May and June that Catholic and other interest groups were continuing to build up strong resistance to the Hyde Park–Kenwood Final Plan. It was also the case that some banks and mortgage houses in the city, who had a stake in the plan, were convinced that the amount of proposed federal expenditures should be reduced, asserting that the total amount of money available for reconstruction in Hyde Park would not be enough to use up the land to be released by the demolition called for in the plan. The administration promptly made its own political "soundings," and then the Mayor called a special meeting of his informal coordinating committee. Commissioner Holland appeared before the committee with suggestions for suitable compromises.

The compromise "cut-back" suggested involved removal from the plan of twelve buildings originally scheduled for demolition and elimination of plans to widen 47th Street, the northern boundary of the planning site. One of the buildings removed from the demolition list was owned by the Chicago Transit Authority. The results of this meeting were announced to the press as decisions made by the Conservation Board at a "meeting called by the Mayor to resolve the impasse which had arisen because of differences among the city agencies involved."

The Community Conservation Board itself assumed responsibility for proposed elimination of the street widening, but its position was strengthened by a letter from the City Department of Streets and Sanitation, stating that it had reconsidered its earlier agreement to this proposal and found it could not "endorse proposed expenditure of department funds for this program at the present time." A letter from the Chicago Transit Authority was also released, announcing that it had reviewed the proposed acquisition of its property on Cottage Grove

Avenue and had decided this property was "essential to its future operations."

News of this proposed compromise was released during the first week in July, 1958. The releases included the explanation that Commissioner Holland had asked for a special session of the local Conservation Community Council to discuss the "cut-back," but that this request had been refused "only hours before the time it [the Council] was slated to convene" (*Herald*, July 9, 1958). Responsibility was thus also redirected toward the local authorities and away from the Office of the Mayor.

The Conservation Community Council finally met on July 21, three weeks after the "cut-back" proposal had been announced. This delay gave all interested parties time to develop their cases and to bring pressure to bear on the Council. It also gave the Mayor's administration a period in which to lay a firm basis for political consensus in the larger metropolitan community.

For example, between July 9 and 20, the Office of the Mayor and various administrative units under it made several announcements in the daily papers.

On July 16 the *Herald* quoted from the city department memorandum:

At a meeting this afternoon, the Chicago Housing Authority Commissioners, who are also Directors of the Chicago Dwellings Association, met to consider the formulation of a policy requesting that sites cleared by the urban renewal program to be made available for low and middle income housing. Alvin H. Rose, executive director of the CHA and CDA, stated it is already a matter of record that the agencies want to engage in middle income housing programs in Hyde Park–Kenwood. The meeting today is being held to establish this view as a matter of official policy and to explore avenues to cooperation with other agencies.

The same news story included reports of plans to build by two other middle-income organizations, the University Neighborhood Homes group and the Cooperative Homes of Hyde Park, Inc.

A week later the CHA announced its achievement of a firm policy agreement to be ready to build low- and middle-income housing in Hyde Park and Kenwood "to such extent as those facilities may be deemed, by the cognizant parties, to be of value in adding to the supply of housing for moderate income residents in the Hyde Park–Kenwood neighborhood" (*Herald,* July 16, 1958; quoted from CHA memo).

In addition, the Community Conservation Board gave strengthened publicity to its actions on behalf of nine designated conservation areas in the city. It publicized the plans for a Near West Side project that were announced as "ready in about a month" for presentation to the City Council. They advertised achievements in several neighborhoods surrounding Hyde Park–Kenwood, including Englewood, where they announced plans to set aside $7 million in federal funds for renewal work, and West Woodlawn, which was newly designated as a conservation area.

Except on the issue of relocation, the municipal administration thus attempted to meet almost every widely circulated objection to the renewal plan. Without direct commitment, it was made apparent that the amount of demolition would be reduced, that public and private low- and middle-income housing would be included, that surrounding neighborhoods would not experience further deterioration because of renewal in Hyde Park–Kenwood, and that other neighborhoods would also receive renewal funds.

The Conservation Community Council met for five hours over the "cut-back" compromise on the evening of July 21, 1958. At the outset of the meeting James Downs, acting as special assistant to Mayor Daley, presented the case on behalf of the cut. After extended exchanges between Council members and Downs, the city government officials present—three Conservation Board commissioners, Assistant Commissioner Donald Hanson, and a few other aides—left the conference, and the Council went into private session. Following the executive session, the Conservation Board Commissioners were called back and presented with the terms the Council had decided upon. Agreement was reached within the Council on a "cut-back" smaller in size than that proposed by the Conservation Board. This was presented to the Board Commissioners, who accepted the compromise agreement immediately by formal vote.

In reaching its decision, the Conservation Community Council noted the letters from the Chicago Transit Authority, which said it could not afford to relinquish its local garage, and the Department of Streets and Sanitation, which said it could not widen 47th Street. David Sutton, Council Chairman, had also distributed copies of twenty-five letters he had received from many citizens and organizations concerning the "cut-back." All twenty-five opposed making any of the proposed "cut-backs."

James Downs had given assurances during his presentation to the Council that 47th Street would be widened by the city eventually, probably as a municipal highway expenditure rather than through the renewal plan. Downs also emphasized—and the Council later recognized the importance of—"saving face for Mayor Daley." Rejection of the proposed "cut-backs," said Downs, would be "politically embarrassing" to the mayor, since he had endorsed them publicly. Commissioner Holland and James Downs both emphasized that if some or all of the "cut-backs" could be accepted, the plan could be "sped" through the city government.

Downs also said a wide variety of opposition had developed against aspects of the Hyde Park–Kenwood renewal plan, and that the proposed "cut-backs" would help to reduce this opposition and to enlist new support.

As one highly experienced respondent summarized the negotiations over the "cut-back": "Of the cutbacks that were accepted, none were of any direct or institutional concern to the members of the Conservation Community Council. They accepted about half of the proposed revisions. The ones they accepted were those they didn't care much about personally."

The original "cut-back" proposal issued by the Community Conservation Board had called for reduction of the total federal and city investment in the amount of nearly $4 million. The formal compromise reached agreed to eliminate $1.8 million from the federal application and $600,000 from the municipal investment—together slightly more than half of the original cut-back suggested.

In summary, we conclude that Mayor Daley and his executive assistants attempted to meet objections to the renewal plan by reducing the size of the project. The "cut-back" was an answer to two objections raised by the opposition: that undeteriorated buildings were scheduled for demolition, and that the project was getting too large a share of the $10 million city bond issue to be used for general city renewal. In addition, to answer the objections that the language in the original plan did not provide sufficient guarantees to protect properties not already slated for demolition, the compromise agreement stated: "Buildings which are in conformance with the city code standards will not be acquired, with the exception of buildings where a public use is contemplated."

Knowing that the Conservation Community Council had earlier voted down proposals by a minority of its own members that public housing should be included in the plan, the administration attempted to meet the low- and middle-income housing issue above the local level, through the Chicago Housing Authority, as we have shown. This question was not reintroduced before the Conservation Community Council.

The Hyde Park–Kenwood Community Conference, the Independent Voters of Illinois, the Northwest Hyde Park Redevelopment Corporation, and other local groups had vigorously opposed the proposed "cut-backs." They were not at all gratified by the compromise, but their activities were immediately redirected after it was announced. Sensing that the plan, reduced but slightly by the compromise, would now have direct support from the Mayor's Office before the City Council, they stopped working to restore "cut-backs" and concentrated on preparation of testimony for the City Council's public hearings. A week after the compromise was reached, the Conservation Board transmitted the proposal to the City Council.

Opposing groups—particularly the Cardinal's Committee, the National Association for the Advancement of Colored People, and the Tenants and Home Owners Association—were equally unsatisfied by the "cut-backs," and they announced their dissatisfaction publicly. The Cardinal's Committee emphasized that the compromise did nothing to reduce "the haste" with which the plan was being forwarded, and nothing about integrating the plan into a comprehensive renewal program for the city as a whole.

Ironically, plan proponents criticized the "cut-back" for one set of reasons and opponents for another; yet the "cut-back" took the political heat out of conflicts between the two sides and to a significant degree neutralized the remainder of the decision-making process. The Cardinal's Committee was neither satisfied nor mollified by the token "cut-back," but the action made their additional demands appear excessive.

Significance of the "Cut-Back"

As a "strong" mayor who was fairly certain of wide and strong local support for the renewal of Hyde Park–Kenwood, Mayor Daley probably could have secured passage of the Final Plan by April, 1958, at the very latest. He had merely to mobilize his administration. The timing of decisions was very largely within his hands. He chose instead to delay the process in an effort to increase city-wide support for the plan and to negotiate to a point where the opposition was effectively neutralized.

This choice of tactic is best understood in two ways. Mayor Daley would be facing re-election (or election for a different office) in the winter of 1959, and in September, one month after the Conservation Council agreement on the "cut-back," he was elected Vice President of the United States Conference of Mayors, where renewal was the primary political business of the day. At the Conference of Mayors, partly through Mayor Daley's leadership, a resolution was passed urging Congress to make urban renewal and slum clearance its first order of legislative business in January, 1959. Thus, the Mayor not only needed to secure passage of the nation's first experiment in conservation renewal; he wanted to secure it with overwhelming support.

To this end, the Office of the Mayor centralized all governmental controls over the Hyde Park–Kenwood proposal. Yet responsibility for actions remained decentralized, and antagonism thus diverted from the Mayor to the various administrative agencies. Issues surrounding the proposal were left to be resolved at the local level, in the hands of the Conservation Community Council. But announcements of compromise and achievement were made by the Community Conservation Board, the Chicago Housing Authority, and other city agencies.

Only once in the "cut-back" incident did Mayor Daley intervene publicly, and he then played the role of resolving differences between his several administrative units through wise compromise. Without visiting the Conservation Community Council, he negotiated through his deputy James Downs. Yet he was quoted publicly on repeated occasions as favoring the Final Plan and its rapid approval.

As a political expedient, the "cut-back" was in one sense a failure: it did not bring to an end the conflcts between supporters and opponents. After its announcement, Mayor Daley had still not completely satisfied the Cardinal's Committee, the Negro defense organizations, and the Packinghouse Workers Union. The questions surrounding inclusion of low- and middle-income housing continued to be posed by supporters and opponents alike, and the relocation issue continued to burn brightly.[9] The most important accomplishment of the "cut-back" compromise was neutralization of two important criticisms: that the proposal called for excessive demolition to the neglect of city housing needs, and that properties left standing were threatened under the language of the proposal by eventual acquisition and demolition. By and large, neither of these complaints was heard loudly again following the "cut-back."

In demonstrating how a strong mayor working in a complex decentralized governmental structure may amplify citizen influence, the story of the "cut-back" is an instructive one. It is true that within Hyde Park–Kenwood the Conservation Community Council held seven public hearings during 1957, preliminary to deliberating over the Final Plan, that the Council also held two additional public hearings before its final vote on the Plan in March, 1958, and that publicity about the renewal plans had been extensive. Nonetheless, the proposal remained a paper proposal of only local interest until it was transferred from the Conservation Community Council to the city hall "downtown."

9. On August 6 and 7, 1958, Eric Lund wrote feature articles in the Chicago *Daily News* entitled "Get Moving! The Story of Chicago's DP's." While it dealt with relocatees generally and with those moved for expressway construction in particular, it struck a very strong note of public sympathy: "This is a story of displaced persons. It's a story of people—Americans—made homeless not by war or communism or disaster but by wreckers. . . . These are Chicago's DP's . . . refugees of the relocation that inevitably accompanies redevelopment. They are people, angry, indifferent, resentful, resigned. . . . In Chicago alone some 131,000 persons will be uprooted this year (by one estimate) and next and forced to find new homes."

At this point the city government was so designed and its strong mayor so constituted that the widest possible public involvement was stimulated without sacrificing the chances for survival of the renewal project itself. Of course, Planner Jack Meltzer had appeared before the joint meeting of the Conservation Board Commissioners and the Conservation Council to explain how each proposed cut would militate against the best planning interests of the project.

But, as Chapter 3 considered in detail, in the matter of public housing—as in a vast array of small plan changes in North West Hyde Park, and as with the content of the plan generally—citizens, institutions, agencies, and mayor alike were centrally identified with the desirability of a renewal project in Hyde Park–Kenwood. Detailed contents of the plan rarely became salient, except in the over-all sense of whether its scope should be enlarged to include public housing or reduced in amount of demolition and schedule for relocation.

Mayor Daley and the Final Hour

The "cut-back" agreement was reached on July 21, with the tacit understanding that the Final Plan would be brought promptly before the City Council. However, conflicts still raged around the issues of housing, relocation, and racial aspects of the project. The Plan was not submitted to the Council by Commissioner J. Paul Holland until September 9, 1958, more than a month later. At that time Commissioner Holland's news release, moreover, stressed that "Thirteen other technical steps must be taken before the renewal program reaches the clearance and construction stage" (Chicago *Daily News*, September 10, 1958, p. 52). He predicted, "it will be at least three months before a final contract is signeed by city and federal officials."

This, then, was a continuation of the tactic of cautious timing. In the Mayor's own release on the same release of the Plan to the City Council, he expressed "hopes the Council can take final action on the project by the end of this month or early October" (*Sun-Times*, September 9, 1958, p. 21), thus making public a new time schedule.

Two new strategic features had been added to the political

situation during August. The United States House of Representatives on August 18 defeated a $1 billion housing bill that was expected to provide Chicago with funds for a six-year renewal and redevelopment program to relieve it of year-to-year project efforts. On August 22 the Department of City Planning released the "Central Area Plan," also known as the "Daley Plan," designed to revitalize downtown Chicago over a period of from ten to twenty years. This $1 billion plan coincided with news releases concerning several other planning projects sponsored by the Mayor, and preceded his departure for the national Conference of Mayors.

Congressional defeat of a new housing bill made it even more imperative that approval of the Hyde Park–Kenwood proposal be secured. While funds for this were already safely earmarked from the 1954 federal legislation and the 1957 appropriation, the chances of obtaining future funds for additional conservation had been severely narrowed for the time being.

This "breathing spell" of nearly two months netted two particularly significant changes in the local political situation concerning the fate of the renewal project. Cardinal Stritch, founder of the Cardinal's Committee on Conservation, died in Rome during the summer. In the period of organizational uncertainty within the diocese that followed, the Cardinal's Committee on Conservation began to lose its power as the single spokesman for the Church on renewal issues. Ambiguities of authority and representation developed from within, while attacks against the views of the committee intensified outside Church circles.

Of lesser importance, the National Association for the Advancement of Colored People dissolved its Hyde Park Chapter and two other neighborhood units on September 6. In addition to continuously opposing aspects of the project, the Hyde Park chapter had a month earlier launched a campaign seeking signatures of local residents on petitions calling upon the Mayor and the city to modify the Urban Renewal Plan. The Hyde Park Chapter called for inclusion of public and middle-income housing and improved relocation regulations.

Theodore A. Jones, Chicago N.A.A.C.P. President, told the press, "The three units . . . frequently operated without complete sanction of the parent branch, and were eliminated so that the board could have a firmer grip on all city-wide activities." Since he had taken office (nine months earlier, in January, 1958) Jones announced, "Some of the neighborhood units failed to cooperate with the parent body by engaging in program activities and releasing unauthorized statements to the press" (*Tribune*, September 7, 1958, part 3, p. 1). Reactions within Hyde Park by members were extremely critical, and several ex-members published letters in the papers asserting that the dissolution concerned the Chapter's actions in opposition to the Urban Renewal Plan.

According to Theodore Jones himself, the point of disagreement with the Hyde Park Chapter was the fact that it made public its views on the Plan without checking with the Chicago Branch. Chapter views and Chicago Branch views, claimed Jones, differed only in that the Hyde Park unit did not make its call for modifications in the Plan precise enough. The Chicago Branch used many of the arguments and most of the facts assembled by the Chapter in its City Council testimony. They too called chiefly for low-income housing and improved relocation regulations. Moreover, the Chicago Branch of the N.A.A.C.P. lobbied with about a fifth of the City Councilmen on behalf of its proposed changes.

From the point of view of city politics, however, N.A.A.C.P. opposition to the Urban Renewal Plan was comparatively neutralized by dissolution of the Hyde Park Chapter. Also, Theodore Jones was a Kenwood resident and a former member of the Hyde Park–Kenwood Community Conference Board of Directors. This suggested to all concerned that one crucial segment of organized Negro leadership could be expected to consent to approval of the Urban Renewal Plan with only minor reservations. Jones' assertion of leadership during the "breathing spell" allowed politicians to make this assumption.

As we shall demonstrate, opposition to the Plan as it was when transmitted to the City Council in September became, as a result of this period of neutralization, so feeble as to be insignificant except from within the City Council and from the Cardinal's Committee on Conservation. Nevertheless, the Mayor maintained a schedule of caution and did not intervene to speed up City Council deliberations. Council review continued from

September through October 21, 1958, involving more than a month of Housing and Planning Committee meetings, public hearings, and debate.

On October 20 Mayor Daley urged approval of the plan "in its present form," adding that "After that there can be negotiation with various agencies for changes to meet objections. . . ." He explained: "The difficulty is, that the city council has not power to amend, but can only reject or approve this. Rejection by the council would be not only a blow to the city, but a setback for urban renewal on a nationwide basis." If the council rejected the plan, Daley claimed, then the "laborious process" of preparing a new plan would have to be started. He added that some way could be found later to provide public and middle income housing for the area (*Tribune*, October 21, 1958).

The Mayor's statement did not specify all the alternatives open to the Council. The Council Committee on Housing and Planning could return the Plan to the Community Conservation Board after the public hearings, but before action of the Council as a whole, with instructions to make changes. It could recommend a joint meeting between the Conservation Board, the Council Committee, and the Hyde Park Conservation Community Council. A legislative body obviously can suggest revisions in proposals of administrative agencies and their advisory councils.

But the statement by Mayor Daley was a signal for decision. It pointed the path to be taken: approval and later negotiation over details. The Mayor had been the first witness to appear before the Council Committee on behalf of the Plan. He was also the last, for on the day following his request for immediate approval, the Housing and Planning Committee voted unanimously to approve the Plan. On November 7, only a few days later (measured in aldermanic time), the City Council voted forty-four to nothing to approve the Urban Renewal Plan, after Mayor Daley had praised the project as a great experiment and promised that "relocation of displaced persons will be handled with humanity" (*Tribune*, November 8, 1958, part 1, p. 3).

The Special Role of the Alderman

With respect to influence, the City Council as a whole was of limited importance aside from completion of its formal task of a vote of approval. Alderman Claude Holman (Fourth Ward, Kenwood), for example, who was not a member of the Housing and Planning Committee, participated publicly at only one point during the two months of deliberations. Before the final Council vote, he spoke for two minutes to endorse the Plan.[10] Lobbying was minimal, and such as did occur was directed for the most part at members of the Housing and Planning Committee.

The Council's Committee on Housing and Planning performed some noteworthy functions on behalf of public involvement, however. They conducted extended public hearings, at which all testimony was received with great dignity, seriousness, and interest. The committee heard from spokesmen for the widest possible range of individual and organizational interests. Public sessions frequently ran from 10:00 a.m. until the late hours of the evening, and Committee members attended session after session faithfully. Five members of the fifteen-man Committee were especially active in questioning speakers, and all were vocal in expressions of interest and concern with particulars.

This drama of democratic, legislative process was so effectively enacted that the Council Chambers where the hearings were held were fairly well filled with Chicagoans—most of them Hyde Parkers—during nearly every session. Both the core of criticisms of the Urban Renewal Plan and the extent of endorsement became perfectly clear during these hearings. The extent of endorsement—roughly three out of four spokesmen testified for approval of the Plan in its present form—indicated that the Plan had extremely substantial backing from metropolitan and local groups and institutions. The core of criticisms concerned appeals for the inclusion of public and

---

10. In September Alderman Holman had been privately active in attempting to secure a low-density, row-house public housing project in the 4th Ward facing Cottage Grove Avenue, adjacent to the Renewal Plan area. Some groups had expected to hear him appeal for inclusion of public housing in his speech of endorsement before the Council.

middle-income housing and improved guarantees on relocation procedures, particularly to prevent relocation into already overcrowded neighborhoods, to prevent administrative neglect, and to avoid discrimination.

The sentiment of the more vocal members of the Council Committee on Housing and Planning also became manifest to any observer during the hearings. They felt the Plan should be modified to meet the core of criticisms, and they appeared to resent the notion that nothing could be done to modify the Plan in this final stage. When spokesmen for the Plan testified in favor of its approval without modification, for example, any one of the five most vocal Committee members would challenge the testimony courteously.

Typical is the instance when Lloyd G. Allen spoke for the Ridgewood Court Block Group (Hyde Park). He recommended immediate acceptance of the Plan without any changes. Alderman William Harvey then questioned Allen about specific houses in the Ridgewood Court block. Harvey asserted that in Redevelopment Project Number One ("A and B") some houses had been demolished and others left standing, though all had seemed to be roughly in the same state of repair and were occupied by their owners. Harvey said he could not approve of owner-occupied houses being torn down for institutional expansion, as was the case in the present plan.

In another instance, Rabbi Ralph Simon, testifying for the Rodfei Zedek Temple of East Hyde Park, stated his congregation supported the plan; he said that the plan would hurt some people but was necessary. He urged that its passage not be delayed further, even if it was imperfect. Alderman Harvey said he agreed that time was of the essence, but then went on: ". . . why can't the Community Conservation Board take care of modifying the Plan in twenty-four hours, simply by further specifying the use of land already scheduled for residential re-use—which would not mean the plan would have to be sent back to Washington?" While we have given examples drawn from Alderman William Harvey's questioning, these represent the tone and intent of questions posed as well by Aldermen Petrone, DuBois, William Murphy, and Leon Despres.[11]

---

11. Alderman Harvey, however, was most critical of the Urban Renewal Plan, or expressed the greatest doubts. When a spokesman for the Greater

On the other hand, testimony opposing the Renewal Plan and demanding certain changes was very courteously and sympathetically received, with Committee members inquiring repeatedly whether inclusion of public and middle-income housing and better relocation guarantees would make approval of the existing Plan satisfactory.

In addition to numerous individual property owners and residents and five block groups, opposition was most coherently and uniformly expressed by the following groups, all of whom shared the criticisms on housing and relocation: The Chicago Urban League, the National Association for the Advancement of Colored People, the Cardinal's Committee on Conservation, the Communist Party of Illinois, the Tenants and Home Owners Association, the C.I.O. Cook County Industrial Union Council, the Chicago Institute of Social Welfare, five community organizations similar to the Hyde Park–Kenwood Community Conference but located in surrounding neighborhoods, and the United Packinghouse Workers Union.

The position taken by Hyde Park Alderman Leon Despres in a way represented the middle-ground criticism of the Plan which developed in the hearings. Three days before the hearings began Despres sent the following letter to Mayor Daley:

In your statement, I know that you will want to anticipate and deal with the serious comments that have been made on the plan, and I would very much like to ask you to do so. I certainly do not refer to the persons who have simply opposed the plan. I refer to the rather widespread comments from a great many fine and reputable sources that the plan should make adequate provision for: 1) *Middle-income housing* by way of Chicago Dwellings Association. I think it would be most helpful to strike an affirmative note about definite arrangements . . . for such property. 2) *Low-income housing.* As you know, there are many people, starting with the Hyde Park–Kenwood Community Conference . . . who feel that there should be scheduled

---

Lawndale Conservation Commission testified that his group intended, as a designated conservation area, to use the Plan as a model, Harvey asked what they would do in Lawndale with "all the people, if all conservation areas lower their populaton densities?" Claude Peck, the spokesman, replied he had been working on a self-help program, and Harvey replied, "That's what block groups did in Hyde Park. These people were duped," since their properties were now scheduled for demolition. "Who then is safe?" Harvey asked.

small, attractive public housing . . . at least as a moral token. . . . I think it would be most constructive . . . if you could deal with this. 3) *Relocation.* I think that you would be able in your statement to cover this extremely well. . . . I know that these questions are going to be brought up, because they have been hammered on so often by so many fine and reputable persons in addition to persons who have used them as a cloak for opposing all urban renewal . . . they have also been brought up in the utmost good faith . . . your support . . . will be enhanced by straightforward dealing in anticipation rather than after the fact.

If Mayor Daley heeded this advice at all, it was only on the matter of relocation, about which he promised effective and humane administration. This letter heralded Despres' own tactics in the City Council and the Housing and Planning Committee. Before the close of the first day of hearings it became clear that Despres was taking every opportunity to press for inclusion of the sought-for housing provisions. Despres persuaded, cross-examined, and challenged speaker after speaker —from Commissioner J. Paul Holland of the Conservation Board, Chancellor Lawrence Kimpton, and Julian Levi to groups opposing the Renewal Plan as a whole. Despres sought tirelessly to obtain verbal agreement on the desirability of writing in additional housing provisions particularly for 200 units of public housing.

Charles Cleveland, political reporter for the Chicago *Daily News,* crystallized the rumors that began to flow from Alderman Despres' championing of low cost and middle income housing during the hearings and committee meetings:

Is Alderman Leon Despres (5th) in trouble in his home ward? He has been one of the sharpest questioners of the Hyde Park–Kenwood redevelopment project [*sic*] and was among those who voted to delay its consideration in Friday's planning committee session. . . . Chief criticism has been that the proposal contains too few public housing units. There are strong arguments on that stand. But, if the plan is defeated it has to go back to the local conservation board [*sic*] and again get federal approval. This time lag could result in junking the project. Despres is taking that risk and the University of Chicago, among others, doesn't like it. Politically this could be important because Despres was elected as an "independent" in 1955 and comes up for re-election next spring. It took special circumstances (a three-way squabble) to put Despres in three years ago; those same circumstances aren't likely to repeat (*Daily News*, October 18, 1958, p. 4).[12]

Despres took risks in dramatizing housing issues surrounding approval of the Urban Renewal Plan, but these placed him in a relatively greater position of influence when the Committee on Housing and Planning began its closed session deliberations over a final vote.

The Council Committee on Housing and Planning

The public hearings concluded, the council committee convened on October 27 for its first deliberative session. In fact, committee members had met informally in advance of this formal session and had discovered a majority favored introducing scattered public housing into the final version of the Urban Renewal Plan. Chairman William Murphy—two weeks later elected to the U. S. House of Representatives and thus under election pressures at this time—asked Despres to write a statement on public housing and to present it at the formal session. Observers predicted the committee would make its decision that afternoon or shelve the plan until after the November elections.

Instead, the first session was spent on an exploration of the authority of the committee. The city's Corporation Counsel office was represented by attorney Handleman, who, with Commissioner Holland and other advisers, sought to clarify the limitations on the authority of the committee. It became clear that the committee could not negotiate directly for changes with the Community Conservation Board and could not make changes in the Plan if it voted approval at this time. Planner Jack Meltzer and an attorney from Corporation Counsel explained that introduction of public-housing provisions in particular would constitute "a major change" in the ordinance

12. In fact, the same circumstances did repeat themselves politically. In spite of great personal concern over the effects of his active standing on public housing, Alderman Despres became the I.V.I. endorsed candidate for re-election in January, 1959, and, against two other Democratic Party candidates, one of whom dropped out, he obtained the endorsement of the Democratic Federation of Illinois, Hyde Park chapter. Most significantly, he won re-election.

and would require repetition of the entire decision-making procedure, including referral back to the local Conservation Community Council and also to the Housing and Home Finance Agency in Washington.

It also became clear that the Urban Renewal Plan itself now included no public housing. The one public-housing project planned for Kenwood, while within the planning area, was not a part of the plan. The desirability and feasibility of public housing were then discussed in detail. D. E. Mackelmann, representing the Office of the Mayor, gave assurances that exclusion of public housing would not necessarily be "precedent setting," and explained that the Chicago Housing Authority and their Chicago Dwellings Association "were standing by" waiting to invest in the planning area at a later time. This did not satisfy several committee members, and pressure accumulated in favor of somehow insuring inclusion of special housing in the Final Plan.

Alderman Despres negotiated seventeen specific but very minor modifications in proposed land uses and site acquisitions in the plan with Jack Meltzer. On most of these, Meltzer indicated that they could be reconsidered sympathetically after approval of the over-all Plan.

The details surrounding guarantees of effective relocation were aired at length, and D. E. Mackelmann provided evidence that a new ordinance was to be introduced into City Council on October 22 to establish a Relocation Bureau to handle all relocation in city projects. Finally, a representative of the Chicago Dwellings Association said his agency intended to participate in the project up to $2 million worth of middle-income construction, and that approval for this was pending with the Illinois State Housing Board. "They are and we are more or less waiting to see what you people will do," the representative said.

No solution on public housing was reached. Alderman Prucinski attempted to gain the floor to introduce some Plan amendments drawn up by the Cardinal's Committee on Conservation, but the Committee avoided confronting these and agreed to meet once again early the following week.

It is interesting that the committee not only seemed sharply limited in the extent of its formal authority but that informally its members felt srongly constrained to reach a decision by the time of the next session of City Council on October 21.

Before its next deliberative session, the committee met in secret session to thresh out the public housing question. There the committee confronted a warning from the Chicago Mortgage Bankers Association that public housing might endanger a promised mortgage pool of $30 million to be used for private rehabilitation in Hyde Park–Kenwood. At the informal session it was agreed that Alderman Despres would suggest a compromise on the issue at the formal meeting.

Thus, when on the afternoon before the City Council vote the Committee convened, Despres opened the session. He said he wanted the committee to recommend that the plan include 120 scattered, row-type units of public housing, one-half of which would be designated for the aged. However, Despres said, this would take too much time because it would mean returning the Renewal Plan to Washington and to the Conservation Board. He said he therefore proposed the Committee recommend to City Council (1) that the Plan include 120 units, as described; (2) that the Conservation Board and the Conservation Council be requested to put this into effect as soon as possible; and (3) that the Council approve the plan.

That one element in the situation had changed since the earlier committee meetings was revealed when the council clerk read from the proposed Renewal Plan about the setting aside of three sites for Dwellings Association Housing. The three sites referred to in the reading were basically different from the sites mentioned in the Plan as it had been submitted to City Council.[13] The "new sites" eliminated the problem of proposing location of public or middle-income housing in any "inner" sectors of the community. Quite apparently, a political difficulty had been negotiated during the week end. A letter from Alvin Rose, Executive Director of the CDA, confirmed the making of these three sites available, and the power of the CDA to proceed with use of these sites.

---

13. The submitted version of the Urban Renewal Plan called for CDA housing at 51st and Drexel Avenue, 47th and Lake Park, and 5200 Kimbark Avenue. The sites read by the clerk were Cottage Grove Avenue near 51st Street, Cottage Grove Avenue between 47th and 51st Streets, and the south side of 47th Street, all of them in the northwest border zone of the planning area and none of them within the community.

Commissioner J. Paul Holland assured questioning aldermen that the Plan would come before City Council once again
for approval of the financial arrangements and that therefore
the committee would have further control over its contents. He
also expressed awareness that failure to comply with the intent
of the committee to include public and middle-income housing in
the execution of the final plan would mean council resistance to
future conservation renewal generally. On this basis, then, the
Committee, with Alderman DuBois absent, voted unanimously
to recommend approval by the City Council.

Thus, guarantees for public and middle income housing were
not secured as part of the ordinance, nor were the specifics of
site locations for such housing settled within the committee.
Instead, the issue was resolved as a matter of trust between the
Council and the administrative units of the city government.
The threat of future disapproval strengthened this informal
arrangement somewhat.

CHAPTER 10

Implications for
Urban Renewal

The central problem of this study has been to assess the contributions of citizen participation to the urban renewal planning of Hyde Park–Kenwood. The importance of this enterprise lies partly in whatever understanding we have been able to give of what was necessarily a very complex series of events. But we hope to make a more important contribution to urban renewal efforts elsewhere in Chicago and throughout the land. This is the primary function of the present chapter— to draw out implications for urban renewal processes in general.

As an intensive analysis of a single case, our study is handicapped. While we want to continue in this chapter our concern with the case of Hyde Park–Kenwood, we also want to transcend the limits of a unique instance. To community leaders in a particular case the unique features of a community are of considerable strategic importance, for special situational elements are often the key to action in desired directions. But the value for other communities of a single case is precisely its common rather than its unique features.

We can hardly generalize from a single case without violating some of the canons of social science research. Yet tentative generalizations are essential, even if hazardous, for they serve to alert others to vital features in cases yet unanalyzed. We will attempt to make such generalizations on the grounds that despite their insubstantial bases they may nevertheless prove of some worth.

Unique Features in the
Hyde Park–Kenwood Case

Renewal planning in Hyde Park–Kenwood occurred in an unusual community at a time when the concept of conservation renewal and the legislation concerning it were new and unprecedented. These are the chief idiosyncratic elements in the case we have presented.

The primitive state of governmental machinery in the city before 1956 made it necessary for the local community to seize the initiative. The South East Chicago Commission and the Community Conference had to provide services and plans which would otherwise have been developed by city agencies.

Placing the Planning Unit under the direction of the Commission (and thus, the University of Chicago) and locating it on the University campus produced very special circumstances: planning was done faster, was negotiated with a closer eye to neighborhood interests, and gave the citizens readier access to the planner himself. That the Planning Unit was not totally under municipal direction meant that it could handle private as well as public proposals, such as the case of planning for private redevelopment of South West Hyde Park.

This approach was not without disadvantages, of course, as the City Council resolution questioning such arrangements in future planning would indicate. The task of defining the public interest in contrast to private institutional interests was made much more problematic. The approach also meant that the University of Chicago, to avoid charges of exploitation and collusion, had to forego gaining immediate advantages from renewal planning. The University had to arrange for its physical expansion through private investments; under the Final Plan no land is to be sold to the University of Chicago. Another penalty may have been the overcautious identification of the Office of the Mayor with the plan. Had the plan been devised within the municipal government, the Mayor and other officials would perhaps have proved less cautious in furthering final passage of the plan.

Decentralization of the technical planning function is unlikely to occur in the future in Chicago or in similar large cities. It may serve, however, as a workable pattern for cities large enough to require conservation programs but too small to sustain renewal planning agencies on a fully staffed basis. Renewal in the middle-sized city is likely to require only an occasional project, and a decentralized planning unit could prove very effective in such situations.

The other unique features of Hyde Park–Kenwood—which were so frequently pointed out in earlier chapters—hardly need repetition here. Particularly important were the characteristics of its population—their prosperity, liberal beliefs and intellectual perspectives, the high degree of organization, and their strong attachment to the community. Certainly the University of Chicago is a neighborhood feature whose likeness would be hard to find elsewhere. Singly or in combination, these are features rarely to be encountered at all and certainly absent in the usual metropolitan middle-class neighborhood.

Properly to assess the contribution of citizen participation we need to find some other community of similar composition facing similar problems of deterioration and change, but without the machinery for participation in which Hyde Park–Kenwood was so rich. To be sure, our two neighborhood case studies show that high citizen participation in North West Hyde Park facilitated planning for that neighborhood in several important ways. Low initial participation in South West Hyde Park contributed poignantly to misunderstanding, conflict, and long delay in execution of renewal. But these neighborhood differences are locked inside our single case study. For true contrasts, we need a second community. While we were unable to make a thorough study of a second area, we were able to make a quick excursion to Morningside Heights in New York City, the community surrounding Columbia University, where since 1948 attempts have been made to renew the area. In the fall of 1958 we collected interviews with community leaders and organization officials as well as documentary materials sufficient to make some superficial comparisons.

Morningside Heights versus Hyde Park–Kenwood

Morningside Heights is the home of more than seventeen institutions, including Columbia University, Union Theological

Seminary, Teachers College, International House, Jewish Theological Seminary, St. Luke's Hospital, Julliard School of Music, Riverside Church, and Cathedral of St. John the Divine. The area comprises about three-quarters of a square mile and housed about 60,000 persons in 1950. Most of the land is used by institutions and the housing consists of high-rise apartment buildings and residential hotels.

Differences between Morningside Heights and Hyde Park as dwelling areas include the fact that the Heights are denser, institutionally and demographically, the dwellings eight to twelve stories high rather than walk-ups, and the commercial boulevards more extremely developed. In some respects these differences are crucial; yet the similarities are imposing. Both communities function as educational islands and as interethnic areas. Both are being progressively infused with increasing proportions of minority populations. Both have very similar occupational bases. It must be stressed that the statements that follow apply to Morningside Heights as of 1958. Since then many changes have occurred that might substantially alter this analysis.

In 1947 most of the Morningside Heights institutions banded together under the leadership of David Rockefeller to form Morningside Heights, Incorporated, an organization functionally very much like the South East Chicago Commission. However no organization comparable in membership or program to the Hyde Park–Kenwood Community Conference exists in Morningside Heights, even though several hundred middle class residents, especially faculty wives, maintain the Morningside Heights Citizens Committee and the Riverside Democratic Club, both of which attempt to speak for the "grassroots."

The interviews and documents we obtained in Morningside Heights drew our attention to several critical distinctions between the progress toward renewal in that community in contrast to Hyde Park–Kenwood. Morningside Heights, Inc. had a head start of more than four years on the South East Chicago Commission; yet an over-all plan for Morningside Heights had still to be created. Morningside Heights, Inc. had stimulated a program of construction of housing which by 1956 amounted to the commitment of more than $136 million to building investments, but no comprehensive and coordinated attack on commercial facilities, traffic conditions, open space, and rehabilitation had been planned as yet.

In fact, as of 1958, the acceptance of planning had proceeded very slowly among the officials of the institutions and the local residents. When specific proposals have been presented, the Morningside citizens have created *ad-hoc* organizations to oppose the plans. The cooperative apartment houses (Morningside Gardens) built under slum-clearance legislation were vigorously opposed by a citizens association, and only the location of a vast public housing project adjacent to these middle-income apartments made the program acceptable at all.

Attempts of Columbia University administrators to repossess University-owned housing to be made available to faculty families and married students have been fought in the courts by organized tenants. In short, the movement from ideas to action has been hampered by widespread local suspicion of the motives of the local institutions and by a lack of acceptance of the concept of planning.

Another critical distinction that caught our attention was that the presence of dominant institutions such as universities is no guarantee that leadership for community conservation will be forthcoming. According to one very well-placed informant in Morningside Heights, movement toward urban renewal had been severely hampered by the lack of responsive and energetic leadership in the administration of Columbia University. Similarly, the policies characteristic of the University of Chicago administration under Robert Hutchins were also unlikely to have stimulated a renewal program.

Indeed, the impetus to the organization of Morningside Heights, Inc., itself came not from the University administration but from "outside" sources. The University had been reluctant to call upon its own faculty for advice and had pursued an extremely conservative policy of committing few funds to neighborhood purposes other than funds for the expansion of the University plant. The vigor of Chancellor Kimpton's administration is a striking contrast.

Hyde Park–Kenwood and Morningside Heights both contain exceptional resources in well-educated adult populations as well as wealthy institutions. The University of Chicago and

Columbia University are both capable of giving form and strength to planning operations. They are also capable of giving a special flavor of public interest to renewal projects, since great universities tend to be regarded generally as public-service organizations. It would seem that such universities would help give urban reconstruction in their environs special priority among projects.

Yet these are merely resources, possibilities that apparently must be treated as such. Priorities are not automatic consequences. For example, the University of Chicago chose to emphasize the deterioration of its total environment and to underemphasize its needs for expansion. This tactic heightened the perception of the institution as performing a role in defense of the general public interest. Even with this approach some misunderstanding arose, and the community relations of the University were often strained. But at least agreement was possible on the problem of renewal. The fourteen institutions comprising Morningside Heights, Inc., chose to give priority to *private needs*—space for expansion and housing for personnel. This tactic contributed directly to the cultivation of local public opposition and misunderstanding, which costly public relations efforts could do little to reduce. Municipal government officials were correspondingly unsympathetic.

Unlike New Yorkers on Morningside Heights, Hyde Parkers are organized into a network of voluntary associations. Both populations have extraordinary reserves of human talent and skill, but Hyde Park–Kenwood has organized these resources. The most vivid distinction between the two communities is that in Morningside Heights no adequate machinery exists that is capable of involving citizens directly. The existence of an organization with the scope and vigor of the Community Conference appears to be a genuine rarity. The lack of an equivalent association in Morningside Heights is the more common situation.

Vigorous civic associations such as the Conference do not evolve in metropolitan university neighborhoods automatically as a response to demographic characteristics, common culture, and the perception of area deterioration. This generalization is suggested by the case of the Morningside Heights Citizens Committee. An elected officer of the Committee, when asked whether it had ever attempted to build a mass-membership organization, replied that there had been discussion of this, but that the leadership had decided against it, as the group lacks any planned program that clearly indicates the need for a mass organization. She also expressed amazement when the authors indicated the kinds of individuals who were active in the Hyde Park–Kenwood Community Conference. She did not believe that persons of comparable stature and position in Morningside Heights possibly could be attracted to join her organization. While in part her statements represent a restricted horizon on the organization's membership potentialities, they also represent severe differences between the two communities in the devotion of its residents. New York offers to its liberal intellectuals a variety of congenial environments, both urban and suburban, and hence the commitment of Morningside Heights residents to the area is slight.

Except for one isolated attempt, as of 1958 the Citizens Committee had made no efforts to develop liaison with Puerto Rican or Negro community organizations in the neighborhood. The informant blamed her group's inertia on failures of Morningside Heights, Inc., which, she said:

Does not understand why its interests might *need* a citizens' organization. Besides, most Citizens Committee members want to remain independent of other organizations generally and free of Morningside Heights, Incorporated, in particular.

What do these contrasts tell us about the contribution of citizen participation? The first lesson to be drawn is that citizen participation provides a means of establishing what is the public interest that must be served by urban renewal. The sources of heaviest strain in the Hyde Park–Kenwood case were those stemming from the poor community relations and socially insensitive practices of the University of Chicago. The inability of Morningside Heights, Inc., and its constituent institutions to move toward urban renewal is at least partly a function of its inability to engage the interest and support of local citizens. Every move toward change in the community has been met by citizen opposition that has seriously hampered quick action.

In other words, citizen support and attention are necessary to successful conservation renewal. Without these renewal in a physical sense may be achieved, but only at some cost—delay, opposition and excessive instability in neighborhood population. The programs of private institutions seeking to conserve their environs must be shown to coincide with the interests of residents if conservation is to be achieved.

Of course, the lack of effective citizen organization in Morningside Heights also coincides with the lack of effective renewal leadership on the part of local institutions. To what extent the leadership of the University of Chicago was led on by the organized citizenry is hard to establish, although it is safe to say that it was easier to contemplate renewal efforts in the knowledge that the population was ready for some drastic action along planning lines. Thus the conservative and cautious nature of institutional leadership in Morningside Heights may partly reflect the uncertainty as to how planning might be met by the citizenry.

In any event, urban renewal planning in Hyde Park–Kenwood was accomplished to the accompaniment of an extensive interchange between the citizens, as organized in the Conference, and the renewal leadership, as represented in the Planning Unit and the South East Chicago Commission. The special advantage in Hyde Park–Kenwood was that renewal efforts could be addressed to an *organized* citizenry. Means were provided (and used) by which consent could be tested and, if found wanting, plans could be modified. Furthermore the two-way exchange provided a way in which the failures of either side—University and Community or Community Conference— did not endanger success of the over-all mission. We predict that without such a complementary system, urban renewal can be accomplished only slowly and against the sporadic opposition of the citizenry. Note that we do not say that urban renewal cannot be accomplished without citizen participation along the lines that developed in Hyde Park–Kenwood, but only that the process will be fraught with conflict and difficult to achieve. Furthermore, by creating a wide gulf between the aims of renewal and the interests of citizens, it is likely that such renewal programs will radically transform the neighborhood composition, leading to ironic results in which a renewed neighborhood may have lost the population for which it was being renewed.

A Closer Look at Citizen Participation

We have now given reasons why citizen participation is essential to a workable program of conservation. In their driest form, the basic reasons are that without citizen participation the public interest cannot be defined and planning efforts must fumble about to work out an acceptable proposal; and citizen organization is especially important in circumstances where the impetus for renewal comes from private institutions. The dialogue between citizen association and private institution gives an essential *legitimacy* to planning. Now we want to look at citizen involvement in sharper outline.

To judge the functions of citizen participation, we must consider separately the different roles an organization such as the Hyde Park–Kenwood Community Conference could play. One is achievement of public acceptance of the idea that the community could be conserved as a desirable neighborhood on an interracial basis. This could only be achieved by a mass-based civic association on the local scene. We do not know precisely how effective the Conference was in disseminating this idea. On the one hand, we know that white residents continued to leave the community between 1950 and 1956. We also know that the idea of interracialism was never widely espoused.[1] On the other hand, the response to the Conference was considerable. The slogan "An interracial community of high standards" fired the imagination of the press and came to epitomize the renewal of the community in the city and in the nation.

To block groups between 1949 and 1954 were remarkably effective in countering the anxieties that arose from changing neighborhood conditions, according to virtually unanimous opinions among very diverse individuals and groups, and judging from the work of Bettie Sarchet and Herbert Thelen in assessing block groups. We do not know any way of measuring the objective consequences of this allaying of anxieties, but

---

1. The minister of the community's most racially integrated church described the progressive disillusionment during the earlier fifties within the Hyde Park Council of Churches and Synagogues. Initial attempts to induce integration of congregations were abandoned, as ministers concluded that interracialism in the churches would have to wait for integration in housing, employment, and commercial services.

it does help to explain why the slogan of the Conference was ultimately so well received.

As Ronald Lippitt, Jeanne Watson, and Bruce Westley have pointed out, a process of planned change can begin only when a problem awareness and a confidence in the possibility of improvement have developed.[2] The Conference slogan symbolizes its acceptance of these change functions. In its first phases the Conference managed to define the problems confronting Hyde Park, and it created a climate of optimism and urgency about doing something about these problems. As such, the Conference demonstrates the first functional potentiality of citizen participation—the stimulation of public awareness of the necessity and practicability of change.

The University of Chicago, the hotel owners and businessmen, and other private institutions responded to the appeal for change sounded by the Conference and to the neighborhood conditions but were unwilling to invest in this civic organization as the group to conduct the task of changing the community. The relationship between the citizens and the private institutions "got off on the wrong foot," as this study has shown in full detail. The South East Chicago Commission was created in the conviction that through a separate organization change could be achieved on safer, speedier terms as far as the private interests were concerned.

Nevertheless, the Community Conference persisted and it achieved a working if rather uncomfortable relationship with both the University and the Commission. Having sparked a movement toward change, the Conference assumed its second important function, that of shaping the general goals to be sought in the planning of renewal in Hyde Park–Kenwood. Again citizen participation played important roles. Citizen activity kept alive the issues of low- and middle-income housing. Citizens maintained vigil over code enforcement and zoning controls. Repeatedly they "humanized" the character of the technical plan, which otherwise might have been too oriented toward institutional, commercial, and traffic facilities.

It is impossible to evaluate precisely the importance of this last function. We can only say that the Conference created a

2. *The Dynamics of Planned Change* (New York: Harcourt, Brace, 1958), p. 131.

climate of opinion within which planning operations took place. This climate shaped many of the hearings conducted first by the Conference and later emulated by the Conservation Community Council.

The third role played by citizens was to function as policy-makers influencing the specific details in the plan. While our case study of North West Hyde Park shows how far organized citizens may go in shaping and modifying technical plans, our evidence as a whole reveals that citizens did not play a crucial part in this regard.

The relative ineffectiveness of citizen participation in this respect must be examined very carefully. In the first place, we must ask the question whether such influence is of top importance? Certainly for particular individuals whose homes may be scheduled for demolition or whose businesses may be relocated, the problem of finding an effective channel for negotiating with the planners is an important one. But a case may be made that such specific details cannot all be negotiated without significantly deteriorating total objectives. At some point a line must be drawn, beyond which the authority of technicians must prevail. Final decisions on the details of the plan must be afforded the planners if the over-all features of renewal are not to be undermined by small concessions that, when aggregated, amount to serious departures from the grander conception. In other words, if we consider the over-all needs of renewal planning, we cannot expect that the citizens should have their way on the details of the plan.

A second related consideration to be borne in mind when reviewing the role citizen organization played in affecting the details of the plan is whether such success should be measured by its effects on the plan or its effects on the citizens? While from the former viewpoint the Conference shows up poorly, from the second viewpoint the Conference does very well. Citizen organization was effective in promoting in instance after instance the idea of a general public interest overriding individual interests. This was the end result of much of the negotiations over specific sites in North West Hyde Park, as we saw in Chapter 7. The Conference, because it was the guardian of many interests, was able to convince some that the general interest would be served by a curtailment of specific benefits.

In the final phases of planning the function of the Community Conference was to create broad popular acceptance of and support for the renewal plan. In the end the Conference had to decide to support a plan that was not entirely in keeping with its own earlier objectives, once primary control had centered in the Commission and its Planning Unit. This role of endorsement, education, and promotion occupied the Conference from 1957 through approval of the Final Plan late in 1958. We suggest that the lack of deep opposition within the community to the plan in its final stage was probably a product of this extensive conditioning of the local population. The South West Hyde Park case shows that where the Conference was not in close touch with neighborhood residents opposition flourished, although this is a concomitant rather than a causal relationship (see Chapter 6).

In performing this supportive function, the Conference acted with distinction and creative success. City officials at all times accepted the Conference as the most authoritative spokesman for the community, and officials in the South East Chicago Commission and the University were made aware of the worth of an accepting enthusiastic public.

Reviewing the successes and failures of the citizen-participation activities of the Conference, it is clear that this organization made its greatest contribution in its passive rather than in its active roles. That is to say, the Conference obtained for the idea of planning and for the plan itself a mass base of support which facilitated the planning process and the acceptance of the Final Plan in the local community and "downtown." At the same time, however, the Conference was unable to modify the plan to conform in all details to the goals the Conference held out as desirable. There can be little doubt that the planning of the conservation and renewal of Hyde Park–Kenwood was materially aided by activities channeled through the organizational mechanisms provided by the Conference. It is also the case that the citizens of Hyde Park–Kenwood felt a sense of participation in the planning process and more confidence in the final outcome of the Planning Unit.

If we take the Hyde Park–Kenwood Community Conference as representing the upper limit of the effectiveness attainable by citizen participation (as we suggested earlier), then we must conclude that the maximum role to be played by a citizen-participation movement in urban renewal is primarily a passive one. Acting through mass organizations, citizens can perform the functions of endorsing or rejecting very general goals, providing solidary support for a plan, reacting to specific details of the plan, and providing an intelligence network for the renewal planner. The experience of participating in these functions apparently provides an important element of mass commitment to a plan, which aids in providing support for the notion of a general public interest overriding individual interests and in preventing the formation of dissident local groups.

Was it possible for the Conference to play any other role in the planning process? Several somewhat disaffected respondents suggested that the Conference might have maintained a greater distance between itself and the planning process, making stronger stands on policy issues through public attacks on the plan and political pressure on public officials. They suggested a role for the Conference similar to that of veto organizations and a disengagement from the "transmission-belt" function.

As an organization representing all interests and viewpoints in the neighborhood, the Conference could not have achieved so wide a base of popular support except by acting as it did. Secondly, the pace of planning may well have been slowed considerably, since without the machinery for testing in advance the popular acceptability of proposals, local opposition would have been more frequent and more vocal. Finally, there would probably have been more attention paid to housing on the part of the planners in an attempt to meet the major demands of the Conference. In short, the consequence of adopting a more militant stand on the part of the Conference would probably have been a reduced membership, perhaps even rival organizations, a plan with greater attention to housing, a slower pace in planning, and a plan which would be more acceptable in its general features but less favorably received in specific details. Of course, there would have been other consequences for the Conference as well. For one thing, foundation support for the Conference activities would have been less likely, as the Conference would have appeared as more of a pressure group than a neighborhood-wide civic association. Another consequence would have been the withdrawal of business support from the Conference, a move further enhancing its sectarian qualities.

Implications for Other Neighborhoods

An urban renewal plan for Hyde Park–Kenwood is now a reality. The Final Plan for the community has been approved all up the line, and although the formidable job of carrying out the plan still remains, the planning process is now over. Already the city's appraisers have set purchase prices on many of the structures to be acquired for demolition, and the sole remaining local concern appears to be that the urgent pace set in achieving passage of the plan may somehow not be maintained.[3] From at least the point of view of strong local support and the considerable speed with which it was accomplished, the planning process in Hyde Park–Kenwood must be considered successful.

What can other neighborhoods learn from this case that could help them in the search for amelioration of their conditions of decline and incipient blight?

As we mentioned earlier, the unique features of Hyde Park–Kenwood urban renewal are partly a function of the historical context of urban renewal in general and partly a function of the particular characteristics of the neighborhood and its institutions. The implications of the case have to be considered against these features.

The major burden of leadership and administration for the planning process was carried by the University of Chicago through its Planning Unit and the South East Chicago Commission. But the functions for urban renewal performed by these organizations are not specific to such organization: in other words, they are functions that can be carried out by alternative arrangements. To be maximally useful to other

---

3. Citizen organizations in Hyde Park–Kenwood have found themselves at the present time in the familiar posture of pressuring municipal agencies to carry through the items presently on the renewal agenda. For example, on June 11, 1959, David L. Sutton, chairman of the Conservation Community Council wired Mayor Daley urging him to press toward rapid acquisition of buildings. "Delays," he wrote, "are seriously destroying community confidence in the feasibility of the entire urban renewal plan." In September, the new Executive Director of the Conference, Harry Bovshaw, complained to the Mayor that only eleven parcels had been appraised and that acquisition was being slowed down to a dangerous extent.

neighborhoods it is important to point up what these functions were and how they could be served by substitute arrangements.

Though there are few middle-aged urban neighborhoods in need of conservation and renewal that have at their cores such reservoirs of talent and wealth as the University of Chicago, there are many that have other types of institutions which might perform similar leadership roles. In Chicago the Catholic Church provides much of the leadership in the Back-of-the-Yards neighborhood, which has done much in the way of voluntary rehabilitation to preserve a working-class neighborhood. The Back-of-the-Yards Council has enough organizational know-how and popular support to provide some large measure of leadership to more formal urban renewal planning for that area. Churches, industrial corporations, business enterprises, and the like could provide much of the same core of leadership if they were so inclined.

However, there are few institutions that have as much of a stake in their environs as a large university. Such a university is firmly rooted in its neighborhood by virtue of the fixed capital represented in its physical plant. At least some of the large metropolitan universities—for example, Harvard, Columbia, the University of Pennsylvania—are beginning to pay more attention to their immediate surroundings as they attempt to find space for expansion and to provide an attractive environment for their staffs and students. In contrast, businesses can more easily move, and factories can rely on mass transportation to bring in their labor force. Churches resemble universities in their close dependence on the neighborhood, but their ability to command talent and resources is ordinarily slight (with the exception of such highly centralized churches as the Roman Catholic).

In the "ordinary" declining middle-aged neighborhood it can be expected that local institutions would be neither willing nor able to supply the same kind of leadership as that provided by the University of Chicago in the Hyde Park–Kenwood area. Leadership, then, must be provided through other organizational arrangements. Two types of organizational substitutes for the arrangements in Hyde Park–Kenwood seem workable. The first is some sort of metropolitan-wide voluntary organization to perform the functions of organizing citizen participation in neighborhood after neighborhood and of serving as a spur to municipal agencies. Several cities have already formed such organizations. For example in Pittsburgh, ACTION-Housing, Inc.,[4] backed by the power and financial resources of civic-minded businessmen and industrialists, has begun the task of stimulating citizen organization in a number of neighborhoods that face problems that may call for urban renewal efforts.

The second type of substitute for the organizational arrangements of Hyde Park–Kenwood would be located within the municipal agencies themselves. In Chicago, for example, the Community Conservation Board would be the agency to supply the staff and leadership functions for local neighborhoods seeking conservation. Indeed, at the present time the Board is attempting to do so.

There are several advantages in relying on metropolitan-wide agencies to supply these functions. First of all, a central agency can to some degree rise above specific local interests. At the least, it would not be suspected, as was the University of Chicago, of serving its own interests exclusively. A second advantage would stem from the kind of specialized staff that such an agency could assemble. It would be impossibly expensive for neighborhood after neighborhood to assemble their own planning units, legal talents, housing and zoning experts, and the like. Furthermore, such staffs could hardly be expected to command as much in the way of talent as could a central staff, which could pay higher salaries and guarantee longer tenure in the job. Finally, as we suggested earlier, such organizations can be expected to command more commitment to its actions from other public officials.

There are particular disadvantages as well. In Chicago, with its highly centralized city government, municipal agencies suffer from not having enough independent authority. Up to this point, the Community Conservation Board appears to have suffered from being too dependent on the wishes and interests of the Mayor's Office to work out its own program and pace of accomplishment. For such an agency to accomplish successfully urban renewal planning for the many neighbor-

---

4. Former Director of the Conference, James V. Cunningham, was hired by this organization to perform the important function of stimulating neighborhood organization in areas scheduled for urban renewal.

hoods in Chicago that are interested at present in conservation, it must have the ability to proceed on its own and have a sufficiently strong position in the city government to command the respect and cooperation of other city agencies (the Building Department and Planning Commission, in particular). This disadvantage in municipally run urban renewal is not necessarily inherent in municipal-agency operations but is characteristic mainly of such operations in Chicago.

Location of the Planning Unit in the neighborhood and its sponsorship by a local institution probably made the Planners more sensitive to local interests and more attentive to local needs. How to build a bridge of communications between the local community and the metropolitan-wide agencies is a problem which will have to be worked out in Chicago and in other urban communities.

The leadership and staff functions provided by citizen organizations in Hyde Park–Kenwood community might be best summarized under three categories:

Stabilization: The reduction of population turnover and the enforcement of local housing and zoning regulations.

Renewal Planning: The drawing up of specific proposals for the renewal of the community.

Obtaining Approval: The obtaining of the support of the local community for the plan and making representations of such support to public officials empowered to make final decisions.

As our analysis of the case of Hyde Park–Kenwood indicates, these functions were performed with some success under an informal division of labor, in which the University of Chicago acting through its Planning Unit and the South East Chicago Commission drew up the plan and handled relations with municipal agencies, while the Hyde Park–Kenwood Community Conference took on the role of building popular acceptance of the concept of planning and publicizing of the specific plans developed by the Planning Unit.

While it is easy to envisage metropolitan agencies, whether municipal or voluntary, taking on the roles played by the University and the South East Chicago Commission, it is hard to see how they can effectively take over the functions provided by the Conference.

For example, a well-staffed and powerful municipal agency conceivably can adequately perform in the areas of law enforcement, providing a staff of professional planners to draw up proposed plans and negotiating with other municipal agencies for their cooperation. Essential to such effective functioning would be sufficient status and authority within the local municipal government to undertake decisions on its own and to command the respect of fellow agencies. Indeed, this is the pattern in other urban areas and the pattern envisaged by federal legislation and Illinois law.

Because the success of the Conference was so closely tied to the pre-existing hyperorganization of the community and the characteristics of its population, it is hard to envisage how metropolitan agencies could take over the functions performed by the Conference. Yet there are many examples of neighborhoods without Hyde Park–Kenwood's particular characteristics that have managed to form very active and vigorous community organizations. In fact, the Back-of-the-Yards Council is one of the best examples of such a neighborhood without most of the favorable characteristics of Hyde Park–Kenwood. Perhaps there are ways and means of stimulating neighborhood organizations that could be successfully employed by metropolitan-wide agencies patterned along the lines of ACTION-Housing, Inc., or by such municipal agencies as the Community Conservation Board. Certainly, the talent commanded by the Conference is not necessarily a monopoly vested only in particular individuals; indeed, much of the know-how of the organization has been incorporated in one or another publication and is now in the public domain.

It seems likely that successful urban renewal in large cities —successful in the sense of widely accepted both within and without the neighborhoods under renewal—will come primarily either in neighborhoods that have an indigenous successful community organization or in neighborhoods in which some outside agency manages to create one. In the absence of such organization physical renewal can be accomplished, but it seems likely that the neighborhood will lose whatever particular flavor it had through loss of essential population types.

An Attitude Survey of
Hyde Park—Kenwood

*E*arly in 1958, a small-scale attitude survey was made of residents of Hyde Park–Kenwood. Dr. James A. Davis,[1] of the National Opinion Research Center at the University of Chicago, conducted a survey to measure the attitudes of citizens toward the community and their involvement in the community organization surrounding urban renewal. The study was conducted by graduate students of the Department of Sociology as part of their training in field-research methods. Interviews were sent to a sample of blocks in which at the time there were organized block groups and instructed to interview a quota of residents.

Because it was difficult to evaluate the worth of the sample of residents so obtained, we have not presented the findings of this survey in the main body of this report. Although some interviews were obtained on all of the blocks originally designated for study, it is not possible to state with any certainty that the interviews conducted on each block were with persons representative of those blocks. Indeed, there is good evidence from the results that interviewers tended to prefer as respondents white, well-educated home owners. For example, half of the sample had completed college and many have had some postgraduate training. Half of the respondents were employed

---

1. We are grateful to Dr. Davis for making the interviews and punched cards available to us. The basic analysis of the materials presented in this appendix was made by Miss Carolyn Huson of the project staff, who was very skillful in discerning the major meanings to be gained from the data.

as professional workers, and 40 per cent of the sample were home owners. Finally, only 31 per cent were nonwhites. Quite clearly, this sample consists primarily of the upper-middle-class, whites, professional group in the Hyde Park–Kenwood community.

Despite the obvious bias in the sample, it is still possible to gain some useful information from the survey, especially in the comparison between different groups within the sample and among different subareas in the community. Furthermore, the bias in the sample is precisely toward those groups who may be expected to be most deeply involved in citizen participation, relatively best informed about urban renewal, and generally among the most vocal segment of the political community. Moreover, there are enough respondents in the sample who do not conform to this characterization so that contrasts, if they exist, may be profitably studied.

Specifically, we shall concern ourselves with three questions: (1) How do the perceptions of the community held by whites differ from those held by nonwhites? (2) Do attitudes toward aspects of the community differ according to a resident's geographical location within it? (3) What are the differences in degrees of involvement in community organization? The reader should bear in mind that we will not be generalizing from the sample to the community as a whole. We will consider the sample as worth generalizing from to the upper-middle-class community, for one thing, and we will look for significant differences by race.

Perspectives on the Community

Hyde Park–Kenwood Negroes are recent arrivals to the community. Only a small proportion have resided in this community for ten years or more. The majority have arrived since 1948 from Chicago's segregated "ghetto," the "Black Belt." For the most part, the remainder are recent migrants from the South, new to the North and new to metropolitan ways of life. Refined data would probably reveal the many ways in which it is a gross distortion to lump the three groups together, for we already know that social attitudes are rarely, if ever, a product of racial factors themselves. But if we look at differences between white and nonwhite[2] perceptions of aspects of Hyde Park–Kenwood (and keep in mind the many differentiating forces within these categories) we may see how the former "ghetto" and southern rural life works upon the nonwhite resident—how it makes him "see" his local world in an especially distinctive way.

Interviewers asked, "Aside from your own apartment or house, how would you rate your immediate neighborhood as a place to live?" Two-thirds answered that they lived in an excellent or good neighborhood. Less than 3 per cent rated their own neighborhood as "bad." The interviewers then asked, "Why do you say that?" Table A.1 shows the differences between the races in the spontaneous answers given to this probe.

Table A.1—Neighborhood Assets, by Race of Residents

Race	Convenience to Loop, Stores, etc.	University & Cultural Resources	Nice, Friendly People	Quiet, Clean, Safe, or Well-Kept	Diversity of Kinds of People	Community-Minded People	Other	(N)
White	57%	53%	51%	20%	11%	10%	15%	(73)
Negro	31	7	34	62	7	10	17	(29)
Oriental	20	60	40	0	20	20	20	(5)

In the view of more than half the white respondents, their neighborhoods were good because they were near the University and cultural resources, because they were convenient places to live (i.e., close to the downtown Loop), and because their neighbors were "nice and friendly." In marked contrast, the dominant and most frequent response given by Negroes (62 per cent) was that their neighborhoods were quiet, clean, safe, or well kept; only 20 per cent of the whites mentioned these conditions as assets. Is it possible the groups do not cue to the same features of their environment?

In a limited way, this question is answered in Table A.2,

---

2. In the case of Hyde Park–Kenwood, "nonwhite" is a misleading term, for the community includes a sizable component of Oriental families, most of them Nisei Japanese who have been in the locale for the past ten to thirty years. None of the Negroes in our sample, in contrast, had resided in Hyde Park or Kenwood for more than ten years. In some tables, therefore, we have separated nonwhites into Negroes and Orientals, even though only nine Oriental respondents were in the sample.

which reports answers to this question: "Here is a list of problems that some neighborhoods in Hyde Park face. Could you give me your opinion as to whether these are a serious problem, a slight problem, or no problem at all?" The table shows responses by race of respondent to a selected number of problems.

Table A.2—Neighborhood Problems, by Race of Residents

Race	Crime *	Smoke & Dirt *	Park-ing	De-terio-ration	Con-ver-sions	Race * Rela-tions	Demo-lition Plans	(N)
White	82%	93%	78%	63%	42%	40%	33%	(73)
Nonwhite	56	59	74	50	29	15	27	(34)

* Statistically significant differences between races are marked with an asterisk.

Of the whites, 82 per cent view *crime* as a neighborhood problem, but only 56 per cent of the nonwhites make the same observation. In the case of excessive smoke and dirt, 93 per cent of the whites in contrast to 59 per cent of the nonwhites consider this a neighborhood problem. And, while 40 per cent of the whites consider race relations a problem, only 15 per cent nonwhites agree. On these three topics racial differences are significant statistically.

To a lesser degree, the pattern of differential perceptions of problems is maintained on all topics. Proportionately fewer Negroes and Orientals view conversions, parking, housing deterioration, or demolition as neighborhood problems. The fact that 40 per cent of the sample was drawn from home-owning house dwellers probably influences views on conversions, as these occur mostly in apartments. Table A.2 indicates, moreover, that the problems of smoke and dirt, crime, and scarce parking space are the three most commonly identified problems among the seven presented to the respondents. Among the whites, deteriorating housing must be added as a commonly defined problem.

If we consider the findings in Tables A.1 and A.2 in relation to one another,[3] we come to this over-all characterization of race differences among community residents. Upper-middle-class whites tend to live in Hyde Park–Kenwood because it is

3. Table A.7, prepared from an independent survey by Donald Bogue and containing a representative and adequate sample, tends to confirm our findings as shown in Tables A.1 and A.2

a University community; because it contains many nice, friendly people (probably meaning many persons like themselves in terms of interests and values); and because it is convenient to the downtown Loop. Furthermore, they live there in spite of its high crime rate, its excessive smoke and dirt, and parking problems and deterioration of properties. In contrast, Negroes live in Hyde Park–Kenwood principally because it is so much better as a living area than others open to them in metropolitan Chicago and because it is better physically than the locales from which they moved. Thus, while they are also aware of lack of parking space, smoke and dirt, deterioration of housing, and crime as local problems, this awareness is significantly less a matter of concern. And, accustomed to greater overcrowding than the whites, less than a third of the nonwhites view conversions as a problem and proportionately far fewer of them consider race relations a difficulty than do the whites. They emphasize the quality of the physical neighborhood as among its finest assets—not sociability, culture, or convenience. Relatively more deprived than white residents in the past, nonwhite residents are apparently thus relatively more satisfied with their present environment.[4]

Residential Location and Attitude Differences

In our report on the community setting (Chapter 2) we divided the community into several sectors and noted the ways in which each was socially distinctive. In examining Hyde Park–Kenwood Community Conference membership distribution geographically (Chapter 5), we noted that members were drawn disproportionately from the University Community, the area immediately surrounding the University of Chicago. The attitude-survey sample, based on the location of Conference block groups as it was, does not include respondents from either East Hyde Park or Kenwood, but it does allow breakdown of

---

4. Another study confirms this difference. Bogue found 81 per cent of the whites liked living in the community in 1956, contrasted with 89 per cent nonwhites—Donald Bogue, *Hyde Park–Kenwood Urban Renewal Survey* (National Opinion Research Center Report No. 58, September, 1956), Table F-VI-1.

responses into three of the five neighborhoods. We have used these to demonstrate the sense in which views toward Hyde Park depend in important degree, not only on race, but on which sector of the community the viewer lives in.

Table A.3—Rating of Quality of Neighborhood, by Neighborhood *

Neighborhood of Respondent	Excellent	Good	Fair	Bad	Don't Know	(N)
University Community	34%	50%	16%	0	0	(38)
Old Village Core	13	36	47	4%	0	(45)
Border Zone	20	20	45	4	8%	(24)

* The differences among neighborhoods are statistically significant at the .02 level.

Table A.3 shows the ratings given to their neighborhoods by the inhabitants of the University Community, a border zone, and the Village Core. The differences obtained are statistically significant. They show that University Community residents tend to rate their living area more favorably than do border-zone or Village Core inhabitants. Differences between the latter two are completely negligible. While 84 per cent of the University Community respondents rate their neighborhood as excellent or good, only half the respondents in each of the other two area groups do so.

Like Table A.2, Table A.4 gives the proportions of respondents who regard each of seven aspects of their neighborhoods as problems. This time the ratings are broken down by the sectors from which the respondents were drawn as residents.

Table A.4—Neighborhood Problems, by Neighborhood Location of Respondents

Neighborhood of Respondent	Crime *	Smoke, Dirt *	Park-ing *	De-terio-ration	Con-ver-sions	Race Rela-tions	Demo-lition Plans	(N)
University Community	90%	86%	60.6%	50%	47.4%	34.2%	36.8%	(38)
Old Village Core	80	86	91.2	71.1	37.7	37.7	27.3	(45)
Border Zone	46	62	75	50	29.1	16.6	29.1	(24)

p <.005   p <.02   p <.01   p <.1

* Items marked with an asterisk are statistically significant at .05 level or better.

Differences by sector location are neither as great nor as clearly patterned as are differences between racial groups. Renewal of Hyde Park will introduce practically no demolition or reconstruction into the sector labeled the University Community, in contrast to the other two types of neighborhoods. Yet the upper-middle-class whites in this sector are comparatively in greater agreement that crime, conversions, and plans for demolition are problems in their neighborhood than are inhabitants of either of the other two sectors. Perhaps most striking as a finding is the great agreement irrespective of sector, that crime, smoke and dirt, and lack of parking space are neighborhood problems. (Only the border-zone respondents are an exception, and then only in the matter of crime.) Taken generally, these, as well as definitions of deterioration, appear to suggest some consensus on critical features of the community regardless of place of residence. Yet the border-zone residents tend to regard their neighborhood—where the greatest renewal is scheduled and where the most severe deterioration, illegal converting of apartments, and the greatest proportions of crime occur—less frequently as problematic than do the other two groups. Crime is viewed most widely as a problem in the sector where least crimes occur.

Crime, smoke and dirt, lack of parking, and deterioration tend to be defined as genuine neighborhood problems throughout Hyde Park. The extent to which they are so defined, however, varies according to the neighborhood in which a resident lives. The more privileged the neighborhood, the more extensively are these aspects of it defined as problematic, with the exception of parking and deterioration. On these two aspects, however, the least privileged neighborhood—the border zone—contains residents who express less concern than those in the Village Core.

Citizen Involvement in Community Organization

The respondents in this sample are a fairly well-informed and community-centered group. Three out of four (78 per cent) claimed to have discussed urban renewal and redevelopment with an acquaintance or to have read about local renewal activities in the papers "in the past couple of weeks." Nearly two-thirds (62 per cent) are regular readers of the Chicago daily newspapers, 45 per cent are regular readers of the Hyde

Park *Herald*, and another 14 per cent read the *Herald* occasionally. Range of social contacts is often used as a measure of both sociability and community involvement, and this sample included 59 per cent who reported knowing between eleven and sixty-one or more families by name within their neighborhoods. Half of these knew twenty or more families—an unusually wide range of associations.

Although spectator interest in urban renewal and neighborhood problems seems fairly high, what about the more active forms in involvement? Nine out of ten respondents knew of a block group in their neighborhoods, indicating that the latter have made their activities visible to almost everyone in the community. About a third of the respondents had actually attended at least one meeting, and two-thirds of this group rated themselves as frequent attenders. Judged by these figures, the block groups have managed to activate and to involve a considerable proportion of the persons on the blocks that they cover.[5]

As one might have suspected from the distribution of Conference membership and from general knowledge on the social concomitants of participation, those who do participate in block groups are of generally higher socio-economic status than the nonparticipants. This finding is supported in several ways: First, among those who participated in block-group activity 80 per cent had attended or graduated from college, while among those who had not participated only 57 per cent had been educated beyond high school. Secondly—excluding University students, none of whom (in this sample) participated —and dividing respondents into blue-collar and white-collar categories, 44 per cent of the white-collar residents and only 18 per cent of the blue-collar residents reported having participated at any time. Finally, if we divide residents into tenants and home owners, 50 per cent of the owners were block-group participators and only 17 per cent of the tenants. Of the three factors education, occupation, and home ownership, then,

5. The reader is reminded that the sample covers only blocks in which a block group was organized at the time of the survey.

Because it requires that only one member of a household be an active member of a block group to tie the household into the block organization, the sample probably underestimates the coverage of households obtained by the block groups.

ownership differentiates most dramatically between those who do and do not become involved in block-group meetings.

Table A.5—Attendance at Block Group Meetings, by Race

Race	Attended	Never Attended	(N)
White	36%	64%	(73)
Nonwhite	23	77	(34)

Note that, although race is highly correlated with educational attainment and occupation level, the amount of participation does not differ much by racial groups. Table A.5 indicates that 36 per cent of the whites as compared with 23 per cent of the nonwhites were participants in block groups. This finding suggests that the block group participants among the nonwhite group dipped lower down in the educational and occupational scales.

Table A.6—Attendance at Block Group Meetings, by Neighborhood

Neighborhood	Attended	Never Attended	(N)
University Community	32%	68%	(38)
Old Village Core	29	71	(45)
Border Zone	33	66	(24)

Finally we may note that there are few differences among neighborhoods in the proportions of residents who reported activity in their block groups. (Of course, it is necessary to bear in mind that these interviews were made with residents in blocks that had active block groups at the time.) In other words, it would appear that where block groups managed to establish themselves, they also managed to involve about the same proportion of residents.

Table A.7—Things Disliked about Hyde Park–Kenwood Area *

In Order of Frequency	White	Nonwhite
1. Noise, Smoke, and Dirt	47%	23%
2. Parking	39	32
3. Police and Fire Protection	25	13
4. Kind of People	20	9
5. Interracial Features	14	1
6. Crime	4	1

* Data selected from Table F-VI-4, p. 156, Donald Bogue, *The Hyde Park–Kenwood Urban Renewal Survey* (National Opinion Research Center Report No. 58, September, 1956).

Summary

Even if one keeps in mind the sample behind this survey was heavily biased toward the upper-middle-class, white, adult population of Hyde Park, it is nevertheless possible to obtain several important clues about the attitudes toward and the degrees of involvement of Hyde Parkers in their community. These are as follows:

1. Most Hyde Parkers assess their community as an excellent or a good one in which to live. Its most frequently cited aspects are, in their order of frequency, its convenience to the downtown Loop, its nice, friendly people, and its proximity to the University of Chicago and related cultural resources.

2. Negro residents agree with this general assessment, but they give first emphasis to Hyde Park's physical advantages. Unlike white residents, they view Hyde Park as quiet, clean, safe, and well kept.

3. While most residents see the community as faced with problems of crime, smoke and dirt, and lack of parking space, significantly fewer nonwhites than whites view these as problems. And significantly more whites than nonwhites regard race relations, conversions, and property deterioration as neighborhood problems. We have suggested that white Hyde Parkers, less deprived in the past than their nonwhite neighbors, tend to see themselves as living in the community in spite of its crime, overcrowding, and racial difficulties.

4. The views residents hold of Hyde Park differ according to the sector in which they live. Those dwelling in the neighborhood of the University rate their locale very favorably but perceive it as problem-ridden, particularly with crime, dirt, and lack of parking space. Those who live in the least-privileged neighborhood, the border zones, tend to rate their area less favorably than those from the better areas; yet they do not view their neighborhood as problem-ridden to the same extent. We suggest the hypothesis that the more privileged the neighborhood (other things held constant), the more favorably the neighborhood is rated generally but the more problems in particular are perceived as noteworthy.

5. Most Hyde Parkers are unusually well-informed citizens,

even given the bias of this sample. They tend to read about and discuss renewal planning, they tend to be regular readers of both metropolitan and local newspapers, and they have wide contacts among families in their own neighborhoods.

6. If one uses participation in block-group meetings as an indicator of community involvement, Hyde Parkers tend to be unusually strongly involved. Nearly all know about block-group programs, and one-third participate to some extent.

7. As in all urban communities, however, neighborhood involvement in Hyde Park depends on a cluster of interrelated considerations. The college-educated, white-collar home owner tends to be the active block-group participant—the individual to whom local improvements, questions of redevelopment and renewal, and neighborhood sociability are bound to prove most salient. The less-well-educated, blue-collar tenant tends, in contrast, to be the least-involved resident of Hyde Park.

8. Our sample was drawn from neighborhoods where block groups had long been in existence. Therefore, extent of participation in block groups is not significantly differentiated from one type of neighborhood to the next.

9. While whites tend to be more involved in block-group participation than do nonwhites, the difference is not statistically significant.

Name Index

Abrahamson, Julia, viii, 5, 61n, 103-106, 143, 145, 189n
Alinsky, Saul, 226n
Allen, Lloyd G., 268

Bach, Ira, 94, 245
Banfield, Edward C., 64n, 241, 248n
Blackiston, Don, 30, 84
Bogue, Donald, 47
Boyd, J. M., 2
Braxton, James D., 197
Breckenfield, Gurney, 234n

Cassels, James, 127n
Cobb, Jessamine, viii
Cunningham, James V., viii, 136-137, 141, 143-144, 233
    North West Hyde Park, 207
    South West Hyde Park, 164, 165, 171, 173-174, 177

Daley, Richard, Hyde Park A and B, 98, 148
    role in urban renewal, 248-253, 261-263, 266
Davis, James A., 293
Dawson, William, 243
Deackmann, Anneta, 252
Denton, Patricia, viii, 156n, 191n
Despres, Leon, 40, 63n, 147, 177, 181, 206, 243, 269-271, 272
Donahue, Elmer, 197
Downs, James, Jr., 77, 87, 98, 244, 250, 258-259, 262
Doyle, Phil, 94, 250
Drake, St. Clair, 165-166, 169
    South West Hyde Park hearings, 172 *passim*

Duncan, Beverly, 10n, 21n
Duncan, O. D., 21n

Eaton, Norman, 157
Egan, John J., Mgr., 226 *passim*, 254
Ernst, C. F., 24

Farr, Newton, 129
Frederick, William, viii, 127n, 161

Goodman, Howard, 157

Hagiwara, Michael, 169, 179-180, 189-190
Hansen, Donald, viii
Harrell, William B., 129, 157
Hauser, Philip M., viii, 70, 127n, 176-177
Holland, J. Paul, viii, 256-257, 270, 274
Holman, Claude, 181, 243, 249, 267
Horwitz, Irving, viii, 160, 163, 167, 169-170, 171, 184
Huson, Carolyn, viii, 293n
Hutchins, Maynard, 39, 67, 68

Isaacs, Reginald, 77, 78, 109, 127n, 128

Jones, Theodore A., 264-265

Keck, William, 127n
Kennelly, Martin, 87, 248, 251
Kimpton, Lawrence, 61, 67, 74, 76, 129, 160, 270
Kreuger, Maynard, 127n, 196

Landrum, Robert, 182, 189

Subject Index

ACTION–HOUSING, INC., 290
AMERICAN SCHOOL, 14
ARCHDIOCESE OF CHICAGO, 6, 225 *passim*

BACK–OF–THE–YARDS COUNCIL, 234-235, 289
BAIRD AND WARNER, 97
BLOCK GROUPS, 108-109, 120-123, 299-300
BORDER ZONES, definition, 18-19
BUILDING CODE ENFORCEMENT, 79, 83n

CARDINAL'S COMMITTEE ON CONSERVATION AND RENEWAL, 225ff. *passim*, 254
CHICAGO CITY COUNCIL, Committee on Housing and Planning, 271-273
general description, 242-244
hearings on Final Plan, 229-231, 267-270
CHICAGO COLLEGE OF OSTEOPATHY, 53, 195
CHICAGO COMMUNITY INVENTORY, 29n
CHICAGO DWELLINGS ASSOCIATION, 273
CITIZEN PARTICIPATION, absence in neighborhood redevelopment, 182-183
impact on Plan, 152-156, 216-219
Morningside Heights, 281-283
role in renewal, 283-288
CITY OF CHICAGO, Chicago Housing Authority, 247
Department of City Planning, 245
Mayor's authority in renewal, 244-245
renewal agency structure, 242-243
see also, Community Conservation

Board, Land Clearance Commission
COLUMBIA UNIVERSITY, 66, 278 *passim*
COLUMBIAN EXPOSITION, 12, 16, 17
COMMITTEE OF FIVE, 72-74, 76
COMMITTEE OF SIX, 129-130, 135, 144-146, 160
COMMUNITY APPRAISAL STUDY, 109
COMMUNITY CONSERVATION BOARD, vii, 77, 86, 245-248
cut-back action, 253-257
CONSERVATION COMMUNITY COUNCIL, 146-147, 257-260
COUNCIL OF CHURCHES AND SYNAGOGUES, 38, 44
CRIME, prevention, 82
rates, 30-31

DAILY NEWS, 270-271
DEFENDER, 151, 179, 254
DEMONSTRATION GRANTS, 2

EAST HYDE PARK, definition, 17-18
ECONOMIC DISCRIMINATION, 51-52

FEDERAL HOUSING ACT OF 1954, 58
FIFTY-FIFTH STREET BUSINESSMEN'S ASSOCIATION, 39, 91-92

GEORGE WILLIAMS COLLEGE, 14, 53, 195
GOLDEN SQUARE, 16

HOUSING AND HOME FINANCE AGENCY, vii, 3
HUMAN DYNAMICS LABORATORY, 106-108
HYDE PARK A AND B, 90-92, 220-222